THAT
GREAT
HEART

THE LIFE OF I.A. O'SHAUGHNESSY
OILMAN & PHILANTHROPIST

DOUG HENNES

BEAVER'S
POND
PRESS

ISBN 13: 978-1-59298-912-6

Library of Congress Catalog Number: 2014915634

Printed in the United States of America

First Printing: 2014

18 17 16 15 14   5 4 3 2 1

Cover and interior design by James Monroe Design, LLC.

Beaver's Pond Press, Inc.
7108 Ohms Lane
Edina, MN 55439–2129
(952) 829-8818
www.BeaversPondPress.com

BEAVER'S
POND
PRESS

To order, visit www.BeaversPondBooks.com
or call (800) 901-3480. Reseller discounts available.

CONTENTS

PART III

PART IV

ACKNOWLEDGMENTS

I want to thank a number of organizations and individuals for making this biography possible.

The I.A. O'Shaughnessy Foundation board approved a proposal for the biography in 2012 and provided funding. John O'Shaughnessy Jr., president of the foundation board and I.A. O'Shaughnessy's grandson, consulted with me throughout the project and edited the original manuscript, and foundation administrator Brenda Freidel assisted on many issues. Larry O'Shaughnessy (I.A.'s son), Patrick O'Shaughnessy (grandson), and Chevonne O'Shaughnessy (great-granddaughter) also reviewed the original manuscript. Patrick provided invaluable insights during interviews about I.A.'s years in the oil industry.

The Minnesota History Center staff assisted on numerous occasions as I sifted through O'Shaughnessy's voluminous papers. Ann Kenne, director of special collections at the University of St. Thomas in St. Paul, Minnesota, provided similar assistance with O'Shaughnessy files there, as did librarians at the University of Notre Dame in South Bend, Indiana; St. Catherine University in St. Paul; St. Thomas Academy in Mendota Heights, Minnesota; and the public libraries in Wichita and McPherson, Kansas. I also am indebted to John Lindley and the late Virginia Brainard Kunz, whose *Ramsey County History* magazine story on O'Shaughnessy in 2004 was a source of significant background information and inspiration.

Tom Kerber, publisher and chief executive officer of Beaver's Pond Press in Edina, Minnesota, and Lily Coyle, director of publishing, ably guided the biography throughout the process. They contracted with two exceptional talents in copy editor Kellie Hultgren and designer Jay Monroe.

Finally, I must thank Karen, my wife. Her steadfast encouragement and incredible patience were a source of strength throughout the project.

PROLOGUE

I knew the rule and the penalty.
I broke the rule and got caught.
They had to fire me.
—I.A. O'Shaughnessy

Ignatius Aloysius O'Shaughnessy had a big decision to make.

It was January 1902, and the sixteen-year-old boy from Stillwater was in trouble. He and two classmates had skipped Sunday vespers at St. John's University in Collegeville, Minnesota, and headed for the woods—and a hidden barrel of beer. They were nabbed upon their return to campus and expelled the next day.

O'Shaughnessy, the youngest of thirteen children, boarded a Great Northern train for the Twin Cities and considered two options. He could transfer trains in downtown St. Paul and head for home, where he surely would face the wrath of his disappointed parents, or he could skip the transfer and pursue something else.

He chose to get off the train at Union Depot. He walked more than six miles through downtown, up the hill past James J. Hill's new mansion, and west on Summit Avenue until he reached the College of St. Thomas in the early evening. Cold, hungry, and scared, he encountered Father John Dolphin, president of the college, on his evening walk around campus.

Dolphin took O'Shaughnessy to the dining room for a hot meal, and the youth told the president about his misfortune. But Dolphin had heard the story already. One of O'Shaughnessy's drinking buddies had beaten him to St. Thomas and asked to be admitted, but Dolphin had turned him down after he said he thought he had been treated unfairly by St. John's. Dolphin asked O'Shaughnessy if St. John's was justified in expelling him. "Absolutely," he replied. "I knew the rule and the penalty. I broke the rule and got caught. They had to fire me."[1]

Dolphin appreciated O'Shaughnessy's honesty and accepted him on the spot.

O'Shaughnessy went on to star on the football team, serve as secretary to Dolphin and his successor, Father Humphrey Moynihan, and graduate in 1907. Ten years later, he founded Globe Oil & Refining Company in Blackwell, Oklahoma, and went on to become the largest independent oil refiner in the United States. He amassed great wealth and gave most of it away, with St. Thomas as the primary beneficiary. He also contributed generously to the University of Notre Dame, the College of St. Catherine, St. Thomas Academy, and hundreds of other organizations and individuals around the world, either through the I.A. O'Shaughnessy Foundation he founded in 1941 or with his own personal funds. No cause was too small, nor any request too insignificant, for his consideration. He reviewed and replied to virtually every inquiry and included, if he had to say no, an explanation.

O'Shaughnessy became the largest benefactor of Catholic higher education in the United States and joked about it. When asked what it felt like to give so much money to Notre Dame, where his contributions included $2.2 million for the complete construction of the O'Shaughnessy Liberal and Fine Arts Hall in 1953, he replied, "It gives you an empty feeling—in your pockets."[2] Money wasn't that important anyway, he said, and if he gave it away, he didn't have to worry about how to spend it. "I've got good health, two suits of clothes and I eat three meals a day. What more do I need?"[3] After seeing the musical *Hello, Dolly!* on Broadway, he said, "You know, that girl has the right idea. Money is like manure. It doesn't do you any good unless you spread it around."[4]

Spread it around O'Shaughnessy did, and in doing so he endeared himself to everyone he met—but not just because he had said yes to their requests. He became their friend and counselor, a wise member of their boards and a thoughtful consultant to whom they turned time and again for advice.

O'Shaughnessy had what Irish poet William Butler Yeats once called "common sense which is genius." Sister Alice Smith made that observation in October 1973, a month before O'Shaughnessy's death, when benefactors of St. Joseph's Hospital gathered to celebrate its 120th anniversary and pay tribute to him. Said Smith, reflecting on Yeats' words:

> What did he mean? A gift for cutting through nonessentials
> and finding what really matters? Is it a sense for the perfect
> timing of a philanthropic action? Is it a sensitivity to the
> needs, the hopes, the aspirations of others? Is it an unfailing
> moral sense in the matter of priorities? Could there be any
> relationship between this most desirable quality and the one
> described by St. James in his Universal Letter, when he speaks
> of the Christian "who looks into that perfect law, which is the
> law of freedom, and dwells on the sight of it, does not forget
> its message; he finds something to do, and does it, and his
> doing of it wins him a blessing." It seems to us that this could
> have been said truly of the good and great man we wish to
> honor tonight. To such a blessing, what can be added? Only the
> promise of our faithful and continued prayers.[5]

James Shannon, president of St. Thomas from 1956 to 1966, paid tribute to O'Shaughnessy in a *Minneapolis Tribune* commentary after his death. "Unique is a strong word. It should be used with the greatest restraint," Shannon wrote. "Having said that, I say that Ignatius Aloysius O'Shaughnessy was a unique human person. He was brilliant, tough, relaxed, determined, incisive, devout, witty, generous and a thoroughly lovely man."[6]

What would have happened to the sixteen-year-old O'Shaughnessy if he had not left the train on that cold January night and walked to

St. Thomas? What if he instead had returned to Stillwater? Would he have gone back to his summer job as a logger on the St. Croix River? Would he have worked in his father's bootmaking shop? Would he have returned to college? And would he have made hundreds of millions of dollars and consequently changed and enriched the lives and livelihoods of so many?

There is no record that Ignatius Aloysius O'Shaughnessy ever looked back on his life to ask himself those questions and wonder, "What if?" But they are interesting questions to ponder, nonetheless.

PART I

1

The Best Man on the Team

He would tell stories about his reckless enterprises as a youth, such as crossing the railway trestle when a train was coming. He and his friends would hang on below the trestle until the train had passed. He had a degree of pride in his derring-do.
—Son Larry O'Shaughnessy

Ignatius Aloysius O'Shaughnessy was born on July 31, 1885, in Stillwater, Minnesota, the thirteenth child of Irish immigrants John and Mary Ann O'Shaughnessy.

The O'Shaughnessys hailed from County Clare and County Galway in Ireland. Legend has it that O'Shaughnessys (O'Seachnasaigh in Gaelic) were kings or chieftains as early as the fourth century and that King Henry VIII knighted Dermot O'Shaughnessy in the early sixteenth century, although no conclusive proof exists that the Minnesota O'Shaughnessys were direct descendants.

As the potato famine wracked Ireland in the 1840s, a bootmaker named John O'Shaughnessy packed up his family and left the country from Limerick in 1848 or 1849. He took up his trade in Milford, Massachusetts, south of Boston. One of his sons, John, became a bootmaker and married Mary Ann Milan of Milford in 1859. They moved to Stillwater, Minnesota, in 1860 to open a boot and shoe company on Main Street and had twelve children before Ignatius arrived in 1885.[1]

Ignatius loved to tell people why he had such an unusual name. "I was the last of thirteen children," he said. "By the time I arrived, mother had run fresh out of all the regular names like John, James and Joseph, and being a good Catholic, she went to the Calendar of Saints. So I became Ignatius."[2]

The custom in those days among Roman Catholics was for a child to choose his or her middle name at confirmation. Ignatius was fond of a St. Michael's School nun whose name was Sister Aloysius, and when she told him that Aloysius was the patron saint of boys, he settled on that for his middle name. Known to close friends as "Nashe" (nayshh), he later joked, "What with Aloysius and O'Shaughnessy, that's too long. They should pass a law that no name should be over five letters."[3]

The O'Shaughnessys lived in a large house with thirteen rooms at 703 Third Avenue South, one block south of St. Michael's Church. The family often took in less-fortunate youth, including an orphaned boy who became a successful New York stockbroker and a young woman who was blind and deaf but sewed for the entire family. John O'Shaughnessy and his friends established an unofficial community relief fund and met in his home to determine which families in town needed aid, taking care to ensure that the recipients' identities would not be revealed. "Not even my mother knew who was being helped," Ignatius later recalled.[4]

There are no records of O'Shaughnessy's first communion or confirmation, nor does the school have any records of his years there because its files date back only to 1901. Fifty years later, however, a former teacher identified as Sister Victoria wrote to congratulate him on a papal award that he had received and remembered him as "a very interesting little boy" at St. Michael's in 1891. She wrote:

> It has always given me great pleasure to hear of the honors
> that have been bestowed upon you and I have often wanted

to write you a word of congratulations, so I cannot let the present occasion pass without doing so. With all my heart I congratulate you on this latest honor. I am quite proud of my little boy. Best of all I am thankful to the good God that you are a loyal son of Holy Mother Church and that you have been able to befriend her and have done so generously. I would love to see you in your new regalia, but I fear that pleasure is not to be mine, as I do not go out anymore. I am quite crippled and must stay indoors. My four score years have left their mark upon me. I pray the great and good God to bless you and all yours, and that He will continue His care of you.[5]

O'Shaughnessy loved to play football as a teenager and said he toughened up for the sport by working six days a week as a lumberjack in a mill on the St. Croix River. He earned $1.40 for a twelve-hour day and developed great respect for married men who raised families on such wages. "It was a great hardship," he said. "They had to get up at 5 a.m. to be at work by 6 a.m. After hours of labor they would go home, eat and go to bed, worn out."[6]

His middle son, Larry, recalled his father's remembrances of Stillwater before the turn of the century:

He would tell stories about log spinners and log spinning contests among people who did that kind of thing. He also told wild stories about how the large sucker fish were so thick at certain periods during their spawning that you could walk across the river on their backs. He loved spinning those tall tales. He would tell stories about his reckless enterprises as a youth, such as crossing the railway trestle when a train was coming. When the train reached the trestle, he and his friends would hang on below the trestle until the train had passed. I assumed he had a degree of pride in his derring-do. He was an enterprising young man, willing to take chances.[7]

Leonard Rogge, a career administrator at the College of St. Thomas in St. Paul, recalled in an oral history for the college a story that O'Shaughnessy once told him about his restless youth. He quoted

O'Shaughnessy as saying, "I did run away from home, and I got down to the railroad tracks, walked along the rails for some distance and as night fell, I proceeded to lie down beside a stack of railroad ties. After a fairly sleepless night and a stomach that became empty for want of something to eat, I decided to head back home."[8]

Others thought of him as just a regular boy. One friend, Ed Boyle, called O'Shaughnessy "a rough and tumble kid, and in a tussle he'd come out on top. But he was a good sport, not a rowdy."[9]

The O'Shaughnessys determined that their sons should have college educations, and several enrolled at St. John's University, west of St. Cloud, Minnesota. Ignatius was sixteen when he matriculated at St. John's in 1901, following brothers Joseph, John, William, and James there. At the time, many "colleges" or "universities" offered courses that resemble high school or community college programs today, and O'Shaughnessy paid $100 per semester for tuition, room, and board. St. John's enrollment totaled 331 students, including 46 seminarians, and students abided by strict rules. Attendance at daily worship services was mandatory, tobacco use was prohibited, and permission had to be obtained to leave the grounds once a month. Visits home were allowed only at Christmas and Easter.[10]

O'Shaughnessy joined the football team when he arrived in the fall of 1901. The sport was new at St. John's, which twice had lost 5–0 to St. Cloud High School in its first games the previous October. The 1901 team fared much better, avenging both losses to St. Cloud before playing the College of St. Thomas for the first time on Thanksgiving morning at Lexington Park in St. Paul. The Johnnies scored three touchdowns (then worth five points each) en route to a 16–0 win.

The *Record,* St. John's monthly newspaper, carried a lengthy account of the game and called O'Shaughnessy one of the stars in the victory. He started as an offensive tackle but carried the ball seven times from scrimmage for seventy-six yards, all in the first half, including runs of twenty, thirteen, and fourteen yards on consecutive carries in one series, and he also ran back a kickoff twenty yards.[11] "When the news of the victory reached St. John's, the campus went wild," states *Scoreboard*, a 1979 history of athletics at St. John's. "It was heady news for the young partisan-minded St. John's fans."[12]

More than a half century later, Father Louis Traufier, the St. John's coach, described the game for *Worship & Work* magazine. The team had taken the train to Minneapolis the night before the game and slept on cots in barracks at St. Boniface Church. After going to Mass on Thanksgiving morning, they took the streetcar to Lexington Park for the 9 a.m. game. He wrote:

> We were called "the hay seeds" so the boys came on the field with hay seeds in their caps. One of the men from St. Thomas had written a poem and set it to song: "When Rueben Comes to Town," and they were to sing and play it during the half. They [St. Thomas] were a foregone conclusion to win and had a paid coach. Our boys had no equipment except canvas jackets and shorts, and no headgear. We led in the first half and won the game. The boys ran over each other for touchdowns. They made a human pyramid so they could run over each other. We returned on the midnight train and had no trouble controlling the boys.[13]

One of O'Shaughnessy's teammates at St. John's was John "The Swede" O'Leary of San Diego. They lost track of each other after graduation, but O'Leary sent O'Shaughnessy a letter in December 1949, and he responded:

> Fifty years is a long time between drinks. I have often thought of you and the many good times we had at St. John's. I have often thought of the boys who were in school with us in those days, but they must be either dead or in hiding as your letter is the first time I have heard from any of the old bunch. Memories of one's boyhood days are perhaps the nicest we have. If we could only get together and rehash the many incidents that happened, it would be worthwhile.[14]

Twelve years later, O'Shaughnessy received a letter from Father Walter Reger at St. John's about O'Leary's death and responded, "It seems that as one gets older he hears of the deaths of his contemporaries. I guess the best thing to do is not get old."[15]

Memories of the first St. John's–St. Thomas game lasted for generations. O'Shaughnessy made a $1,000 contribution to a football stadium expansion at St. John's in 1957 and received a thank-you letter from Father Dunstan Tucker, faculty representative for athletics:

> I will treasure your letter as coming from one of our first
> lettermen and a player in that legendary first victory over
> St. Thomas. I was not aware that you had played in that game.
> It gave me a good feeling to learn that you considered it your
> good fortune to have had a part in it. We have had many a
> good battle since that time and I assure you they have always
> been for keeps. I coached baseball here for some fifteen years
> and can report that the competitive spirit has not deteriorated
> through the years.[16]

In 1962, a St. John's librarian came across issues of St. John's *Record* stories and sent copies to O'Shaughnessy. Father Benjamin Stein mused in a letter to O'Shaughnessy that the team lineup in 1901 "seems particularly odd to a present day football fan" and wondered why he played tackle and "carried the ball as much or more than any other man on the team! Were these all Statue of Liberty plays or did you just decide to rotate in the office of carrying the ball?"[17] O'Shaughnessy had the answers: "Like many others, you were not around watching football games in those days. The question has often been asked of me why men in the line ran with the ball. The original lineup in those days was what is called the T-formation now. It was a very close formation and if the guard as well as the tackle or end wanted to, he could drop back and receive the ball from the quarterback and run with it."[18]

O'Shaughnessy also noted in the letter to Stein that the St. John's Alumni Association chapter in Minneapolis offered a Meerschaum pipe to the player making the longest run in the St. Thomas game. "I happened to be the one who won the pipe," he said. "However, in those days, if a student was caught smoking a pipe, he was immediately sent home—so you can see how times have changed."[19]

The authors of *Scoreboard* concluded their review of the 1901 season with a few comments about O'Shaughnessy, writing, "It is still a subject for jestful comment at St. John's the fact that the future great philanthropist, the generous endower of Catholic schools, colleges and universities, did not remain at St. John's. He transferred and graduated from the College of St. Thomas. Fr. Walter Reger, O.S.B., once jokingly remarked, 'Someone goofed at St. John's.'"[20]

O'Shaughnessy may not have been expelled from St. John's for smoking a pipe, but his dalliance with that keg of beer in January 1902 did lead to his expulsion and his enrollment later the same day at St. Thomas.

He wasted no time in becoming a star on the St. Thomas team. After a 1904 season in which St. Thomas outscored its opponents 63 to 6, the campus newspaper, the *Collegian,* called him "perhaps the best all-around man on the team" heading into 1905, when he would be captain. "O'Shaughnessy will hold down his old position at right half although an injured shoulder may keep him out of some of the games," read one story. "He is a hard, conscientious worker, and well-fitted in every respect to lead the Purple and Gray to victory."[21]

The *St. Paul Pioneer Press* agreed. "Capt. O'Shaughnessy will hold his old position at right half," the newspaper said in a preseason story. "This is his fourth year at St. Thomas and it is expected that he will be better than ever, although [since] the very first year he has been one of the best players, whether at tackle, full or halfback."[22]

St. Thomas won the state championship in 1905 (the Minnesota Intercollegiate Athletic Conference did not form until 1920). Years later, a fellow alumnus from that era recalled O'Shaughnessy's outstanding play and his drive on the field. "I can only visualize you as one of the hardest guys on the football field, and the dirtiest and most torn when you came off," wrote Dr. Will Donahue, a Sioux Falls, South Dakota, physician, to O'Shaughnessy in 1940. "Maybe that new field fence of yours will just about compensate for all the old purple and gray jerseys you ruined."[23]

O'Shaughnessy followed the St. Thomas football teams—academy as well as college—for the rest of his life. The St. *Paul Dispatch* published football photos of O'Shaughnessy and his oldest son, John, under the headline "Son is Following in Father's Footsteps" after John was elected captain of the academy team for the 1926 season.[24] The *Purple and Gray*, a student newspaper at St. Thomas, published its own photo and story about the father-and-son football connection. "That the captain elect is a 'chip off the old block' is peculiarly evident as he is the son of I.A. O'Shaughnessy, captain and star of the championship 1905 St. Thomas College grid team," the story said.[25]

In 1948, O'Shaughnessy attended the first meeting of the college's Monogram Club, joined by three hundred men who elected him as its president and presented him with an *ST* monogrammed blanket. The club held a dinner that December for the undefeated football team, which played in the Cigar Bowl on January 1, 1949, in Tampa, Florida. O'Shaughnessy helped to underwrite the trip and paid for a radio broadcast of the game. "I should also like to tell you how much [the players] enjoyed the experience of playing in the Cigar Bowl, an experience which would not have been possible if not for you," public relations director Dan Herget wrote to him. "The boys are still talking about it, and already they have set their sights on a return bid next year."[26]

O'Shaughnessy also was known to make an occasional wager on a game. One bet was with Donald MacGregor, vice president of the First National Bank of St. Paul and the father of Bob MacGregor, captain of the Macalester team that upset St. Thomas 20 to 13 on October 10, 1953. The two men attended the game and watched MacGregor score Macalester's first touchdown when he scooped up a St. Thomas fumble and ran fifty-four yards. But O'Shaughnessy did not pay up that evening.

"I would think you would sleep much better when you've taken care of this obligation, which has been hanging over you for all these years," the elder MacGregor wrote to O'Shaughnessy in 1964, eleven years after the game. "Moreover, it won't cost you anything, as all I want is a check which I can frame and hang in my den with the other trophies, souvenirs and mementoes of the past. Kindest personal regards in spite of the unconscionable delay."[27]

Two days later, O'Shaughnessy enclosed a brief reply with the check: "I give up. My conscience has begun to bother me."[28]

The check was for $1. MacGregor framed it and later passed it on to his son, who served on the Minneapolis City Council and as president of the Minnesota Center for Ethical Business Cultures at St. Thomas. The *Minneapolis Star Tribune* wrote about the wager in 2007, in a story headlined "I.A.'s checkbook still doesn't balance."[29]

~~~

In addition to football, O'Shaughnessy "also led a well-rounded student life," Rogge said in his St. Thomas oral history. "In those days boys were not adverse to having a drink of whiskey or a few beers. I remember one occasion described to me when he [O'Shaughnessy] and several of his friends proceeded to steal a couple of chickens and to prepare them for roasting, only to ultimately discover that barbecuing chickens over an open fire was not quite as easy as he thought."[30]

O'Shaughnessy also caught the eye of Father Dolphin and was appointed the president's private secretary in March 1903. Dolphin resigned that spring because of ill health, and his successor, Father Humphrey Moynihan, retained O'Shaughnessy as a secretary. Among the young man's duties was overseeing the purchase of military uniforms for all students after the United States War Department classified St. Thomas as an official military school. O'Shaughnessy also was listed in the 1902–3 college catalogue as librarian for the Literary and Debating Society, and a half century later he was asked by a University of Minnesota graduate student writing a history of the St. Thomas library what he might remember. Those times, O'Shaughnessy replied, were "so remote that I would be unable to give any light upon the information which you are seeking."[31]

O'Shaughnessy became a bookkeeper-secretary during his senior year. "It was somewhat unusual for a student approaching graduation to become part of the college administration team," Monsignor Terrence Murphy, president of St. Thomas from 1966 to 1991, later commented. "However, St. Thomas was a small institution then and money was scarce."[32]

O'Shaughnessy graduated in 1907, and his experience led to his hiring that February as secretary of the St. Paul Amateur Athletic Association, the forerunner of the St. Paul Athletic Club. "He has secured a position that pays $1,200 a year, which is a pretty fair start for a young man," the *Stillwater Weekly Gazette* reported.[33] The St. Thomas *Collegian* reported that his many friends on campus "regret his departure and wish him all success in his new field. Mr. O'Shaughnessy, while a student, decided many a close gridiron battle by his prowess."[34]

2

Feeling Like a Millionaire

One evening he said, "May I kiss you?" I said,
"But we're not even engaged!" And he said, "Okay, then,
will you marry me?" And that's how I caught him.

—LILLIAN SMITH

During his years at St. Thomas, I.A. O'Shaughnessy attended St. Mark's Catholic Church a few blocks east of campus, and on the evening of August 13, 1903, he took a church-sponsored boat cruise on the Mississippi River. It was there that Father William Hart of St. Mark's introduced him to sixteen-year-old Lillian Smith, the daughter of Charles and Honora Smith of St. Paul.

O'Shaughnessy eventually moved into the Smith home at 1952 Ashland Avenue, also within walking distance of St. Thomas, and paid for room and board. A romance developed between Ignatius and Lillian, who later loved to tell the story of their courtship: "One evening he said, 'May I kiss you?' I said, 'But we're not even engaged!' And he said, 'Okay, then, will you marry me?' And that's how I caught him."[1]

11

He borrowed $600 and the couple—Ignatius at twenty-three and Lillian at twenty-one—married on October 7, 1908, at St. Mark's, with Hart performing the ceremony. The groom's mother had died the previous year, but his father (who died the following January) attended the wedding. The St. *Paul Pioneer Press* published a story three days later:

> The bride entered the church accompanied by her father, and her dress of antique slipper satin was made on Empire lines, with a long train. The bodice had a Princess Lace yoke with high collar. The sleeves were long with points over the hands, and the puffs on the shoulders were made of the satin in folds fagotted together. The front panel of the dress had Princess Lace trim. Small pearl buttons were used down the back of the dress. The underskirt was made of soft nainsook with a deep flounce of net banded in satin. The veil was French Illusion made in cap style and fell to the end of the train. Her almost black hair was pulled to the back of her head, where it fell in three curls. The Bride carried a spray of white roses and lilies-of-the valley tied with white ribbons. Her only ornament was a diamond and pearl brooch, a gift of the Groom.[2]

And O'Shaughnessy? The newspaper account had only two sentences about him: "The groom wore a Morning Suit, gray vest, pearl buttons and gray cravat. His brown hair was parted in the middle."[3]

After the ceremony, a wedding breakfast was served at the home of the bride's parents.

The *Pioneer Press* also reported that the newlyweds would live in Houston, where Ignatius had joined his older brothers John and William in the insurance business after leaving the St. Paul Amateur Athletic Association.

John had been involved in politics in Minnesota and ran the successful 1900 gubernatorial campaign of John Lind, a former three-term congressman, teacher, and lawyer who rewarded him with an appointment as state insurance commissioner. Lind failed in his reelection bid in 1902, and by 1905 John was a vice president of the Minnesota Mutual Life Insurance Company (known today as Securian). He left that position to move to Houston and work in the insurance industry.[4]

"He told me to come on down to Texas and he'd set me up with my own insurance company," O'Shaughnessy later told the *Minneapolis Tribune*.[5] He used a $500 wedding gift from John to buy a car and set out for Houston. He encountered early success, reportedly earning $10,000 his first year. He felt "like a millionaire," his son John, who was born in 1909, later recalled. "He never went back to see a prospect because there were too many others to see."[6]

O'Shaughnessy's brother set his eyes on expanding his business to Mexico and reportedly attempted to negotiate a deal with President Porfirio Díaz and his government for the exclusive rights to sell life insurance for Minnesota Mutual in that country. But a series of revolutions engulfed the country in chaos, and one popular leader, Pancho Villa, crossed the border into New Mexico and looted the town of Columbus. Several citizens died, President Woodrow Wilson dispatched General John J. Pershing to deal with the uprising, and the O'Shaughnessys' dreams of a Mexican life insurance empire vanished.[7]

O'Shaughnessy chose to end his business relationship with his brothers and organized the Bankers' Trust Company in Dallas in 1913. That same year, Lillian gave birth to their second child, Eileen. She often was ill as a toddler, and in 1914 the family moved to Denver and a climate drier than humid Texas. O'Shaughnessy organized the Farmers' Life Insurance Company there and also worked for Gates Tire Company, but the couple soon were on the move again, this time to Wichita, Kansas, where they had their third child, Marian, in 1916.

While in Wichita, O'Shaughnessy "organized and put on a sound basis" the Mid-Continent Tire Manufacturing Company and leased a factory to make tires to sell to the federal government. It was "the largest tire manufacturing company in the West," one newspaper later reported.[8]

But before long, O'Shaughnessy had his eye on another line of work. Oil had been discovered near Garber, Oklahoma, south of the Kansas border, and O'Shaughnessy decided to try his hand in the business that would make him his fortune.

3

A Good Industry to Get Into

He couldn't do it [build the Blackwell refinery]
on his own because he had no cash, so he got people to invest.
Then when the money came in from refinery sales,
he could pay people back or buy them out.
—GRANDSON PATRICK O'SHAUGHNESSY

To this day, it remains unclear exactly why—and even when—I.A. O'Shaughnessy decided to enter the oil business.

The Lario Oil & Gas Company website says he formed Globe Oil & Refining Company in 1916 in Oklahoma, as does a story published in the *American Oil & Gas Reporter,* but that may have been when he came up with the idea. Other sources have reported 1917 as Globe's first year. As for why, O'Shaughnessy once told a reporter that someone had asked him to move to Wichita "and organize an oil company. So I figured it was a good industry to get into."[1]

Around this time, O'Shaughnessy met William Hamann, who had executed oil and gas leases near Blackwell, Oklahoma, twenty miles south of the Kansas border and just east of today's Interstate 35. The two men and three others—Lee Boyd, O.F. Hawkins, and H.C. Beneke—signed a contract on January 31, 1917, "to commence the drilling of an oil and gas well" by March 15 of that year.[2]

A separate agreement, also dated January 31 and handwritten on the back of stationery from the American Hotel in nearby Enid, Oklahoma, states that Roy Walter gave O'Shaughnessy an eighty-acre lease in Garfield County. O'Shaughnessy agreed to pay $200 in cash on January 31, $200 on July 15, and $500 each thirty days thereafter until $5,000 had been paid. The agreement also stated that O'Shaughnessy and two other partners would organize a stock company, give Walter $2,000 in stock, and sell him $1,000 in stock.[3]

The agreement did not identify the two partners, but a 1957 Globe history written by Francis L. Jehle indicated that O'Shaughnessy, A.N. Bontz Sr. of Wichita, and Dr. D.S. Smithhisler of Enid founded Globe on February 2, 1917.[4] Bontz knew Jehle and contacted him in search of someone who could serve as bookkeeper and stenographer for the new company. "I was offered and accepted the position," Jehle wrote, "and was told to arrange to leave early Monday morning, February 5, for Enid," forty miles southwest of Blackwell. Jehle became a trusted and hardworking associate of O'Shaughnessy's, advanced to vice president of Globe companies by 1933, and remained with Globe until his retirement in the 1950s.

"The train left Wichita some time between 5:00 and 6:00 and there for the first time I met Mr. O'Shaughnessy," Jehle wrote. "We proceeded to Enid on the Rock Island train and upon arrival Dr. Smithhisler showed us a couple of rooms in the First National Bank Building which he thought would be satisfactory for the office of the company.... The next thing we did was to go down to an office supply store and buy some furniture and record books."[5]

O'Shaughnessy's original intention was to focus on converting crude oil to usable fuels and oils. He later realized that involvement in the exploration process, including drilling, would be beneficial because successful wells would provide a steady supply of oil for his refineries. Some newspaper writers later would call O'Shaughnessy "king of the wildcatters," but he disliked the name because it misstated his role in the oil business. A wildcatter explored and drilled for oil in untried or unproven areas, while O'Shaughnessy primarily operated refineries, especially in the early years, and always was judicious about tracts of land where he might drill for oil.

His initial plans were to construct a refinery near Enid, a town of about 15,000, where drilling had occurred in several area fields. "Globe Company Buys Site for Large Refinery," stated the page one headline above the nameplate of the *Enid Morning News* on July 22, 1917. "Plant to Have a Big Capacity," read one sub-headline, with a daily capacity of 5,000 barrels (210,000 gallons). The story went on to speak enthusiastically about Globe's aspirations and O'Shaughnessy's business moxie:

> The site selected by Mr. O'Shaughnessy is one of the very
> best that could be secured for a big refinery near Enid, and
> by reflection and close observation [of] Mr. O'Shaughnessy
> since he started operations with the Globe Oil and Refining
> Company it will be noted that nothing but the very best will
> satisfy the management of this growing oil refining industry. It
> is certainly a big step forward in the industrial life of Enid and
> too much cannot be said or done to help boost this institution
> in its present stage of development.

Success with the tire company in Wichita "speaks very highly of Mr. O'Shaughnessy's ability as a builder of big institutions," the story continued, "and the News predicts big success from the start for this new refinery."[6]

Globe obtained several leases in the Enid area, Jehle recorded,[7] and O'Shaughnessy contacted L.J. Dixon of Houston, a friend with experience in drilling wells, to see if he would be interested in drilling for Globe. Dixon arrived and spudded a well early that summer, but it was abandoned as a failure. "It soon became apparent that our major problem would be to locate the necessary crude oil with which to operate the proposed refinery," Jehle wrote.[8] O'Shaughnessy revisited the Blackwell area and decided to build the refinery there because of better potential oil supplies and a location on branch lines of the Santa

Fe and Frisco railroads.

In those early years, O'Shaughnessy typically spent his weeks in small Oklahoma and Kansas towns where his oil interests were located and returned to Wichita on the weekends. On one train ride from Wichita, O'Shaughnessy and Jehle met Carl B. Haun, a young engineer who worked for a different refining company. O'Shaughnessy liked Haun and hired him to build the Blackwell refinery and serve as its general superintendent. Haun later became a Globe vice president and general manager.

O'Shaughnessy often grabbed a room wherever he could find one when he was on the road. Bob McDowell, an early Globe employee in Blackwell, recalled that O'Shaughnessy lived in the McDowell home for a period of time and was a welcome guest. "I am sure you know that my father and mother thought that 'Mr. I.A.' was all right in every respect," McDowell wrote to I.A. and Lillian O'Shaughnessy in 1958. "In addition to being Presbyterians and rock-ribbed Republicans, my folks bordered upon being teetotalers, but the fact that I.A. O'Shaughnessy had liquor in his room never occurred to them as being wrong."[9]

The Blackwell refinery opened February 22, 1918, with a daily capacity of 1,500 barrels furnished via a four-inch pipeline from oil leases owned and operated by B.E. LaDow of Fredonia, Kansas, and the National Union Oil & Gas Company of Blackwell. "We were able to manufacture aviation gasoline," Jehle wrote, "and much of it was shipped to various Army airfields. The company was successful and showed a nice operating profit in the beginning, although it was necessary to pay a premium to obtain a supply of oil."[10]

I.A.'s grandson, Patrick O'Shaughnessy, long-time chairman of Lario Oil & Gas and associated with the company for more than four decades, said his grandfather took a risk even in building the Blackwell refinery. "He couldn't do it on his own because he had no cash," Patrick said, "so he got people to invest. Then when the money came in from refinery sales, he could pay people back or buy them out. The relationships he established years earlier paid off. You can see the pattern."[11]

Most refined products were shipped in railroad tank cars provided by buyers, including the Santa Fe Railway, but "early in 1920 it became almost impossible to secure sufficient tank cars to move our products," Jehle wrote.[12] Globe also grappled with other challenges, including a glut of gasoline on the market in the early 1920s. "It was, indeed, difficult to make money in the refining business. In fact, in those years usually for every profitable year the company experienced we would have at least one bad year and several times two. This was prevalent throughout the entire industry."[13] Globe also had an occasional drilling misadventure. One prospective well, drilled to a depth of 3,290 feet in Grant County, twenty miles west of Blackwell, was abandoned as a dry hole in 1920. Cost: $50,000.[14]

Such setbacks never deterred O'Shaughnessy, who kept pressing forward and always sought to take advantage of the latest technology in refining crude oil. In 1922, Globe took out the first commercial license to use the Cross cracking process for the Blackwell refinery. The process, developed by Dr. Walter Cross, a professor of chemistry at the University of Kansas, and his brother Roy, found that higher pressure produced a substantially greater number of barrels of gasoline—and at a cost of $1 less per barrel than conventional methods. O'Shaughnessy was one of the first to use a rotary drill developed by Howard Hughes Sr. (father of the famous aviation pioneer) instead of conventional cable tools, which literally pounded holes in the ground.

The typical workweek was six days, Jehle wrote, "and on Sunday it was the custom to go the post office to pick up the mail and take it to the office. Since I was unmarried, my Sundays were usually spent with Mr. O'Shaughnessy at the office. . . . We would spend part of our time in the shade of the office throwing a baseball back and forth. We even had a bat and would do a little hitting."[15]

The Blackwell refinery expanded in 1922, to 5,000 barrels a day, to handle crude oil obtained through a Globe pipeline to the Tonkawa field fifteen miles south of Blackwell. Globe routinely contracted with major oil companies to obtain a steady supply of crude while O'Shaughnessy continued to explore drilling opportunities in the region. A partnership in 1923 with Clark Denny and Harper Poling led to the acquisition of the eighty-acre Door Step Pool lease, northwest of Blackwell, which Jehle described as a "nice gas producer."[16] The Blackwell plant expanded once again, to 8,000 barrels a day.

A 1926 partnership led to the development of perhaps the most successful lease in Globe's history. O'Shaughnessy had provided funds to Tom Palmer, a wildcat oil driller out of Ponca City, Oklahoma, and obtained a one-half interest in a lease near the Oxford pool in Sumner County, Kansas, north of the Oklahoma border. Palmer struck oil, and O'Shaughnessy was emboldened to expand his own exploring and drilling efforts. He incorporated Lario Oil & Gas Company in Delaware in July 1927 as an exploration and development company to ensure that Globe would have ample supplies of crude for its refineries, and O'Shaughnessy, Jehle, and Palmer became directors of the new company. Lario was named for O'Shaughnessy's middle son, Larry, and the same year O'Shaughnessy incorporated Don Oil Company, named after his youngest son, Don, to drill for oil in the Blackwell area.

One of Lario's early ventures was to further develop the Oxford pool. Two deep tests drilled north of Oxford resulted in dry holes, but on December 24, 1927, a third lease—the Bertha Wenrich on an eighty-acre site southwest of Oxford—"blew in a large producer," in the words of the *Daily Republican* of McPherson, Kansas. Fifteen wells drilled on the lease produced 2.5 million barrels of oil over the next six years, with the Oxford pool growing to eighty acres and twenty-eight wells and reaching the largest recovery per acre of any lease in Lario history. (The lease produced 5.5 million barrels through 1970, and as of 2014, four wells on the site produce twelve barrels of oil a day. Patrick O'Shaughnessy says the lease still is profitable with oil prices at $100 a barrel; he points out they were 32.5 cents a barrel in 1927 and $3.54 a barrel in 1970.)[17]

When crude oil supplies became tight around Blackwell, O'Shaughnessy found other sources. Jehle recalled one purchase of a trainload of crude oil with a high sulfur content from the Panhandle area in Texas, but refining yields were low and of poor quality, "and the terrible odor emanating from the plant during the run caused many complaints from people living in the vicinity," he wrote. "The result was that we were subjected to a number of lawsuits."[18] One plaintiff alleged damages to his home and injuries to his health, but the jury returned a verdict of $1 each on two of three counts. "While this might appear as a victory," Jehle wrote, "we could not consider it as such . . . and there was always a possibility that a jury would return a sizable verdict if other trials were held." A $5,000 settlement was worked out to cover all the lawsuits.[19]

O'Shaughnessy formed another company—Globe Oil & Refining of Delaware—in 1928 to acquire crude oil from Shell Oil and refine it at a 10,000-barrel Sinclair Oil plant in Cushing, Oklahoma, west of Tulsa. "A deal was made whereby the plant was leased for a period of two years at a rental of $5,000 per month," Jehle wrote, "and arrangements were completed with Shell for the purchase of a quantity of crude and the sale back to it of the light ends. . . . The transaction proved profitable from the very beginning."[20]

That same year, Globe began to use a new "thermal" cracking process developed by the Winkler-Koch Engineering Company of Wichita to increase the percentage of gasoline that could be refined from crude oil by eliminating the formation of coke. Standard Oil of Indiana subsequently sued Globe and other refiners, alleging they had infringed on Standard's patent for cracking and should obtain a license from Standard to use its process. Globe refused, and after a two-month trial in 1934, a federal judge in Chicago dismissed the lawsuit because the Standard Oil patent didn't cover the Winkler-Koch method. There were other lawsuits, including one filed by Chicago-based Universal Oil Products in 1934 alleging infringement on Universal patents in operating Winkler-Koch pipe stills, and the final lawsuit was not resolved until 1955.

Chicago law firm Thiess, Olson, Mecklenburger, Von Holst & Coltman represented Globe for nearly thirty years on the cracking process lawsuits. O'Shaughnessy was known to be impatient with lawyers but always appreciated the diligence demonstrated by the Chicago firm. "After fighting this case all these years and finally coming out victorious," he wrote in a 1944 telegram to J. Bernard Thiess, "it gives one a feeling of great satisfaction. Hats off to you and your gang, for a job well done and one that will always be remembered by me." Other cases dragged into the 1950s, and a federal appeals court unanimously affirmed a lower court's decision in favor of Globe in 1955. "We take this occasion to express our appreciation for having the privilege of acting as your counsel over this period of twenty-eight years," the law firm wrote to O'Shaughnessy in 1955. "Your confidence and pertinacity even when (in one case) we had apparently lost will always be for us, as lawyers, a very happy memory."[21]

⁓⁓⁓

Buoyed by the success of his Kansas and Oklahoma operations, O'Shaughnessy cast an eye in 1929 on the lucrative Chicago market and the opportunity to distribute refined products in the Upper Midwest. He formed the Globe Oil & Refining Company of Illinois and purchased a 3,000-barrel refinery in the Chicago suburb of Lemont from the Lemont Refining Company. Starting with an expansion to 6,500 barrels a day in 1933, O'Shaughnessy increased capacity to 48,000 barrels before selling the refinery in 1954.

At the time O'Shaughnessy purchased the Lemont refinery, some of its crude oil came from fields in Muskegon, Michigan, "and it was to be transported across Lake Michigan to the plant by barge," Jehle wrote. "I had never seen an oil barge before but was at Muskegon when the first barge, an old wooden scow, arrived to transport the first oil to Lemont. It reminded me of pictures which I have seen depicting Noah's Ark."[22]

Jehle and George Woodruff, a Shell manager who joined Globe's Lemont operation, were dissatisfied with the Michigan crude oil and the low-quality gasoline refined from it. O'Shaughnessy took matters into his own hands, visiting Houston in 1930 to negotiate a contract with the Texas Company for the purchase of Oklahoma crude oil that would be transported to Chicago through a pipeline jointly owned by the Texas and the Empire Oil and Refining Companies. "We were not only the first customer outside of the owners of the line," Jehle wrote, "but perhaps also the first independent who was able to tender crude for shipment to a pipeline owned by a major company or companies. With this supply of crude and the completion of the Winkler-Koch cracking facilities at Lemont, the plant began making money."[23]

Subsequently, refined products were distributed from the Lemont refinery to Globe dealers and gasoline stations throughout the Midwest and Canada. The Minneapolis-based Barber Company marketed gasoline, kerosene, burning oils, turpentine, and lubricating oils and greases under the Globe trademark to six hundred locations in more than a dozen states, including Minnesota, Wisconsin, and Illinois. Globe also provided financing to, or became part owners in, companies that sold its products and wanted to expand, but lacked capital. One such partner, Southside Petroleum, had seventy-five gasoline stations in the Chicago area, each selling 3,000 gallons of gasoline a day. "Our interest in these companies provided us with an unusually fine outlet," Jehle wrote, "and over the years proved to be a very profitable investment."[24]

Globe sold more than just oil products. An advertising and merchandising plan from that era also offered independent gasoline stations the opportunity to buy and sell everything from uniforms, dust cloths, and road maps to balloons, book matches, baseball caps, and pencils—all with the Globe insignia, of course. The merchandising plan read:

> In 1917, Mr. I.A. O'Shaughnessy organized the Globe Oil &
> Refining Company in order to give the independent jobber
> a reliable source of supply that would not compete directly
> or indirectly with him. That the independent jobber would
> be competitive in the marketing of better products, the
> policy of manufacturing the highest quality merchandise
> was inaugurated. These two basic policies have never been
> veered from and today Globe stands almost alone as a source
> of supply, selling exclusively through independent outlets.
> Because of this marketing plan, the welfare and interest
> of the jobber is always foremost. The success of the plan is
> truly exemplified in the phenomenal growth that Globe has
> made during the past few years. Every Globe account is given
> personal attention and consideration. There are no "cut and
> dried" methods, no Board of Directors or other stumbling
> blocks to slow down the handling of questions affecting Globe
> customers.[25]

Texas and Empire weren't the only major oil companies to arrange deals with O'Shaughnessy. Jehle noted that, in 1930, Shell owned land in the Ritz-Canton oil pool in eastern McPherson County, Kansas, between Wichita and Salina, but was not interested in carrying on an extensive drilling campaign.[26] O'Shaughnessy obtained a "farmout" option in which Shell retained an overriding royalty interest, and Lario went into the area "and became the most active operator and largest producer" in this "giant" field. The farmout allowed Lario to expand drilling on Ritz-Canton, and by September 1931 O'Shaughnessy had acquired twelve leases and was operating twenty-two wells with a potential production of 33,654 barrels a day. [27]

The explosion of activity in Ritz-Canton meant one thing: O'Shaughnessy needed another refinery, fast, and he needed it close to all of those wells.

4

A Real Believer in America

He typifies that true spirit of American ability, courage and resourcefulness. While thousands of others were yielded to the popular fallacy that business was going to the eternal bow-wows, I.A. O'Shaughnessy was driving full steam ahead.

—McPHERSON (KANSAS) DAILY REPUBLICAN

In 1931, the McPherson Chamber of Commerce approached I.A. O'Shaughnessy about building a refinery in the central Kansas town. It proved to be a perfect match, and it came at a very unusual time in our nation's history.

During the height of the Great Depression, the building of the refinery would create 350 construction jobs. The chamber liked O'Shaughnessy—and the prospect of working with an aggressive and successful independent refiner with the potential to become the town's largest employer. O'Shaughnessy appreciated both the chamber's entrepreneurial generosity—it furnished a location a mile south of town for the refinery—and the opportunity to develop a full-service operation

25

that would meet Globe's refining needs for years to come.

He formed the Globe Oil & Refining Company of Kansas in 1932 to construct and operate the $1 million refinery, which would have a capacity of 10,000 barrels a day. Ground was broken on July 12, and construction took only six months. The facility's one hundred new workers quickly adopted a tenacious bulldog as their mascot. "With millions of people out of work in the United States, we received applications from many parts of the country," Jehle wrote.[1] The chamber asked Globe to honor the region's prevailing wage scale; consequently, Jehle wrote, "common labor was employed at 35 cents an hour and the work day was nine hours. This is the cheapest labor that we have ever hired in the history of the company. Increases, of course, were given after reasonable length of time, but we could have employed thousands of men at this rate had we been able to use them."[2]

The McPherson project even made headlines in St. Paul, where the St. *Paul News* published a story in August 1932 stating that the refinery "makes Mr. O'Shaughnessy the largest individual refiner in the United States." O'Shaughnessy said he believed his ability to remain independent and his development of a network of independent dealers were the ingredients for what the newspaper called "his phenomenal success."[3]

"The rapidly increasing demand for higher octane anti-knock gasoline has necessitated the construction of the refinery at McPherson, Kansas," O'Shaughnessy told the *News*. "Many innovations in refinery operations and equipment will be employed in this modern plant and no expense will be spared in our efforts to continue production of the finest gasolines and oils for the modern motorist."[4]

By the time the refinery opened in March 1933, Lario had a 30,000-barrel potential in 2,040 acres under lease in the area and enjoyed "the unusual record of not having drilled a dry hole since it came to McPherson County," reported the *McPherson Daily Republican*. Globe's expansive operations involved much more than the refinery building; they also included a tank farm with a 370,000-barrel capacity (165,000 for crude oil and 205,000 for refined products), a pumping station with two 10,000-barrel tanks to move crude oil to the tank farm, pipeline connections, Missouri Pacific and Rock Island sidings to unload materials and ship refinery products by rail, and switching facilities with the Santa Fe and Union Pacific railroads. The refinery even boasted a laboratory with nine chemists.[5]

The Chamber of Commerce celebrated the opening with a five hundred-person dinner the evening of March 14, 1933, in the town's convention hall. W.J. Krehbiel, publisher of the *Daily Republican*, welcomed O'Shaughnessy and saluted his courage "to spend more than a million dollars in the face of opposition. We appreciate his nerve and applaud it heartily."[6]

O'Shaughnessy told the dinner audience that friends either questioned his sanity, having undertaken the project during the Great Depression, or considered him a trailblazer. He continued:

> It is overwhelming to me to receive this wonderful outburst of enthusiasm. It is impossible for me to express my appreciation in words for this wonderful reception you have given to me and my association. I am grateful for what the community has done for us. It is indeed a great happiness for me to be here. As soon as you get in this county the Depression disappears. There is happiness and contentment here. We have been well pleased at every turn we have made. You have helped us at every moment. When I decided to erect the plant at McPherson, my friends wanted to know if I was crazy, for the entire United States was shut down. But I could see the wonderful opportunity at McPherson and I could not resist the temptation to build the plant. Now I am sure we are at the threshold of a new era. We have gone through the worst of the storm. We are looking forward to the most wonderful period of prosperity the United States has ever seen.[7]

The following day, the *Daily Republican* published a special "Globe Refinery Edition" with stories covering more than a dozen pages. One story advised readers that O'Shaughnessy's career should serve as a "real inspiration" to young Americans:

> He typifies that true spirit of American ability, courage and resourcefulness, which drives steadily forward to the ultimate

goal—asking no favors, recognizing no obstacles. While
thousands of others during the recent past were yielded to
the popular fallacy that business was going to the eternal
bow-wows, I.A. O'Shaughnessy was driving full steam
ahead. . . . I.A. O'Shaughnessy is a real believer in America—
that type of man whose handiwork has been the real cause
of America's progress through all the generations since the
signing of the Declaration of Independence. With such men as
he at the helm of American business, the future is assured.[8]

In a statement published in the *Daily Republican,* O'Shaughnessy
said he was convinced that even in poor economic times, a business
"can be carried on profitably, regardless of seeming obstacles." The
McPherson refinery, he said, would demonstrate "an enduring faith
in the soundness of the American business structure, and a supreme
confidence in what the future holds."[9]

The *Daily Republican* was not the only Kansas newspaper to praise
Globe and O'Shaughnessy. The following month, the *Wichita Sunday
Eagle* published a special section with several stories about the company's investment at McPherson. The newspaper called the refinery
"unquestionably the most modern and complete in the entire Southwest," representing "a stupendous accomplishment" during such uncertain economic times:

I.A. O'Shaughnessy's dreams have come true—his vision has
blossomed into solid accomplishment. Because of his genius
and abilities, hundreds of families are enjoying a steady
income, living happy and contented lives. . . . In the short space
of 16 years, this man has risen from obscurity to the front
ranks of American's industrial leaders—one of, if not the very,
largest individual and independent producers and refiners of
petroleum products in the entire country."[10]

The *Sunday Eagle* also credited Jehle, a Wichita native. In a story
headlined "Humble Start No Handicap to Francis Jehle," the newspaper told of his rise from a clerical job to the vice presidency of Globe.
"His whole life, his heart and soul, are bound up in the activities of his

companies," the story read. "His is a success questionably founded upon sheer merit, hard work and faithfulness to every task assigned to him."[11]

Eighty years later, Patrick O'Shaughnessy reflected on the risks his grandfather took in constructing the refinery during the height of the Great Depression. It may not have been as risky as some suggested, Patrick said, because "the country is run on energy—even in a depression. The cost to build was relatively low. Labor was cheap, and the town was supportive. He had a bit of oil, so let's get a refinery in here. Opportunistic? Yes, more than crazy. He knew he had a gold mine."[12]

〰️

Four months after opening the McPherson refinery, Globe responded to President Franklin Delano Roosevelt's appeal to business and industry to participate in the National Industrial Recovery Act and put people back to work.

O'Shaughnessy announced Globe's adoption of a new staffing plan, effective August 1, for its refineries in McPherson, Lemont, and Blackwell, saying they would convert from three eight-hour shifts to four six-hour shifts and that no wages would be cut. The move would provide two hundred new jobs on top of five hundred existing jobs and would be the second time in three years that O'Shaughnessy had juggled employee shifts, having run two twelve-hour shifts until 1930.

"I have always believed in and advocated shorter working hours," O'Shaughnessy said in a July 21 *Wichita Beacon* story headlined, "Globe is First to Adopt New Recovery Plan." He continued, "Shorter working hours and fair and just wages for workers will afford the solution which the nation is seeking. The federal government, three years ago, should have led off on a plan of this kind and the industries of the country would have followed the government's example."[13]

Patrick O'Shaughnessy was not surprised that his grandfather made such a bold move. It was characteristic of the way he looked out for two interests—his own and that of his employees. "He could absorb the costs because the refineries were profitable," Patrick said, "and he knew it was the right thing to do—to help out the areas where he had his operations and to help out the country."[14]

The owner of Globe and Lario called on other corporations to follow his lead, emphasizing that unemployment and its lack of buying power were the roots of the nation's economic malaise:

> When the gigantic corporations, as well as the lesser ones,
> are satisfied to pile up less profits and the money is put into
> the hands of their employees, the real remedy for our ills will
> have been found. These workers will spend the money for their
> needs. It will immediately flow into circulation. The products
> of our machine age will be consumed. They will be bought and
> used for the comfort and happiness of the people and business
> will be restored.[15]

O'Shaughnessy also got personally involved in a new collaboration between the federal government and the oil industry. Roosevelt appointed him to the Planning and Coordinating Committee of the Petroleum Administration Board in Washington, DC. He would work closely for a dozen years, through the end of World War II, with Secretary of the Interior Harold Ickes, who served as committee chairman.

~~~~~

The lingering depression and losses of $700,000 at the McPherson and Blackwell refineries in 1934 prompted O'Shaughnessy to make one of the most difficult decisions of his career: to close the Blackwell refinery late that year.[16]

Carl Haun, the engineer who had overseen construction of the Blackwell plant for O'Shaughnessy seventeen years earlier, had left Globe in 1925 to go into business for himself. As president of the Blackwell Chamber of Commerce in 1934 and 1935, he appealed to O'Shaughnessy to spare the community:

> I know it is not necessary for me to detail to you the blow
> it is to this town to have your refinery not operating. . . . I
> know . . . it is impossible to operate a plant when you are
> losing money. . . . I know you realize that your payroll is the
> only payroll in this town which is of any particular benefit as

your employees receive sufficient money to indulge in some
of the luxuries of life as well as live on a higher plane than the
ordinary laborer or worker.[17]

In his response to Haun, O'Shaughnessy lamented how operating
under the National Industrial Recovery Act "has proven anything but
profitable for the independent refiner." Globe could have met all of its
gasoline refining needs for 1934 at the McPherson plant, he wrote:

But rather than shut down our Blackwell plant and throw a
lot of men out of employment, we elected to take our chances
in the hopes that conditions would get better each month so
that we would at least break even. This was a wild dream on
my part, and had I exercised a little common sense I should
have closed the plant down last January [1934]. However, after
having men working for you for 17 or 18 years it is not easy to
just walk away from them, after they have given you the best of
their services.[18]

A year later, O'Shaughnessy closed the Globe sales office in Blackwell and moved its personnel to Wichita, telling Haun that the decision to leave Blackwell was difficult. "With reference to our carrying
a substantial account at the local bank, you need have no fear of our
reducing the amount for quite some time, I am sure," O'Shaughnessy
wrote. "If at any time you feel as though you would like to have the
amount increased, let me know and I will see what I can do. Your boys
have accomplished a very wonderful job of reviving this bank."[19]

Haun again expressed his disappointment in a letter to
O'Shaughnessy. "To us, it is like the parting of old friends who are,
naturally, unable at this time to fully realize the significance of this
move, and of the very great loss we will suffer and Wichita will
gain. . . . In reality, we hardly know how to express in words our real
feeling of appreciation and the personal friendship we have had for
your organization. But, inasmuch as you are moving, we want you to
know that you have our best wishes."[20]

O'Shaughnessy also had noted in his letter to Haun, "You can rest
assured that I will always have a warm spot in my heart for Blackwell."

He continued to support causes there for many years, including a 1938 donation of $10,000 for the construction of a Catholic church, but with a caveat: it had to be matched by the end of the year by community members. "All say it is hard to raise money on short notice," Father Stephen Leven wrote to O'Shaughnessy in November, "but they have set about raising it with a spirit which makes me confident you will have the pleasure of being robbed of ten thousand dollars by us."[21]

Twelve days later, Leven reported pledges of $10,205. "It looks as though you have done a very good job, and apparently the parishioners there are anxious to have a new edifice," O'Shaughnessy wrote to Leven on December 7,[22] but the pastor knew where the true credit was due. "It has been the quietest fundraising campaign I have ever seen," he wrote to O'Shaughnessy before Christmas. "That it has raised the required amount is due almost entirely to your subscription . . . and we can never be sufficiently grateful to you."[23]

O'Shaughnessy later contributed another $3,500 to make the parish debt-free on completion of the church and a $1,000 match to purchase a rectory. In 1946, he made a donation to a new $300,000 hospital in Blackwell, and another donation followed in 1952.

~~~~~~

The early success of the McPherson operation continued throughout the 1930s. "M'Pherson Globe Refinery Is One Of Best In Country," stated a July 1935 headline in the *Wichita Eagle*, boasting that Globe "has become one of the Southwest's leading industrial units" and "has expanded into one of the largest independent oil refining units in the entire nation."[24] The refinery workforce had grown from 100 to 140 people in two years, and other operations on the 160-acre Globe parcel had expanded, including a tank truck loading dock that could handle up to 287,000 gallons of gasoline in twenty-four hours and would process 6 million gallons that month alone. The newspaper reported that "Globe products, which include four types of gasoline, three kinds of tractor fuel, grease, oil distillate, gas oil and fuel oil, are transported to Kansas, Nebraska, North Dakota, South Dakota, Iowa, Missouri, Colorado, and Oklahoma by the hundreds of trucks which load up at this bulk plant each day."[25]

Less than two months later, a *Wichita Eagle* headline read, "Old Oxford Oil Pool Gives Kansas Its Greatest Gushers," and the story told of oil shooting out of a 2,882-foot hole and over the countryside at the rate of 820 barrels an hour. The story calculated, based on a three-hour test of 2,725 barrels, that the well on land owned by Oxford Mayor Otto Wenrich had the daily potential of 21,799 barrels—or double the capacity of the McPherson refinery. A map showed dozens of leases held by Lario, Shell, and other oil companies in the Oxford pool.[26]

The growth of Lario and Globe also provided opportunities for advancement in the management ranks, and one who took advantage was John O'Shaughnessy, I.A.'s oldest son. He had joined Lario on September 1, 1932, after graduating from Georgetown University and studying for a year at Harvard Law School. He didn't receive any parental favors at the outset, according to his younger brother, Larry, who recalled that their father "was very basic in his way of doing things. He said, 'You've got to learn the business from the ground up,' so he put John on an oil rig where he was with the roughnecks; they were called that for good reason. They were hard-nosed guys, capable of treating a young man pretty roughly, especially an educated man, which they weren't. My mother used to worry about that."[27]

John eventually became a scout and learned more about leases and drilling. He worked in the Oklahoma City office before becoming vice president and general manager of Lario in January 1936, succeeding Jehle, who continued as vice president and general manager of Globe. John "is a young man of engaging personality," the *Wichita Eagle* wrote in January 1936. "He is extremely popular in the oil fraternity, and his friends predict for him a successful career as an oil man."[28]

"He was very bright," Patrick O'Shaughnessy said of his father (John), who established a comfortable working relationship with I.A. over nearly four decades. Their personalities complemented each other. "Dad was an introvert—smart and able, and he respected Granddad immensely," Patrick said. "Granddad was an extrovert—the life of a party, always joking and kidding, yet very serious when it came to business.[29]

Under John's "aggressive management," Jehle wrote, "an almost entirely new organization was formed" and operations continued to expand throughout Kansas.[30] New discoveries were made in the mid- to late-1930s in northwest Kansas, and Lario acquired leases in the Bemis-Shutts (Arbuckle) field in Ellis County in western Kansas, opening a field office in Hays. In 1936, Lario became the first company to discover oil in Barber County in south-central Kansas, but Patrick O'Shaughnessy referred to media references to "hot streaks" as "a little bit of hype. We were successful over time by taking good risks—and being lucky," he said. Some strikes were "serendipity."[31]

Deep Rock Oil Corporation, based in Tulsa, Oklahoma, was among Globe's crude oil suppliers, and its vice president, B.L. Majewski, corresponded regularly with O'Shaughnessy on both business matters and their work together on the Petroleum Industry War Council's marketing committee. The two men liked to bet on college football games, with $5 usually in play, although on one occasion Majewski won higher stakes and thanked his friend in a note: "I am attaching hereto paid invoice from my tailor covering the finest full dress suit ever tailored in Chicago. This is a suit of tails, one that I never would have purchased myself. I am grateful to you for it and if there is any satisfaction in losing a bet, please be consoled by the fact that I will not only give my daughters away in marriage in that suit, but will likely be buried in it."[32]

Globe also had an opportunity to explore oil territory in eastern Montana and western North Dakota. The Hole Brothers Refinery in Shelby, Montana, contacted O'Shaughnessy in 1937, but he responded that he had no interest. Shelby executives continued to write to him, and in January 1938 the Chambers of Commerce in Williston and Minot, North Dakota, informed him that oil journals had reported Globe was considering construction of a refinery in Shelby or in North Dakota. "For the present, we would not be interested," O'Shaughnessy wrote, "but can assure you that if anything should develop in the near future which would bring us into your territory, we will most surely get in touch with you."[33]

Nearly sixty years later, Lario began to assemble an 185,000-acre position targeting oil in the Williston Basin and in 2014 had what it defined as "a working interest" in more than 600 wells across Montana and North Dakota. The Williston Basin accounts for about half of Lario's oil sales today. "With Williston, Lario is an investor in different plays, and most are hitting," Patrick O'Shaughnessy said. "Wells are expensive to develop—up to $10 million each—but Lario has had only one dry well."[34]

———

With success, however, also came legal challenges.

In addition to dealing with lawsuits tied to the Winkler-Koch cracking process, Globe found itself under the federal government's scrutiny in 1936. A federal grand jury in Madison, Wisconsin, returned an indictment in July charging twenty-three oil companies, three trade publications, and fifty-eight oil company executives with antitrust violations, including conspiracy to fix tank car prices of gasoline in the Midwest. O'Shaughnessy and the Globe companies in Oklahoma, Kansas, and Illinois were among the defendants. A second indictment returned in November named twenty-four companies and forty-eight individuals, including the three Globe companies and O'Shaughnessy, and alleged they had conspired to fix jobber margins and adopt uniform jobber contracts.

"We, as well as the others named in the indictments, were surprised and shocked by this action," Jehle wrote. "A meeting was held and it was unanimously agreed that since, in the opinion of those indicted, no violation of any law had occurred that the matter would be fought to the last ditch."[35] Patrick O'Shaughnessy later found the charges hard to believe: "The government told them what to do," he said, referring to directives that came out of the Ickes committee, "and then sued them for doing it!"[36]

The defendants retained a New York law firm headed by William "Wild Bill" Donovan, a flamboyant lawyer who had successfully handled earlier cases for other companies. Trials began in October 1937 in Madison, and the following January the court found sixteen companies and thirty individuals guilty of violating the Sherman Act of 1890 by conspiring to fix prices, and levied $5,000 fines on each. The defendants appealed, and in July 1939 an appeals court reversed the district court decision. The Justice Department appealed, and in 1940 the US Supreme Court upheld the Madison court's decision.

The first set of indictments against O'Shaughnessy and Globe of Kansas was dismissed for lack of evidence, but Globe of Illinois and Globe of Oklahoma paid $5,000 fines in 1941. The second round of indictments against O'Shaughnessy and three Globe companies was dismissed in 1940.

5

Independent in Every Sense
of the Word

I was aware that to be an "O'Shaughnessy man"
was a signal mark of distinction in oil circles. I have come to realize
that your reputation was no accident, but based on your reputation
for fair and honest dealing and your willingness to listen to the
other fellow's views.

—EMPLOYEE H. GEORGE DONOVAN

I.A. O'Shaughnessy always knew one of the keys to success was a productive—and happy—workforce, and he took numerous steps throughout his ownership of the Globe and Lario companies to ensure that would remain the case.

In the process, he gained a reputation as a fair and progressive boss and "always enjoyed splendid relations with labor," Francis Jehle wrote, with employees knowing they had the freedom to take grievances directly to O'Shaughnessy. "Very few complaints ever were reported to him as every consideration was given to the employees if they felt they were being treated unfairly."[1]

Shortly after the Blackwell plant opened in 1917, O'Shaughnessy began to give turkeys to employees at Thanksgiving. He instituted paid vacations in the early 1920s—one week after one year, building to four weeks after twenty-five years—and took out group life insurance policies on all fifty-two Globe employees in 1924 after a refinery explosion and fire resulted in a death of a worker whose family had no insurance.[2]

Annual bonuses began in 1935, and a pension plan was instituted in 1950. Employees with a year's seniority received a half-month's salary for a bonus at Christmas, and those with ten years of service received a full month's salary. A December 1938 *Wichita Eagle* story, reporting a total of $100,000 in bonuses to six hundred employees, said Globe was "the first firm in the Middle West to give a bonus to its employees at Christmas." The story quoted O'Shaughnessy as saying that despite an unprofitable year and chaotic conditions in the industry, "we feel our employees should be taken care of for their loyalty to the company."[3] Jehle said that in lean years, the bonuses "were hardly justified, but in keeping with the unusually liberal policies in effect in our organization, they were always forthcoming."[4]

It was a philosophy that O'Shaughnessy maintained until the end of his life, grandson Patrick said, knowing that a content workforce also would be a productive workforce. "He believed in the concept of bonuses as recognition of performance, not necessarily as incentives. You also need to be fair to people. It wasn't out of generosity—it was out of fairness and what's the right thing to do."[5]

Employees especially appreciated the Christmas bonuses. Ralph Pierce, a Lemont refinery superintendent, wrote to O'Shaughnessy in January 1949 on behalf of sixty-five employees, saying, "A great many of the men have told me how much it meant to them and to their families and how much they had counted on it. [They] have come to me with a list of names which they would like to have me attach to my own letter as their means of saying, 'Thank you, Mr. O'Shaughnessy, for your kindness and generosity to us.'"[6]

Another Lemont employee, foreman Jerome Paddock, wrote

to O'Shaughnessy in 1951 to thank him for his Christmas bonus and turkey:

> In addition to bolstering the family budget when demands upon it are greatest, it gives one a feeling of satisfaction to know that he is working for an individual [who] takes more than just a cold business-like attitude towards his fellow man. Many do not feel, as I myself previously felt for the past thirteen years, that propriety will allow them to thank you by note, still one regularly hears words of praise and thanks passed between employees for your generosity.[7]

H. George Donovan of Chicago wrote thank-you letters to O'Shaughnessy for more than thirty years. Donovan went to work for Globe in 1939 and said in December 1950, after receiving a Christmas bonus, "It is good to be known as an O'Shaughnessy man!" He repeated those words in a 1958 letter congratulating the O'Shaughnessys on their golden wedding anniversary:

> Before I became associated with your company, I was aware that to be an "O'Shaughnessy man" was a signal mark of distinction in oil circles, and it was indeed a proud day in my life when I finally made the grade. Since then I have come to realize that your reputation was no accident, but rather it was based on . . . your reputation for fair and honest dealing and your willingness to listen to the other fellow's views.[8]

As he neared retirement in 1971, Donovan wrote, "I can truthfully say that I have never yet met with an ex-Globe employee who did not speak fondly of his days with [the company], and I for one can understand why. I want you to know that I have always appreciated your friendliness and kindness over the years." In a final letter, on the occasion of O'Shaughnessy's eighty-seventh birthday in 1972, Donovan wrote, "I [am] writing to you to congratulate you on a most successful life both in the matter of business success but more important your generous contributions to the welfare of your fellow man. May this bread which has been cast upon waters be returned to you one-hundred fold in health, happiness, and continued longevity."[9]

The benefits and bonuses had their desired effect, according to a *National Petroleum News* profile on O'Shaughnessy in November 1944. "That psychoanalyst the big Irishman from St. Paul had on the company payroll for nearly a year a couple of summers ago also helped several employees find more contentment, 'tis being said," the profile stated.[10] Patrick O'Shaughnessy laughed when asked whether his grandfather really hired a psychologist, and wondered if the writer made the comment tongue in cheek. "*Granddad* was the psychoanalyst," Patrick said.[11]

Yet O'Shaughnessy also knew where he had to draw the line with employees and money. A Globe employee in Chicago asked him in 1934 for an $18,000 loan to buy a house but was turned down because O'Shaughnessy didn't want to set a precedent. "You can readily see if I would make an advance to one employee I could hardly refuse the next man without causing some unpleasantness," he wrote. "I believe that every man should own a home and admire your thoughts, and am certainly sorry that I cannot come to your assistance at this time."[12]

One consequence of the National Industrial Recovery Act, which the US Supreme Court ruled unconstitutional in 1935, was an effort to unionize more workers. An operating engineers union targeted McPherson to become the first independent plant in the Mid-Continent area to fly the union banner. Union organizers claimed they signed a majority of Globe employees but could not offer proof, and a majority of employees "felt they were being treated better than others in similar positions and had no desire to join any union," Jehle wrote. "Several came to me and told me of intimidation and threats made to them if they did not join."[13]

A 1937 *Wichita Eagle* story reported that 100 percent of Globe's 130 employees in McPherson signed a petition expressing approval of the company's methods in dealing with "the labor situation" at the plant and would not seek representation with an outside organization. The petition stated that Globe's management practices prove "that we can accomplish more by dealing direct with our employer than through some outside agency or organization." E.J. Macy, superintendent of the McPherson refinery, told the *Eagle* that O'Shaughnessy felt "gratified at this splendid expression of faith."[14]

Management and employees subsequently agreed to form the Globe Employees Benevolent Council, and workers initially paid dues of 50 cents a month that were matched by the company. The proceeds provided for sick benefits and loans. "We were never bothered again with any indication of unsatisfactory labor conditions as long as we operated the McPherson plant," Jehle wrote.[15]

Workers at the Lemont refinery formed an independent union, apparently in the late 1930s, and the AFL-CIO intensified efforts to enlist them. What Jehle called "unrest and unsettled conditions . . . encouraged by a small minority of the workers" led to a contract with the CIO in 1946, and on May 3, 1952, the Lemont employees followed the lead of unions at other refineries around the country and went on strike. "We were told by our employees that if they did not walk out, a picket line manned by strikers from other plants would be established which might result in injury to our men," Jehle wrote. The strike was settled twelve days later and "on terms which had been offered to the union before the work ceased. This is the only strike that we experienced in our entire business career."[16]

O'Shaughnessy said little publicly about the union votes and the strike, and Patrick O'Shaughnessy later would say only that his grandfather was "disappointed" in what had transpired.[17]

O'Shaughnessy and his companies generally received deferential, if not positive, coverage from area newspapers and trade publications—perhaps because he was effective in controlling messages, if not the media themselves. One exception of sorts occurred when Earl Lamm, a writer for the *National Petroleum News,* set out to write a profile on O'Shaughnessy. Lamm did not manage to line up an interview with O'Shaughnessy but wrote the story anyway.[18] Nearly seven decades later, Patrick O'Shaughnessy reacted to Lamm's numerous observations in the November 1944 story:[19]

Lamm wrote that O'Shaughnessy, at the age of fifty-nine, "retains his vigorous 'bark' when he gets into action . . . particularly when something irritates him." Patrick said he never saw the "bark," but that his grandfather had a "quick wit" that some people might misunderstand.

The profile described O'Shaughnessy as "an aggressive individualist . . . who bears the reputation of always operating as a lone hand and under his own steam and yet delegates practically all operating authority once he has a business or refinery set up and put 'on stream.'" Patrick said his grandfather was aggressive "in the sense he was forward thinking. He saw things others didn't see. Whether it was risk taking or foresight, I don't know, because he wasn't a gambler. He was an entrepreneur."

"He is seldom in any of these offices and then never seemingly to operate his business," the profile reported, stating that he kept in touch by phone and spent winters in Florida. "Only one or two men in his whole organization have any conception of the overall picture. He is one of the country's largest independent oil operators—and the word 'independent' as applied to him carries its full meaning. I.A. O'Shaughnessy runs I.A. O'Shaughnessy's business to suit I.A. O'Shaughnessy." Patrick's response: "He kept his own counsel. I don't think he went out and said, 'What do you think?' But he listened closely to his associates' advice."

"Once he hires a man, he never fires him," Lamm wrote, "but if he does not fit in the job for which he was hired, he is shifted about until he finds a niche into which he does fit." Patrick said that tendency simply was his grandfather hewing to his philosophy: "He had loyalty to people."

O'Shaughnessy "is an ardent believer in free enterprise and acts upon that belief," Lamm wrote. "He is not backward about telling people where they get off." Patrick quibbled with the "get off" characterization, calling his grandfather "conservative, candid, and forthright—but not offensive."

Lamm wrote, "He maintains his separate St. Paul office afar from the field as an aid in preserving a clear, unbiased, level-headed outlook upon his many business interests." There was truth to that observation, Patrick said, but his grandfather also favored St. Paul because it kept him and Lillian close to their family and friends.

When the story hit print, Lamm sent O'Shaughnessy a copy with a note. "I thought you would be interested in the story concerning your activities," he said, adding that it represented material "gathered from various sources. I hope you like it."[20] O'Shaughnessy responded:

> I was very much surprised when I read your article. About a
> year ago you called at my St. Paul office asking for a story. At
> the time I told you I was not looking for publicity. Apparently
> you have lots of ways of finding out things as there was news
> in your article that I myself had quite forgotten. However, now
> that the damage has been done I should be writing you a letter
> of appreciation. Anyway, I am sending you my best wishes for a
> very Merry Christmas and a Happy New Year.[21]

Lamm replied, "About that article. I did what I imagine you would have done under the circumstances—got it the hard way when the easy road was closed. However, I also imagine you could give me some interesting additions to the story if you should decide to do so."[22]

~~~~~

One theory in the Lamm story—that O'Shaughnessy "never takes a financial interest in anything he does not control"—had been put to the test several years earlier.

O'Shaughnessy, O.H. Ingram, and Fred Koch of the Winkler-Koch Engineering Company of Wichita formed the Wood River Oil & Refining Company in December 1939. They planned to open a $2 million refinery in 1941 in Hartford, Illinois, north of St. Louis on the Mississippi River, near its confluence with the Missouri River and close to several transcontinental pipelines. The 15,000-barrel refinery's location made it possible to draw crude oil from almost anywhere—by pipeline and tank cars or from barges on the Mississippi, Illinois, Ohio, and Missouri rivers.

In a December 1939 letter to O'Shaughnessy and Ingram, both of whom lived in Minnesota, Koch wrote that while he expected their business venture "would work smoothly, fairly, and harmoniously," he was concerned about a potential conflict of interest between Globe and Wood River:

While the Globe employees are very experienced and capable of purchasing crude, nevertheless it is only to be assumed that if any particular bargains in crude oil come along that they will be used to go to [the Globe refinery at] Lemont. It seems to me that it should be understood now that the Wood River company is to have an equal opportunity in the purchase of cheap crude with any of the other Globe companies, and that Mr. O'Shaughnessy should not put any stones in the way of the corporation taking the necessary steps to accomplish that end.[23]

Koch went on to say that "Mr. O'Shaughnessy, with his superior experience and business judgment, should undoubtedly have the largest voice in controlling the business policies of the organization, but on the other hand he should make some concessions for the wishes of the other stockholders."[24]

Koch frequently sought O'Shaughnessy's advice on a number of management issues. They had a respectful but occasionally testy relationship, and Koch frequently wrote to his partner about a variety of concerns. In October 1941, for example, he thanked O'Shaughnessy "very kindly for the salary check. It will help pay the grocery man, also the bartender and the income tax guy. However, you are getting short-changed in this business, and I would feel a lot better about it if you would take a good salary and a good rate of interest for the money that you have advanced."[25] In his reply, O'Shaughnessy suggested the Wood River employees receive turkeys at Thanksgiving, and Koch later wrote:

As you know we have had the devil's own time with labor at Wood River. The class of people there plus the way they have been pushed around in the past has created an attitude of sullen rebellious hatred toward industry. This has been capitalized on by so-called labor leaders to build the union setup. The turkeys you sent on Thanksgiving did a world of good. [We] received some very touching letters and one of the welders said, "By God. I've been working for thirty years and this is the first time anybody ever gave me something for nothing.'"[26]

In December, Koch asked O'Shaughnessy how he might handle Jehle's opposition to $500 Christmas bonuses for several managers whose salaries ranged from $250 to $300 per month. "These men have been very loyal and have worked long hours and over weekends without compensation," Koch wrote. "Quite a number of men under them make more money than they do due to overtime. This is bound to create dissatisfaction unless we compensate for it in some way. Francis agrees with this but thinks we should raise their salary." Koch ultimately recommended $500 bonuses for five managers and $100 bonuses for two: "This $2,700 will pay big dividends in loyalty to the company. . . . The two weeks bonus for the rest of the boys is going to do wonders if the turkey deal is any indication."[27]

In October 1942, O'Shaughnessy wrote to Koch on a number of matters, including Koch's concern that the federal government was putting "great pressure" on Wood River to complete an alkylation plant as soon as possible. Said O'Shaughnessy, "First, I am sure it is not necessary to be waving the flag about patriotism to me. For your information, I have devoted not only a lot of my time, but a lot of money in assisting the war effort in every possible way, and for this I have never received any fees."[28]

O'Shaughnessy and Koch also exchanged letters about how to handle a manager Koch felt wasn't needed at Wood River. It's not clear what O'Shaughnessy did, but a frustrated Koch unloaded in a letter to him:

> If you had come directly to me . . . it would have saved me some
> embarrassment. Frankly speaking, if you continue to follow the
> same practise [sic] of going directly to the men at Wood River
> then I cannot function any more in connection with this plant.
> I seem to have the unhappy faculty of keeping you in an uproar
> about half the time. In addition, there seems to be someone
> who continually carries tales to you regarding me, nearly all
> of which are distorted. Having been an independent agent for
> seventeen years, this gets a bit tiresome . . . In view of your

highly autocratic and overbearing nature, and my own equally peculiar characteristics, it seems to me that we would all be happier if you and Hank were to take me out of Wood River.[29]

O'Shaughnessy apparently grew weary of the conflicts. In July 1944, he offered to sell to Koch and Ingram his interest in the Illinois refinery as well as a Wood River gasoline and oil terminal on the Mississippi River in St. Paul and the Globe Oil Barge Company. The two men accepted the offer.

Patrick O'Shaughnessy suggested that his grandfather's unwillingness to supply the Wood River refinery with more oil from the Texas-Empire pipeline, which was furnishing the Lemont plant, ultimately ended the partnership. "They wanted a piece of it," Patrick said, "and he wasn't going to do it. As far as I know, it was the first time he had business partners, and he did the refinery as a favor to Ingram. I suspect he thought Ingram would be on his side. When he wasn't, Granddad sold out."[30]

6

"To Hell with the Profits. We Have a War to Win."

That's when I coined the slogan, "Gasoline is ammunition, use it wisely." You see, I didn't say not to use it. Hell, we tried that with Prohibition!

—I. A. O'SHAUGHNESSY

The Wood River project may have tested I.A. O'Shaughnessy's patience, but he couldn't have been more pleased with operations in Kansas as Globe and Lario entered a new decade.

The *McPherson Daily Republican* heralded the eighth anniversary of the groundbreaking ceremony for the refinery. A 1940 story reported that employment had more than doubled, to 225, and that the refinery had processed 27,414,000 barrels of Kansas crude oil—an average of nearly 4 million barrels a year—with much of the oil coming from wells in the McPherson area. Globe had paid $1.9 million in salaries over the last eight years, the newspaper added.[1]

Less than a year later, the *Daily Republican* announced that Globe would build a 225-mile, 6-inch products pipeline from the McPherson refinery to Council Bluffs, Iowa. The project would have the capacity to expand to 15,000 barrels a day, depending on the number of pumping stations, and would cut the refinery's tanker trade in half.[2] The $2 million pipeline opened in December 1941, with a storage capacity of 375,000 barrels at the receiving tank farm.

Earlier in the year, on March 27, Globe and Lario had moved its Wichita headquarters from the Union National Bank Building into new offices at 301 South Market Street in Wichita to deal with the growth of the companies. (The building remains the home office of Lario today, with Patrick O'Shaughnessy working there; his cousin Michael O'Shaughnessy has offices in Denver.)

Another Globe expansion project was announced in November 1941 to help deal with shortages of aviation gasoline needed for the war effort. Globe submitted a proposal to the federal Petroleum Administration for War to construct a 1,000-barrel, 100-octane gasoline plant as an auxiliary to the Lemont refinery, but was informed of a more immediate need for cumene and codimer, two aviation gasoline components. The plant went into production in October 1942, more than two months ahead of schedule. "It was an entirely new venture and we had to learn the know-how as we went along," Jehle wrote. "We immediately exceeded the hoped-for production both in quantity and quality and by the end of the war had more than doubled the original output. On different occasions the Petroleum Administrator for War wrote congratulating us for our phenomenal increase in production and expressing sincere appreciation for our cooperation and contribution to the war effort."[3]

Jehle's enthusiasm notwithstanding, Globe was disappointed in its inability to win federal approval for a 100-octane aviation gasoline refinery. "I realize fully your acute desire to have an installation at Lemont and feel a very deep regret in not being able to recommend such an installation, particularly in view of your long and extremely helpful efforts to find a place in the 100-octane aviation gasoline program," wrote George Parkhurst of the Petroleum Administration for War in a May 1943 letter to Globe's George Woodruff in Chicago. Two days later,

Globe chemist C.K. Reiman wrote to O'Shaughnessy, "This business of [the feds] always saying 'no' to Globe is beginning to get me down."[4]

In spite of such setbacks, O'Shaughnessy and Globe pursued other opportunities with the Roosevelt administration, well aware of the war's virtually insatiable appetite for petroleum products. Globe produced an all-purpose Army-Navy gasoline and a special diesel fuel for the Navy (and later produced jet engine fuel during the Korean War).[5]

"That's when I coined the slogan, 'Gasoline is ammunition, use it wisely,'" O'Shaughnessy later told a newspaper reporter. "You see, I didn't say not to use it. Hell, we tried that with Prohibition!"[6]

Aside from its federal contracts, Globe found it difficult to secure enough crude oil to operate the Lemont refinery, which had expanded to a daily capacity of 25,000 barrels. Oil had to be obtained from south Texas and delivered to the plant on river barges or shipped from Wyoming in tank cars. "The freight rate on this latter oil was so high that the operation proved unprofitable," Jehle wrote, "but Mr. O'Shaughnessy thought that it was better to operate the plant at capacity as a contribution to the war effort even if part of the operation was uneconomical and unprofitable."[7]

O'Shaughnessy's philosophy on the war may have best been described in a quote that led off a 1942 St. *Paul Pioneer Press* story. "To hell with the profits," he said. "We have a war to win." He described his efforts as chairman of the Minnesota petroleum industry's scrap rubber collection efforts and encouraged employees in Kansas and Illinois to recover scrap metal, buy war bonds, and write letters to soldiers—all in the quest for victory. "Where else in the world can we build our own lives, select our own wives regardless of blood strains, raise our children to worship the God of their own choice in such manner as they wish?" he said. "I offer my own boys. They are precious to this old man. Precious far beyond what I can tell. Yet unless this ideal country is maintained, there is nothing for these boys and my grandchildren."[8]

O'Shaughnessy also felt strongly about his involvement in war activity in the nation's capital. Secretary of the Interior Ickes had appointed him in November 1941 to the newly created Petroleum Industry War Council, a think tank of sixty-six executives, and to its Refining Committee. "He had to do things like that," Patrick O'Shaughnessy said. "The independent refiners wanted him to be present because they knew he was smart and able and had connections in Washington."[9]

O'Shaughnessy admired Ickes but worried that he might be reassigned to other duties in the Roosevelt cabinet. Responding to newspaper stories, O'Shaughnessy sent a telegram to Roosevelt in November 1942 saying that oil industry leaders were "very much alarmed" by rumors that Ickes would be moved to the Department of Labor. "In my opinion, Secretary Ickes is perhaps the most capable man in public office to handle the affairs of the oil industry because of his past experience," O'Shaughnessy wrote. "May I respectfully request that Mr. Ickes be retained as Oil Coordinator for the duration? A change at this time might prove disastrous." Ickes remained as petroleum administrator.[10]

While O'Shaughnessy sought to cooperate with the war effort, the federal government's actions vexed him at times. He was not shy about letting Washington bureaucrats know how he felt, as indicated by a December 1943 letter:

Responding to your recent decision not to allow any compensatory adjustment for high rail costs to get west Texas crude to refineries in District Two to those who are desirous of keeping their plants operating or increasing their runs if they should happen to be in the excess profit bracket, to say that I was shocked is putting it mildly. . . . What we had in mind, and I am sure I can speak for others, was to put idle refinery capacity to use during these critical times when petroleum products are so urgently needed. First, for the war effort and secondly, for civilian consumption. While the war itself is paramount in our minds, we must not lose sight of the fact that our whole economy has been built up around mobile transportation. If that were to collapse then we would be in for real trouble. . . . Millions of people are literally starving for more petroleum products, which we can give them if our refineries could be run to capacity. Don't you think your decision needs reconsideration?"[11]

One of O'Shaughnessy's colleagues on the federal committee during World War II was Bob McDowell, whose parents had provided O'Shaughnessy with a room during his early refining years in Blackwell, Oklahoma. McDowell was vice president of the Mid-Continent Petroleum Corporation in Tulsa, Oklahoma, in the 1940s, and he told O'Shaughnessy in a 1958 letter that he would always "remember vividly and value highly" their work during the war:

> You contributed much to the welfare of our industry and
> to our country because of your g/ood judgment and your
> unselfish and courageous attitude with respect to the necessity
> of maintaining a healthy atmosphere in which the "little
> fellow" could live, grow and prosper. I shall never forget the
> time that . . . you came to my rescue and that of my company
> by simply stating that "if Bob McDowell says he is in trouble,
> I know he is, and if this board refuses to take action, my
> company will help him out."[12]

Yet the war discouraged even O'Shaughnessy, the stoutest of patriots. "During these troublesome times, one finds it very difficult to think of Christmas in its true light," he wrote to a friend after the Japanese attack on Pearl Harbor. "With the world on fire, the Son of God has been cast aside. Let us hope and pray it will be for but a short time so that, when Christmas comes again, we can truly say 'Peace on Earth, Good Will toward men.'"[13]

~~~~~~

McDowell's Mid-Continent Petroleum was one company that O'Shaughnessy considered in 1943 when he decided to sell the McPherson refinery, which had expanded to 20,000 barrels a day—double its original capacity—and 265 employees.

The August 1 sale to the National Cooperative Refinery Association of North Kansas City, Missouri, for a reported $5 million, surprised many in the industry because, in Jehle's words, "the plant was in first-class shape, was operating on a profitable basis, and with the products pipeline [to Council Bluffs] was able to compete from a sales standpoint." But Jehle also acknowledged that two other concerns—lack of a long-term dependable source of crude oil and O'Shaughnessy's "personal affairs"—were influential in the sale.[14]

The latter apparently had to do with inheritance and estate tax consequences that, in the event of O'Shaughnessy's death, "might virtually have wiped out his entire estate," wrote Keith Fanshier, editor (and later publisher) of the *Oil Daily* newspaper, in an August 1943 editorial headlined "Salute to the Inevitable." While O'Shaughnessy was only fifty-eight at the time—and would live another thirty years—he suggested to Fanshier in an interview that the funds generated from the refinery sale would provide the resources to handle any onerous tax demands if he died. "I feel the day of private initiative is passing," Fanshier quoted O'Shaughnessy in the editorial. "Certainly individual enterprise is being subjected to increasing pressure and if the present trends continue it will become virtually extinct."[15]

Fanshier sympathized with O'Shaughnessy's predicament and tried to refute speculation in the oil industry that he was preparing to retire. "He has no thought of quitting the oil business," Fanshier wrote, "nor of disposing of any other of his still extensive holdings in the industry. . . . Today this man of intense loyalties and energetic character is continuing his career vigorously."[16]

It should have been no surprise that Fanshier spoke highly of O'Shaughnessy in his editorials. He sought both O'Shaughnessy's advice and his money over the years, and O'Shaughnessy served on the newspaper's board of directors for a time. He guaranteed six-figure loans from the First National Bank of St. Paul to the *Oil Daily* in 1953 and again in 1957,[17] and Fanshier sought assistance with potential oil industry advertisers. "I don't know how far you may wish to go in suggesting to these people that they should cooperate with the *Oil Daily*," he wrote to O'Shaughnessy on one occasion. "I think telephone calls to them [if] you know them would help."[18]

McDowell, too, understood O'Shaughnessy's decision to sell the McPherson refinery, and he urged his friend to remain active:

> Although the sale of your refinery ordinarily would bring forth
> a lot of sentimental gush about one of the patriarchs of the

industry passing from the picture, I rather feel that this is not at all the case in this instance but that you are just a little like the sailor who wisely "trims sails" before heading into a storm. I sincerely hope that you will continue your active interest in all industry affairs for a long time to come because you have carved a place for yourself . . . that cannot easily be filled.[19]

On July 31, the evening before the sale became effective, the refinery's new owners held a dinner in the McPherson Convention Hall to assure employees their jobs were safe and their wages and benefits would not change. A telegram from O'Shaughnessy was read during the dinner:

> Probably the toughest decision that I have ever been forced
> to make was the sale of this plant . . . and it was done only
> after several months deliberation and your assurance that the
> present employees would be retained in their present positions.
> As you no doubt know, the welfare of those who have worked
> for me has always been foremost in my thoughts. These men
> and women have been very loyal to the Globe organization,
> and you will find them just as loyal to yours if they continue to
> receive the same treatment that they have received from us.[20]

After the refinery sale, which also included Globe's Council Bluffs operation, O'Shaughnessy received a letter from employee E.L. Beeman thanking him for the way he treated employees:

> All of the employees in the truck department have asked
> me to express their appreciation for the bonus checks they
> received. . . . I am sure that I am expressing the sentiment
> of everyone when I say that it has been a great pleasure to
> work for you. I do not believe that any of us have ever been
> connected with a company that seems to always go out of
> its way to make things more pleasant and agreeable for the
> employees and it is with extreme regret that we sever our
> connection with the Globe Oil and Refining Co. All of us will
> always have a warm place in our hearts for you.[21]

The McPherson refinery remains in business to this day—more than eighty years after O'Shaughnessy built it. CHS Inc., a farm and energy cooperative based in Inver Grove Heights, Minnesota, purchased the refinery from the National Cooperative Refinery Association in 2011. Two years later, CHS announced a $327 million expansion from 85,000 barrels to 100,000 barrels.[22]

‒‒‒‒⁓‒‒‒‒

The McPherson sale, followed by the Wood River sale the following year, would allow O'Shaughnessy to focus on Globe's refinery operations in Lemont and Lario's exploration and production efforts, the *National Petroleum News* speculated in November 1944. The newspaper cited Lemont's expanded capacity, to 27,000 barrels a day, and the recent opening of branch production offices in Oklahoma City, Oklahoma; Midland, Texas; and Jackson, Mississippi.[23]

O'Shaughnessy also joined several independents in exploring whether to form a company to obtain an interest in a neutral zone between Saudi Arabia and Kuwait in the Middle East. A 1947 meeting in the offices of Phillips Petroleum Company in Bartlesville, Oklahoma, resulted in the formation of the American Independent Oil Company, which agreed the following year to pay $7,250,000 for a concession with a land area of 2,500 square miles, plus a royalty of $2.50 per ton on all oil produced. Globe and Lario together owned 6.5 percent of the company and sold half their interest in 1950 for their earlier total investment. Oil was discovered in the Middle East in 1908, and American Independent later received about four-tenths of one percent interest in Iranian oil fields and a refinery.[24] Lario sold its remaining interest in American Independent in the early 1960s.

O'Shaughnessy incorporated another company, American-Canadian Oil, in Kansas in 1949 and opened offices in Calgary, Alberta. Lario and AmCan merged in March 1952.

Capacity at Lemont grew to the point where Globe began to process crude oil there after World War II for Pure Oil Company. The original quantity was "only a few thousand barrels a day," Jehle said, but gradually increased to 12,000 barrels, or 25 percent of the refinery's

48,000-barrel capacity. In 1953, Pure approached O'Shaughnessy with a proposal to purchase the Lemont plant:

> They informed us that if they were unsuccessful in completing the deal, they would quite likely build a new plant in the general vicinity of Chicago. They were familiar with the plant and its operation and were satisfied with its condition. It was not an easy matter to agree to let the plant go. In fact, Mr. O'Shaughnessy said it was the hardest decision from a business standpoint that he had ever been called upon to make.[25]

The sale occurred July 31, 1954, but rumors had begun to circulate earlier. Jehle and Pure representatives met a few days before the transaction to share the news with Globe's supervisors. "Many of the men said they hated to see the sale made," Jehle wrote, "but generally they expressed themselves as being thankful for the opportunity to have had the privilege to work for as fine and understanding a man as Mr. O'Shaughnessy."[26]

Oil Workers International Local No. 517 thanked him for his "ceaseless effort" to improve working conditions for employees. "Your splendid cooperation and willingness to meet with our committees on any and all our problems have been deeply appreciated," a letter from Local 517 officers stated. "It is the sincere wish of each of us that your future will be one of good luck, health, and happiness."[27]

One grateful employee was Archie Abrams Jr. of Lemont. He retired that August and later wrote a long letter to O'Shaughnessy, thanking him for providing employment for him and his two sons. "I know that in building the Globe organization you had many tough problems, headaches and sleepless nights and it was not a bed of roses," Abrams said, "but you have shown exceptional ability, determination, sound judgment and unquestionable character . . . yes, you have done a wonderful job and it will stand as a landmark in this community for many years to come."[28]

In his reply to Abrams, O'Shaughnessy wrote, "It is a source of great satisfaction to one when he receives such a letter as yours from a former employee. It makes one feel that perhaps one's life is not wasted when those who have worked for him will take the time out to write such a nice letter as you did."[29]

The growth of the Lemont operations over the quarter century that O'Shaughnessy owned the refinery was stunning: from fifty to sixty employees and a 3,000-barrel daily capacity in 1929 to seven hundred employees and 48,000 in barrels in 1954. The sale also effectively signaled the end of Globe Refining, thirty-seven years after O'Shaughnessy opened his first refinery in Blackwell, Oklahoma. The focus now would be on exploration and development.

Patrick O'Shaughnessy mused that the Lemont sale was similar in some respects to the McPherson sale a decade earlier in that his grandfather knew he was not getting any younger, plus he was more interested in attending to his philanthropic interests: "He was sixty-nine years old, and there would be a changing of the guard. He sold his refineries and terminals because he may have been ready to retire. He was older, [George] Woodruff was older, Francis [Jehle] was older, and John and Don were involved in E and P [exploration and production], not refineries. He never looked again at the refining business after the 1950s because it's too cyclical."[30]

O'Shaughnessy never forgot the city where he built part of his fortune. Eight years after he sold the Lemont refinery, he received a request from the Lemont Teen Club for a donation to its new building, which would cost $17,000. "We are presuming upon your past association with the Village of Lemont, its adults, and its young people," a club member wrote. "We feel that you always have been, and will be, a part of the community to whose future you contributed so much. . . . We are asking if from the kindness of your heart you would make a donation to our Building Fund."[31] He sent a check for $1,000.

Despite the exit from the refinery business, Globe kept active for several years in supplying Chicago-area jobbers such as Southside and Perfect Power with refined products. Globe contracted with Pure to process 12,000 barrels of crude oil a day and with the Texas Company for 3,000 barrels a day at its Tulsa plant. Standard Oil Company of New Jersey purchased Southside and Perfect Power in 1956, and Globe received Standard stock for its interest.[32]

As much as O'Shaughnessy was involved in oil deals that amounted to millions of dollars, he also kept a close eye on every penny that came across his desk. In a November 1959 letter to the president of Aberdeen Petroleum Corporation in Tulsa, he wrote, "I am returning check #34956 for 35 cents which has been sent to me by mistake. To my knowledge I do not have any stock in the Aberdeen Petroleum Co." The company responded with a letter stating that he was the registered owner of five shares of stock and thus was entitled to the 35-cent dividend. The company later offered to buy the stock, and in January 1961 O'Shaughnessy wrote, "If the offer is still open, I will be glad to sell."[33]

Jehle's history of Globe ended in 1958, and shortly thereafter he retired. He stayed in touch with O'Shaughnessy, who occasionally sent money to his first employee and his wife, Helen. Two such checks, each for $3,000, arrived in Jehle's mail in August 1961, and he responded the following day: "These gifts, of course, are greatly appreciated. Once again, I was reminded of the many things you have done for me and my family during the past 44 years. They started on the day I met you and have been continuous ever since. We certainly shall never forget these many, substantial favors. Our fondest wish is that God may continue to bless you with good health and that you will live to enjoy many more years."[34]

Four months later, O'Shaughnessy sent a Christmas present to the Jehles, and Francis again responded with gratitude. "I was agreeably surprised to learn of your gift of 30 shares of Lario preferred stock to each Helen and me," Jehle wrote to O'Shaughnessy. "This, in addition to the Christmas bonus, makes a very outstanding present. Many thanks for remembering us in this manner. As I have told you before, over the years you have been most kind and liberal to me and my family. You may rest assured that you will always have our gratitude."[35]

O'Shaughnessy's Christmas gifts to the Jehles continued. He sent the couple $6,000 in late 1963, and Jehle expressed his thanks. "You have always been very generous to us," he wrote. "The outstanding thing in my life has been my association with you for almost 47 years."[36]

During the 1950s and 1960s, Lario's primary exploration efforts targeted Oklahoma and west Texas, with Donald O'Shaughnessy—I.A.'s youngest son—managing the office in Midland, Texas, beginning in 1952. Lario began to participate in 1969 in joint ventures in Alberta with companies such as Koch Industries, Chevron, and ExxonMobil; an exploration office opened in Calgary in the early 1970s and remained active until 2011, when the Canadian operations were sold as part of a larger strategy to consolidate assets and activities in the United States.

O'Shaughnessy kept tabs on Lario activities well into his eighties, and that was at times a distraction to sons John and Don, who each served as president in turn, respectively, from 1952 to 1966 and 1966 to 1985. "After my father 'retired,' so to speak, if he entered a room, all attention would be on him and not John, the company president," son Larry said. "Both my brothers said that the most distasteful aspect of being in the business was being given authority to make decisions, but my father would frequently overrule, or say, 'Don't you know what you're doing?'"[37]

John O'Shaughnessy remained active in Lario until the early 1980s and died in 1987. His son, Patrick, graduated from Notre Dame in 1965 and moved back to his hometown of Wichita to work in the investment business before joining Lario in 1969 to manage its stock and bonds portfolio. By the early 1980s, Lario ownership was highly fragmented within the family and its five branches, each represented by one of I.A.'s children. The John and Donald branches founded O'S Companies and bought out the Larry, Eileen, and Marian branches in 1985. Patrick became president and Donald's son Michael ran the company's Denver operation, where he had moved in 1977 to open an exploration office to pursue Rocky Mountain and Williston Basin opportunities. Michael remains in Denver today and Patrick is in Wichita.

Lario has interests and operations in Kansas, Oklahoma, Texas, New Mexico, Colorado, Wyoming, Montana, North Dakota, Ohio, and California, with a fluctuating breakdown of 75 percent oil and 25 percent natural gas. The primary focus for investments is in horizontal drilling in North Dakota, with working interests in more than six hundred wells in the Bakken/Three Forks play in 2014, according to the company's website:

> So as it was in I.A.'s day, Lario is still identifying and pursuing
> select opportunities with innovation and hard work. . . . In its
> 87-year history, Lario has flourished during the good times
> and stoically weathered many industry lows with the help
> of experienced management and dedicated employees, all of
> whom take great pride in the company's success and longevity
> in an industry where both can be elusive. As Lario moves
> toward the end of its first century, the O'Shaughnessys are
> already looking ahead to a second century of success.[38]

PART II

7

Home and Family: A Refuge

Mom was afraid, at first, that he would lose his money, so she was
always very careful. She thought he was extravagant. At one time
she said, "Can't you just earn enough money to pay our bills?" He
replied, "Should I then just turn off the faucet?"
—Son Larry O'Shaughnessy

As much as I.A. O'Shaughnessy thrived on his success in the oil business and found great joy in giving away tens of millions of dollars, his highest priority was his family. He took great pride in the five children he and Lillian brought into life and raised, and that pride later manifested in his grandchildren and great-grandchildren. Family was the center of his life.

The O'Shaughnessys bounced around the country during their early years of marriage—first to Houston, then to Dallas, Denver, Wichita, and finally Blackwell, Oklahoma—as "Nashe" (as Lillian called him) moved from one job to the next. Lillian tired of the moves, which she managed, and she saw how difficult it was for their children to change schools so often. "In addition, family members recall, she was uncomfortable in what was for her an alien environment, the roistering oil patch communities of the southwest," stated a 2004 *Ramsey County History* profile on O'Shaughnessy. "Blackwell, Oklahoma, was not sophisticated, cultured St. Paul, Minnesota, with its broad boulevards, its well-built houses, its theaters, and its shops. She was afraid, according to family stories, of the recently affluent Indians who flooded into town. In short, Blackwell wasn't for her."[1]

Lillian finally put her foot down in 1918, according to her middle son Larry, who later recalled the conversation as passed down over the decades: "Nashe, I can't raise a family like this, I need to go home." He agreed to bring her back to Minnesota, where their oldest son, John, reportedly asked, "Now can we stay here forever? Can I go to school here forever?"[2] John later recalled that the family moved so much in the early years, he spent the third grade in three different cities.

The family settled first in Minneapolis before buying, in the early 1920s, a house at 1705 Summit Avenue, about a mile east of the College of St. Thomas and St. Thomas Military Academy. O'Shaughnessy would live in the Summit house (as well as in Florida) until his death in 1973.

His business was in Oklahoma and later Kansas, and he was gone for long stretches of time. Lillian took care of the family and enrolled the children in Catholic schools. "Mother used to lock herself and Eileen, Marian, and me in the bedroom at night and put the chair against the knob when Dad was out of town," John later recalled. "We used to walk to school rain, snow, or shine. Later Larry and Don had a chauffeur (softies)."[3]

St. Mark's was within walking distance, as was St. Thomas Academy, where John, Larry, and Don attended high school. Marian and Eileen went to Ladywood School in Indianapolis. The children enrolled in different colleges—John at Georgetown in Washington, DC; Marian at the University of Minnesota; Eileen at St. Mary-of-the-Woods in Terre Haute, Indiana; Larry at St. Thomas and then Yale; and Don at Notre Dame and then St. Thomas.

The O'Shaughnessys were devout Catholics. I.A. never "wore it on his sleeve," grandson John O'Shaughnessy Jr. said, "but his faith was very deep. I once was in his office at the top of the First National Bank building in downtown St. Paul, and he asked me, 'You go to church? Why?' I said, 'Because I choose to.' That was his way of probing if my Catholicism meant something to me."[4]

John Jr. and Larry both recalled Lillian as a quiet person who focused her energy and attention on her children. "She was a big, warm grandmother—you know the type," John said. Larry said that it took time for the socially shy Lillian to adjust to her husband's style: "Because my father was out of the city so often during his early career, she didn't make many new contacts in St. Paul, beyond her immediate family. He was doing well in business but many others who built homes and fortunes here were 'old money' and did not always welcome 'new money.' My mother attended only those events, civic or social, that my father felt were necessary for her to attend."[5]

Larry, the only child of I.A. and Lillian living today, said his father came to see home as a "refuge" where he could relax and not have to be the center of attention. There was "a startling contrast with how he behaved and spoke in the family setting as to when he'd be in an organized setting such as a business or philanthropy or at a dinner, where he always was the life of the party."[6]

The O'Shaughnessys had a close marriage, Larry said, but they were not demonstrative. "They seldom were seen kissing one another or otherwise being affectionate," he said. "I'm guessing that had a lot to do with the culture at the time, not that either of them was shy about their relationship. I know they loved each other."[7]

The family went on summer vacations, including trips to Glacier and Yellowstone parks in 1926, to Europe on a 1935 cruise and a tour of England, France, Norway, Sweden, Denmark, and Russia, and around South America in 1938.

O'Shaughnessy took his sons on fishing trips to northern Minnesota and Canada, and in the late 1940s he and John bought four cabins on Lower Cullen Lake, near Brainerd, Minnesota. Leonard Rogge, a family friend and career administrator at St. Thomas, recalled accompanying John and Lillian to Brainerd to see what was on the market: "There was one spot that Mrs. O'Shaughnessy liked. . . . I said, 'To the best of my knowledge, it is not for sale.' I proceeded to forget about the matter until about three weeks later when Mrs. O'Shaughnessy said to me, 'Remember that place that you said wasn't available—on Lake Cullen?' I said, 'Yes, I remember.' She said, 'Well, it still isn't for sale. I just bought it.'"[8]

Aside from the time he spent in Florida on the *Marileen,* his sixty-five-foot yacht, fishing and hunting provided the best opportunity for O'Shaughnessy to get away from the day-to-day pressure of the oil business and World War II. He occasionally participated in October pheasant hunts sponsored by the Minneapolis, Northfield and Southern Railway, on whose board he sat in the 1930s and 1940s.

"With the state of the world, and perhaps more particularly the state of the oil business in its present shape (if it can be called shape) it is, more than ever, important that individuals, like yourself, from time to time, absent themselves completely from the grind," railway president George Wright wrote to O'Shaughnessy in 1942. "This is, as you have probably surmised, merely a preamble to my annual announcement to you that the pheasant season will be with us shortly." O'Shaughnessy replied he would participate, but Wright didn't, and O'Shaughnessy rubbed it in. "You missed the time of your life by not being with us last week," he wrote. "Without question, I believe it was the best hunting trip we have ever had." The trip recurred in 1943, and Wright's invitation was succinct: "We have sufficient ammunition, in liquid as well as solid form, to take care of your party. This includes all gauges, as well as most brands."[9]

Lillian managed the O'Shaughnessy family finances. Her husband never carried a wallet but did carry cash, so when she needed money, "she'd raid his pockets," Larry said. "He never missed it." He got in a financial jam on one occasion and told Lillian about it: "She said, 'How much do you need?' He said, 'About $5,000.' She said, 'Well, that's about how much I've got right here.' Imagine in those days, $5,000 accumulated over a period of years. She was always afraid, at first, that he would lose his money, so she was always very careful. She thought he was extravagant. . . . At one time she said, 'Can't you just earn enough money to pay our bills?' He replied, 'Should I then just turn off the faucet?'"[10]

O'Shaughnessy was careful with his investments, eschewing Wall Street and the stock market for tax-exempt bonds or individual companies in which he would take an interest. "He thought that what was going on in the company economically shouldn't be determined by Wall Street and stock prices treading back and forth," Larry said. "He had the old-fashioned idea that 'the only way to make money honestly is to produce something and sell it.'"[11] In response to an acquaintance's 1940 suggestion that he consider purchasing real estate, O'Shaughnessy replied, "For the past several years I have confined all my investments to municipal bonds which, as you know, are non-taxable. Under my setup a 3% non-taxable bond is much preferable to a 6% or even higher interest rate on taxable securities."[12]

As his oil businesses flourished in the 1930s, O'Shaughnessy became increasingly generous in helping individuals and organizations, always mindful of the way his own father had helped the poor in nineteenth-century Stillwater. He gave mostly small sums—$100 here and $200 there—until 1939, when he contributed $400,000 to construct a new athletic building at St. Thomas, where his sons had received their high school educations.

He preferred not to publicly divulge the size of his gifts, but as he grew older he freely shared his philosophy of giving. He told the St. *Paul Pioneer Press* in 1956 that "a man with money has responsibility of putting it to good use" and that "money is not the most important thing in life. Food, shelter and clothing can be bought with money, but the important things, health and happiness, cannot." He also recalled a conversation with his attorney about business issues, and the attorney's laughter as he said, "'You're hooked. You can't quit until you die.'" O'Shaughnessy's response: "Oh, yes I can. I can go to Russia."[13]

On a more serious note, O'Shaughnessy once reflected how "the Lord has been good to me, so I figure I might as well spread some of my money around where it will do some good. I came into this world with nothing and I figure I'll go out the same way."[14]

One thing O'Shaughnessy never needed to worry about was a lack of interest in his money. "All I have to do is furnish the money," he told the *Minneapolis Tribune*. "You know the definition of a promoter: He's the guy who'll furnish the ocean if you furnish the ships. So I furnish the ships!"[15]

He established the I.A. O'Shaughnessy Foundation in 1941 to help him address estate tax issues and bring organization to his philanthropy, although for the rest of his life he continued to make contributions to organizations and individuals with personal resources, often in the form of Globe and Lario stock.

~~~~~~

O'Shaughnessy loved to tease people and play practical jokes, and it made no difference to him who the victim was. "Granddad was always joking with you," John O'Shaughnessy Jr. said. "When we would visit them in Golden Beach [Florida], he'd tell you about the jellyfish he had on his toast for breakfast. We thought he was kidding, but we always kind of wondered. He did that with everybody—whether it was people in business or his grandkids."[16]

"My father once said he was a bugle boy in the Spanish-American War," son Larry said. "He never told me exactly where he bugled. I was just a kid, so I didn't press him."[17]

O'Shaughnessy had nicknames for his grandchildren when they were young, calling Don's children "Meat Bone" (Stephen), "Hamburger" (Mike), and "Lamb Chop" (Karen).[18]

He would make up stories to get his children to pay attention. Larry recalled a schooner trip on Lake Michigan and how his father was looking out to sea. "We kids were busy doing something else when we heard him say, 'Oh, I've never seen a white shark in waters like this before.' Of course, we all ran to the side to see it, but it was gone, and he just smiled in that certain way when we asked him about the shark."[19]

Tongue in cheek, O'Shaughnessy chided the St. Paul branch of the Catholic Daughters of America after they asked him to support a 1959 fundraising event that included raffles on donated items. He told a caller that he couldn't be expected to contribute because he didn't gamble, and she took him seriously. The event organizers persisted with a written request. He sent $200 but advised them, "I do hope that you good ladies will be able to keep out of jail, as gambling is a bad business."[20]

He also groused impudently about a 1941 request for a $100 contribution toward a monument to Father Lucien Galtier, who had founded the first Catholic church in St. Paul in 1841. O'Shaughnessy sent a check earmarked to help "to erect a statue of some foreigner."[21]

O'Shaughnessy once recalled meeting a Roman Catholic cardinal who had come to Notre Dame to give a graduation speech: "We got talking about the celibacy law and the priests leaving and all that. He felt just like I do. These monkeys—they knew what the deal was when they went in. They weren't forced in, so they ought to carry out the rules. We were talking very sincerely about it. When we were going out, I said, 'It was a great pleasure, Your Eminence, to have met you, and by the way, when are you gonna get married?' You should have seen the look of horror on his face."[22]

On another occasion, O'Shaughnessy recalled attending a luncheon with George Meany, the longtime union leader, and Meany told him that they looked alike. "I said, 'George, then I'm ready to die.' On the way out, I was away from Meany, so I put my arm around this top guy from the New York electrical union and said, 'Listen, it's about time you did something for those fellas of yours up there. They're only getting $15 an hour. Don't you think you ought to do more for them?' The guy never knew I wasn't Meany . . . at least then!"[23]

His second wife, Blanche, was a landscape and mural painter, and O'Shaughnessy took up painting to keep her company. "Actually, I've been painting for years," he confided to *Minneapolis Star* columnist Barbara Flanagan in 1967, and he asked if she had seen any of his works in the Minneapolis Institute of Arts. She got a puzzled look on her face. "You may not have realized they were my paintings," he said. "You see, I sign them with the name 'Rembrandt.'" He laughed, and "so did I," the gullible Flanagan wrote. "What else can a sucker do?"[24]

On the day her column ran, Flanagan wrote to O'Shaughnessy to thank him for his "Minnesota hospitality" during their cruise aboard the *Marileen*. "I do hope you'll have a pleasant winter," she said, "and I look forward to attending an O'Shaughnessy art exhibition—perhaps

His as well as Hers—sometime here this year."[25]

He also enjoyed being the target of practical jokes. Nebraska Governor Val Peterson wrote to him in 1949 to inform him that he had been appointed an admiral in the Great Navy of the State of Nebraska: "Your commission is enclosed. As you no doubt know, there is but one rank in our Navy. We are all admirals and enjoy the same privileges. There is no one from whom we must take commands, nor is there anyone to whom we may 'pass the buck.' The morale of our organization is very high, and I am sure you will find your new duties most pleasurable."[26]

O'Shaughnessy was pleased with the appointment. "I have always been a naval man and one of my great ambitions was to become an admiral," he wrote to Peterson. "Now that my ambition has been attained, I have no other worlds to conquer."[27]

An admiral's cap actually would have fit O'Shaughnessy nicely in Florida, where he docked the *Marileen*. He and Lillian bought property in the early 1940s and lived on Ocean Boulevard in Golden Beach, north of Miami, where they spent up to six months a year. Living in Florida "gives you a chance for longevity," he once said. "Up in Minnesota you have to be afraid of getting out and walking in the winter, and I walk a lot. You could fall up there. Here, I get out anytime."[28]

He sold the Golden Beach home in 1970 after burglars locked Blanche and him in a closet. They spent his final three years in an oceanfront hotel in Bal Harbour, north of Miami Beach. A hotel employee once asked a *Minneapolis Tribune* reporter how O'Shaughnessy really had made his money; he had insisted to the hotel staff "that he had run the nation's most prosperous chain of houses of ill fame."[29]

8

The Skipper

It is always intellectual stimulation, restful relaxation
and solid good fun to man one position in the firing line as the four
of us lob shells into the enemy camps (and a few into our own).
God bless you for the unfailing hospitality and kindness
which you have always shown to us.

—FATHER JAMES SHANNON

One of I.A. O'Shaughnessy's fondest avocations during his more than thirty winters in Florida was jumping on the *Marileen* for a cruise along the east coast, north of Miami. The excursions gave him a chance to unwind, to enjoy life on the water, and—more often than not—to entertain legions of friends and family members and engage in conversations both serious and trivial. He was a different man at sea than on land.

The *Marileen* was not O'Shaughnessy's first boat. He leased the *Blackhawk*, a fifty-four-foot schooner, in the mid-1930s, but in 1939 he began to correspond with Henry C. Grebe & Company, a Chicago boat manufacturer, about a new boat. O'Shaughnessy retained Charles

Roach, president of a yacht design firm, in 1947 to prepare plans for a yacht to be constructed by Burger Boat Company of Manitowoc, Wisconsin, but he ultimately signed a contract with Grebe for a yacht that would cost $95,000. The *Marileen*—named for daughters Marian and Eileen—launched in November 1948.

As early as 1949 and throughout the 1950s, O'Shaughnessy received inquiries about selling the *Marileen*. He always said no, with a standard reply that "if at some time in the future I decide to get rid of this boat, I will get in touch with you." He looked at specifications for a seventy-five-foot Grebe yacht in 1960 but always chose to stay with the *Marileen*.[1]

R. Getchell Comstock was a longtime captain of the *Marileen* and occasionally wrote letters to O'Shaughnessy about the boat when he was in Minnesota. "Dear Boss: It is full moon time again and outside of a few squalls and a little hotter than usual, the weather is perfect," Comstock said at the beginning of a three-page letter in 1960. "When the moon is full like it is now, it seems as if we should be coming up the lower Biscayne Bay with you all on the forward seat."[2]

While O'Shaughnessy used the boat primarily for pleasure, he also looked for ways to write off some costs as business expenses. During its construction, he explained to one acquaintance that the *Marileen* "belonged" to Globe Oil & Refining Co., but he was unsure how much the Internal Revenue Service would allow him to write off. "The government agreed to allow me $18,000 for the *Marileen,* which is about half what I have in it," he wrote in one letter. "I suppose one must be a loyal American and forget about such things. However, when one sees the billions of dollars they are spending, and a great deal of it foolishly, one wonders what it is all about."[3]

Austin Black became the *Marileen*'s captain in the mid-1960s and, like Comstock, he kept O'Shaughnessy up to date. Always an eagle-eyed stickler for details and, some might say, a penny-pincher on expenses, O'Shaughnessy sent letters to the captain in 1969 inquiring about $85.82 spent on gasoline: "I note in your letter that you consumed this amount on your vacation. I was unaware that boat owners were accustomed to pay for gasoline for employees on vacation. As I recall that before I left Florida I made a present to you of $500 and I think this is rather unusual, too, but I do know that you had extra expenses on account of the death of your wife."[4]

~~~~~

Among the many guests on the *Marileen* were the priests who ran the University of Notre Dame and the College of St. Thomas. O'Shaughnessy delighted in the company of men such as Fathers John Cavanaugh, Theodore Hesburgh, and Edmund (Ned) Joyce of Notre Dame and Fathers Vincent Flynn and James Shannon of St. Thomas. They couldn't resist the chance to escape Midwestern winters for a few days on the *Marileen*. "Here we are, after the days of blue skies, warm sunshine, luxurious golf, and regal hospitality from your hands, back in the day to day living on the snow and ice," Cavanaugh, president of Notre Dame from 1946 to 1952, wrote in 1950.[5]

Hesburgh, Joyce, and Shannon all wrote to O'Shaughnessy in March 1958 to thank him for their week at sea. Joyce, executive vice president of Notre Dame under Hesburgh, wrote, "Yes, it was a perfect week—superb food, excellent drinks, scintillating conversation, moderate exercise, complete relaxation."[6] Hesburgh, president of Notre Dame from 1952 to 1987, said, "I always come down feeling like something out from under a damp rock and return, after our few days together, feeling something like a human being again. . . . I marvel at the way you are able to stay so young in your point of view and to keep three of us on the run at once."[7] Shannon, president of St. Thomas from 1956 to 1966, wrote:

> As I settle down now to the steady work of running St. Thomas, I have every reason to thank almighty God for the welcome friendship which you have both extended to me so generously. Believe me, that friendship is an encouragement which I cannot evaluate. One consolation, however, which I do have in the sacred priesthood is that when my limited powers of appreciation and of expression prove inadequate I can ask our blessed Lord at my Mass each morning to speak for me and reward such friends as you with the unlimited rewards you so richly deserve.[8]

Another letter from Shannon, written in 1960, called the *Marileen* week "a high point" of his winter every year. "It is always intellectual stimulation, restful relaxation and solid good fun to man one position in the firing line as the four of us lob shells into the enemy camps (and a few into our own)," he told O'Shaughnessy. "God bless you for the unfailing hospitality and kindness which you have always shown to us and the magnificent support your friendship has given to our apostolate in the service of the Church."[9]

Joyce once called his time on the *Marileen* "idyllic," allowing him to return to Notre Dame and "attack university problems with renewed energy. . . . The week spent with you was once again the highlight of our year. It was not only restful, but it was great fun. Our admiration for the Skipper of the *Marileen* knows no bounds."[10]

Ever the football fan, O'Shaughnessy entertained new Notre Dame Coach Ara Parseghian and his staff on the *Marileen* in December 1965. "It is always a pleasure to visit with you in spite of your 'needling,'" Parseghian wrote O'Shaughnessy. "After we had left the boat and returned to the hotel, it dawned on me why you had been able to over-come your hospital [stay]. I don't think the Good Lord is ready for your kind of 'needling!' I would guess you are going to be with us for a long time."[11]

The trips became less frequent in the late 1960s as O'Shaughnessy grew older and spent less time on the *Marileen*. In March 1969, Hesburgh wrote to Shannon, who had left the St. Thomas presidency three years earlier, with a request that he change his schedule and join the group on the *Marileen* at the end of the month: "These are the only three days in the whole year when we can reconstitute the Church, the world, and the universe. We can't do it without Jim Shannon, and I do hope that somehow it will be possible for you to change your schedule and be with us. If not, I will jump in the Venetian Canal and probably drown. You don't want to go through life with this on your conscience, do you?"[12]

O'Shaughnessy used the *Marileen* until his death in 1973. Bob Short, a Minneapolis businessman, bought the boat and kept it for about ten years.

9

The Most Excellent Oranges

We'd rip those things apart and go at it.
The color on the skin was green, but they'd be ripe on the inside.
They were delicious.
—GRANDSON JOHN O'SHAUGHNESSY JR.

If I.A. O'Shaughnessy had a hobby in his life, it may have been growing oranges.

Yes, oranges. As busy as he was, running and expanding Globe Oil
& Refining and Lario Oil & Gas in the 1920s, O'Shaughnessy somehow
became owner of an eighty-acre grove in Florida. For the rest of his life,
he kept track of everything from expenses to per-acre yields to who
should receive boxes of oranges as gifts.

Patrick O'Shaughnessy said the story he heard is that his grandfather
bought the orange grove—two, actually—as a tax shelter. "He bought
a grove, met a neighbor and said, 'I have the best orange grove in the
county.' The neighbor pointed out the grove was in a valley, and that's
where the frost came. So he sold it—and bought higher on the hill."[1]

Throughout the fifty years that he owned the grove in Polk County, east of Tampa, he always seemed interested in selling it—but only for the right price, of course, and even when that price met with his approval he would pull back and say, "Not now." It wasn't until January 1973, ten months before his death, that he sold the property to the family that had managed the grove for more than forty years.

Records indicate that O'Shaughnessy purchased the grove in 1922 from a Mr. Yarnell, who employed M.C. Dopler. It's not clear what O'Shaughnessy paid for the eighty acres, but correspondence indicated he received offers over the years as low as $500 an acre and as high as $4,000 an acre.[2]

A 1931 letter to W.A. Varn, who managed the grove, demonstrates O'Shaughnessy's interest in the operation. Varn had sent him a telegram projecting a harvest of 8,000 boxes of oranges, but in his response O'Shaughnessy instead questioned him about $9,000 in fertilizer costs, if too much ammonia had been used and if more potash should be applied. "[I] do not suppose there is a market for citrus fruit properties at this time," he wrote. "If you happen to hear of anyone that might be interested in purchasing my grove, I will be glad to hear from you."[3] Several months later, in response to an inquiry, O'Shaughnessy suggested $1,500 an acre but got no takers.

O'Shaughnessy loved to send boxes of oranges as gifts to friends or as rewards for employees and jobbers with whom he had contracts. They were effusive in their thanks, writing dozens of thank-you letters.

"They are by far the most excellent oranges I have ever tasted," wrote Steve Loken, manager of the Kenyon Cooperative Oil Association in Kenyon, Minnesota, in 1938.[4] "No doubt some of them will be used in making whiskey sours, and I assure you that each time they are put to that use, we will at least give you a kind thought!" said a secretary at Jobbers Oil Products of Oshkosh, Wisconsin.[5] "The juice from these oranges is so good that I doubt if gin would improve it," wrote Curtis Anderson of Wichita.[6]

"Daddy, this isn't Christmas. We did not see Santa Claus," said the daughters of L.M. Foster of Lakeside Lubricants in Chicago after he received a case of oranges one June. "When you have two little girls cutting teeth," he wrote to O'Shaughnessy, "the value of good orange juice is unlimited."[7] Arthur Haley, director of public relations at Notre Dame, said in a 1942 thank-you note, "The Polk County Orange Growers' Association of Florida really has something and that is the knowledge of how to grow what I think are the finest and sweetest juice oranges I have ever tasted."[8]

And grandson John O'Shaughnessy Jr. recalled contests that he had with his brother to see who could eat the oranges the fastest. "We'd rip those things apart and go at it," he said. "The color on the skin was green, but they'd be ripe on the inside. They were delicious."[9]

The attention sat well with O'Shaughnessy, who always was kind and even generous in his replies. "I am very glad that you like the oranges that I sent you and as per your request I am notifying my man in Florida to send you four additional boxes," he wrote in 1938 to M.L. Rawlings, who owned an ice company in Lincoln, Nebraska. "There will be no charge for this as I am always glad to find someone who appreciates and enjoys good oranges."[10]

~~~~~~~

O'Shaughnessy began a relationship with Highland Park Groves in Lake Wales, Florida, in 1932, when M.C. Dopler wrote to make him aware of two small groves for sale. O'Shaughnessy's response was terse: "I am not in the notion of purchasing any more groves in Florida."[11]

The following August, he wrote to Dopler and questioned $125 charges for pruning, calling them "an exorbitant amount for this character of work. I was wondering if this was possibly a mistake of your auditor." Dopler mentioned hurricane damage in his reply and that up to 10 percent of the crop could be lost, but higher prices should offset the losses.[12]

A December 1934 freeze damaged 30 percent of the O'Shaughnessy orange crop, and Dopler recommended that heaters should be installed. O'Shaughnessy apparently said no, and Dopler renewed the request six years later after the crop was damaged by what he called "the worst freeze in the past sixty years." O'Shaughnessy again said no, deciding to wait for a year.[13]

He kept an eye on his competition, and in 1936 he questioned Dopler's estimate that they would get only $1 a box for oranges when a friend had sold seedling oranges for $1.75 a box. "With this knowledge in mind it is very difficult for me to understand why we should not secure a better price for a Valencia orange," O'Shaughnessy wrote. "It has always been my understanding that seedling oranges sold for a much less price than Valencias. Have about come to the conclusion that it is very foolish for me to continue marketing my oranges on the present basis."[14]

O'Shaughnessy always was a stickler for detail in reviewing crop and financial reports. He wrote to the Lake Wales Citrus Growers Association in September 1940 about a receipt: "My records show $170.03 received instead of $284.50, according to your records."[15] He once noticed an error in a letter regarding production—he calculated 44,110 boxes vs. 25,801 in the letter—but was pleased with revenue exceeding $87,000. "In my opinion," he said, "this is an excellent return."[16]

When sales seesawed in the 1940s, O'Shaughnessy challenged Dopler. "Was very much surprised to hear of the short crop," he wrote in July 1941 after reviewing sales of 11,600 boxes. "I notice that a good part of the crop was picked during the month of July. I was wondering if this was not rather late and if it would not hurt the trees." Dopler responded that he carried out a July harvest "because of the continued jumpy condition of the market." The 1944 harvest dropped from a projected 30,000 boxes to 24,000 boxes after an October hurricane, increased to nearly 30,000 boxes in the 1947–48 season, but fell by half the following two years. One of the best seasons was 1963–64, with a harvest of 48,000 boxes.[17]

O'Shaughnessy continued to receive inquiries about selling the grove, and he always pretended to be clueless about its value. "As I have no knowledge of what my citrus grove would be worth," he said in an October 1949 letter to one real estate agent, "I should be at a loss to suggest a price under the circumstances. If you have any ideas along that line, I should be glad to receive them from you."[18]

He decided to formally list the grove in 1966 with John Brennan, a Lakeland real estate agent who had approached him. A 1968 appraisal stated the property's value at $280,000, exclusive of fruit on the trees. When O'Shaughnessy finally sold the grove in January, the buyer was Dopler Groves, and the price was $320,000, or $4,000 an acre.[19]

10

Olympic Gold Medalists

The McPherson version of a layup shot left observers simply flabbergasted. Those giants left the floor, reached up and pitched the ball downward into the hoop, much like a cafeteria customer dunking a roll in coffee. No team ever played at such breathless pace and with such furious drive.

—New York Times sportswriter Arthur Daley

When most sports historians speak about the importance of the 1936 Olympics, they refer to how African-American sprinter Jesse Owens stole the spotlight from Nazi leader Adolf Hitler, host of the Berlin games, with an exceptional performance that earned four gold medals. But another American entrant also sparkled in the 1936 Olympics, the first to host competition in basketball, and I.A. O'Shaughnessy and his Globe Oil & Refining Company had a lot to do with it.

Globe opened a refinery in McPherson, Kansas, in 1933 and decided to sponsor the McPherson Globe Refiners basketball team. The Refiners won the national AAU basketball championship in 1936 and joined forces with their archrivals, a team sponsored by Hollywood Universal Pictures, to represent the United States and win the first Olympic basketball gold medal.

In the process, the Refiners drew international attention to tiny McPherson and helped to raise the profile of the company that O'Shaughnessy—a Minnesota collegiate football star three decades earlier—had founded in northern Oklahoma in 1917.

The National Basketball Association was still more than a decade from appearing on the sports scene in the 1930s, when AAU "industrial" leagues were popular because players could retain their amateur status. Companies sponsored teams and provided players with jobs, allowing them to make ends meet while still competing at the highest level after their collegiate careers ended.

The McPherson Refiners played a modest schedule in the 1933–34 season, finishing with a 16–8 record, and turned to Gene Johnson to take the team to the next level the following year. Johnson had been a star forward at Emporia State Teachers College in Kansas, coached at Wichita University from 1928 to 1933, and led the Wichita Henrys to their first national AAU title before moving to Globe to turn the Refiners into a national power.

"When I organized the team I went to the head man of the company [O'Shaughnessy] and he thought it was a great idea, but the sales manager thought I went over his head and he never forgave us," Johnson told the *Wichita Eagle-Beacon* in 1986.[1] Nonetheless, the team became a primary marketing tool for the fledgling refinery, according to Rich Hughes, author of *Netting Out Basketball 1936: The Remarkable Story of the McPherson Refiners, the First Team to Dunk, Zone Press and Win the Olympic Gold Medal*:

> In the midst of the Great Depression, Globe Oil decided
> to take the plunge and 'go national.' . . . It was not a trivial
> decision, assuming the responsibility of financing a basketball
> team. There were no guarantees for success for any business
> ventures in the 1930s. The case could be made that sponsoring a
> national industrial team was an extravagant expense . . . but the
> necessity of selling large volumes of gasoline forced the issue."[2]

The Refiners were accepted into the Missouri Valley AAU League and played teams from the region, including the Wichita Gridleys, Kansas City Stage Liners, Hutchinson Western Transit Renos, Chicago Fast Freighters, Tulsa Diamond Oilers, and Denver Pigs. Johnson recruited outstanding players from around the country, and they worked in O'Shaughnessy's refinery. "The basketball Refiners were hired to work long hours in a hot and smelly refinery, play a tough schedule, and win as many games as possible," Hughes wrote. "Globe Oil, the players and McPherson would share any glory."[3]

As many as 1,200 fans would crowd into the McPherson Convention Hall and pay 40 cents for general admission seats to watch the team that was billed as "the tallest team in the world." They were tall, indeed. The starters were center Joe Fortenberry (6' 8"), forwards Willard Schmidt (6' 9") and Vernon Vaughn (6' 6"), and guards Bill "Galloping Ghost" Wheatley (6' 4") and Francis Johnson (6' 1"). They made an impression wherever they played because of Gene Johnson's pioneering full-court zone press and a relentless fast break called the "Fire Department" offense. Arthur Daley, a *New York Times* sportswriter, saw the Refiners practice at Madison Square Garden before the Olympics and was amazed that five players could dunk the ball at a time when few other players did:

> The McPherson version of a layup shot left observers simply flabbergasted. Joe Fortenberry and Willard Schmidt did not use an ordinary curling toss. Not those giants. They left the floor, reached up and pitched the ball downward into the hoop, much like a cafeteria customer dunking a roll in coffee. . . . No team around here ever played at such breathless pace and with such furious drive as the Refiners. They never stop digging. Long passes, short passes, the pivot play, make them the scoring combination they are.[4]

In Johnson's first year as coach, the Refiners finished 24–10 and lost the AAU national title game 45–26 to the Kansas City Stage Liners. The average scores of games were lower than today because the ball was returned to midcourt for a center jump after every basket.

The 1935–36 Refiners started slowly, with a 4–4 record, but ran off a seventeen-game winning streak in compiling a 23–6 regular season record. They won the AAU national tournament with a 5–0 record, including a 47–35 victory over Universal Pictures in the championship game, but lost to Universal 44–43 in the Olympic playoffs after Johnson agreed not to use the zone press.

Johnson and the Universal coach combined their squads for the fourteen-member American team that played in Berlin. Only seven players were allowed to suit up for each game, so the United States used platoons, with Universal playing one game and the Refiners the next. The Americans cruised to easy wins over Estonia, the Philippines, and Mexico to advance to the championship game against Canada. Of the six players in that game, four were Refiners, one was from Universal, and one was a collegian. Slowed by steady rains that turned the outdoor clay and sand court into a virtual swamp, according to one report, the United States took a 15–4 halftime lead before two thousand soaked fans and held on for a 19–8 win.

As successful as the Refiners were at the Olympics, the company decided not to sponsor the team in 1937, and years later Johnson still was disappointed. "It's a hell of a note to come home with a world championship basketball team and have to disband it," he told the *Wichita Eagle-Beacon* in 1986. Several players left Globe to work for other companies and play on their teams, and a few players remained at Globe to play what the newspaper called "a low-key brand of ball in 1937, but things never were the same." Johnson coached at Kansas Wesleyan for six years after leaving Globe before going into the insurance business.[5]

Thirty-six years after the Olympics and one year before his death, O'Shaughnessy still vividly recalled the Olympics and how he was glued to the radio during the games. "Every one of those boys back in 1936 worked for me," he told the St. *Paul Pioneer Press.* "They were a fine team," he said, and he credited their success with sparking the growth of the game around the globe. "Every country is playing it today. Did you notice that Brazil almost beat our boys? Those other countries are getting better and better."[6]

O'Shaughnessy wrote to Sid Hartman, sports editor of the *Minne-*

apolis Tribune, in 1972 to share information about the Refiners in hopes he might publish a story about them. Hartman wrote to O'Shaughnessy after the Olympics and explained that the newspaper had decided not to publish a story because of the controversial way the US team lost in the 1972 gold medal game to Russia. "As things turned out," Hartman told O'Shaughnessy, "the finish of the Olympic basketball finals was such that we didn't think it would be advisable to dwell on it anymore."[7]

The team was honored in 1972 when McPherson celebrated its centennial and held a Basketball Hall of Fame luncheon, and again in 1986, during a fifty-year reunion. Hughes published his book in 2011, and the McPherson Convention and Visitors Bureau produced a film, *Oil and Gold: The McPherson Globe Refiners Basketball Story,* in 2012.

11

Win That Pennant or Else

I.A. O'Shaughnessy always loved football, going back to his days as a star on the college gridirons at St. John's and St. Thomas, and he regularly attended Notre Dame games as an adult.

So it came as something of a surprise in February 1956 when O'Shaughnessy joined five men to form the Cleveland Indians Baseball Company and buy the American League franchise. There is no record indicating why he decided to jump into professional sports, but it's possible that railroad magnate William Daley, a longtime friend, persuaded him to join the venture. The purchase also may have been O'Shaughnessy acting on a whim at seventy. He had sold his last refinery, in Lemont, Illinois, two years earlier and had turned over day-to-day operations of Lario Oil & Gas to his oldest son, John.

Cleveland newspaper reports said the group paid $3,961,400 ($2,044,400 in cash and $1,917,000 in ten-year promissory notes bearing 5 percent interest) and that O'Shaughnessy held the third-largest number of common shares (400) behind Daley (1,350) and general manager Hank Greenberg (1,200), a Hall of Fame slugger. Capital stock of 6,000 shares at $50 per share was authorized, with 3,300 shares held by the new shareholders and 2,700 shares available to stockholders of the Cleveland Baseball Company (the previous owner).

O'Shaughnessy became acquainted in the 1940s with Daley, then an executive with the New York, Chicago and St. Louis Railroad Company, also known as the Nickel Plate Road. O'Shaughnessy owned stock in the company and served on its board from 1948 to 1964, when it was merged into the Norfolk & Western Railroad.[1]

O'Shaughnessy followed the Indians' fortunes closely in his first year as an owner and board member. They had won the American League pennant in 1954 with a record 110 wins (against only 44 losses) but lost to the New York Giants in the World Series. The Indians finished second by three games to the Yankees in the American League race the following season, and it was clear the new minority owner expected a return to the top in 1956. He wasn't shy about criticizing the team's lax play in July when it trailed the Yankees by 10.5 games.

In a *Cleveland Press* story headlined, "Win That Pennant or Else, O'Shaughnessy Tells Tribe," writer Al Ostrow quoted O'Shaughnessy as saying, "I don't believe in being No. 2. I want those boys to get in there and fight like hell to win a pennant this year." He also complained how "the Yankees are winning too many games. We aren't winning enough. Something's got to be done about it . . . and done fast. We need someone to hit that ball. That's our weakness—hitting."[2]

Ostrow went on to call O'Shaughnessy a "fighting Irishman" willing to open his checkbook to purchase better players, "but we need some hustle right now more than money," the owner said. "A lot of things can still happen. A lot of things had better start happening."[3]

Another Cleveland newspaper, the *Commercial Dispatch,* chided O'Shaughnessy for his "the Indians will do better than this, or else" comments. "As a rich man, he knows that money can do many things, and thinks that if it fails, it is only because enough has not been poured in," an editorial stated. "His threat implies that if no improvement comes soon, there will be a new manager and new players." The editorial encouraged him to develop the Indians' farm system because "the stars on other teams are not for sale, as he may be astonished to find out," and even those who spent freely "have never shown a great deal for all their spending. If O'Shaughnessy finds out why, he will be well on his way to a baseball education."[4]

The *Cleveland Press* published a Lou Darvis cartoon of O'Shaughnessy spanking a player held over his knee. O'Shaughnessy wrote to Ostrow, who had sent him matte copies of the cartoon, and said, "You wanted to know what I am going to do with them [the cartoons]. . . . Perhaps I can crown you with them someday. The next time I am in Cleveland I will give you a ring and find out if you are responsible or irresponsible. Do not be surprised if I should take a punch at your nose. It would all be in fun. Anyway, I do appreciate your sense of humor."[5]

O'Shaughnessy sat down for an interview with the *Cleveland News,* which said he was "disturbed over what he termed 'irresponsible reporting' in another newspaper" (presumably the *Press*). He had no intention of interfering with the Indians' operation, he said, and he had "the greatest respect" for Greenberg as a general manager and Al Lopez as manager. "I called Hank Greenberg today to explain to him that I had not made the remarks attributed to me," O'Shaughnessy said. "Greenberg told me he had already had a call from Daley telling him that he knew I would never make such statements because I'm not that kind of a guy."[6]

Several fans wrote letters to O'Shaughnessy. "Congratulations on your blast at the Indians," said Emily Fitzgibbons of Lakewood, Ohio. "Someone has to do something about them." Another fan suggested that O'Shaughnessy buy out Greenberg, "who brought in all these banjo-hitting oldsters. Then I'd fire Al Lopez [and] bring up Rocky Colavito and Russ Nixon from the minors." The fan went on for four more paragraphs before concluding about his plan: "I don't think we'll ever know what would happen if it were carried out, and it would probably make the Indians worse than they are, which is pretty bad already. But at least that crew would have some spirit, unlike the listless team now. And perhaps we fans would take these struggling youngsters to our hearts."[7]

The Indians finished in second place with an 88–66 record, nine games behind the Yankees. Lopez resigned as manager and took the same job with the Chicago White Sox, and Kerby Farrell was hired as his successor, possibly at O'Shaughnessy's behest. "Farrell OK with Iggy," shouted a *Cleveland News* headline, and the story quoted Daley on O'Shaughnessy: "He's tickled. He lives in St. Paul and Kerby beat his team, among others, to win the American Association title. During the past few months he'd call me from time to time and ask if we had a manager yet. When I'd say no he'd ask, 'What are you fellows waiting for? You've got a man down around here named Farrell who keeps winning everything.'"[8]

The Indians struggled on the field in 1957, finishing sixth in the eight-team league with a 76–77 record and 21.5 games behind the pennant-winning Yankees. O'Shaughnessy appears to have stayed out of the newspapers during the season, but as it concluded, speculation began about whether the club would leave Cleveland.

Cleveland News columnist Sidney Andorn described Daley and O'Shaughnessy as the club's "money men . . . well versed in financial wizardry," and he wondered why they were standing pat. "Daley and O'Shaughnessy know that by cutting down on a top-heavy list of front-office executives with duplicating duties they could probably save enough to turn deficit into break-even," he wrote. "They know their general manager [Greenberg] is in disrepute with the fans, that a change here would prove profitable. They make no changes. Appears as if they're trying to alienate a fandom which holds all-time attendance records. Could it be a planned kiss-off to enter the enticing embrace of Minneapolis-St. Paul, where resides co-owner O'Shaughnessy?"[9]

Greenberg was fired as general manager the following month.

Andorn's reference to the Twin Cities alluded to separate efforts of government and business leaders in Minneapolis and St. Paul to land a Major League Baseball franchise in their cities. The mayor and city council approved a resolution on September 25, 1958, urging the Indians to move to St. Paul and play in the newly constructed Midway Stadium, which had 10,250 seats with options to expand to 50,000. Minneapolis area officials had followed a similar strategy in courting other teams, including the Giants, having constructed Metropolitan Stadium in suburban Bloomington (and in 1961 the Washington Senators moved to Minnesota and became the Twins).

St. Paul faced competition for the Indians from the Houston Sports Association, a group of businessmen. "As I told you on the telephone, the Houston group is well organized and ready to move immediately," Lawrence J. Kelly wrote to O'Shaughnessy in September. "They have done considerable spadework over a two-year period. As for the stadium, we are assured of its completion for the 1959 season. Houston, now with a population of 1,195,000, is the largest city in the United States not in the major leagues. With no race tracks here and a shortage of amusements for a working force of about 470,000 persons, Houston is more than ready to support major league baseball."[10]

St. Paul continued to press. H.E. Schell, president of the Roe-James Glass Company and chairman of the Major League Baseball Committee for St. Paul, wrote to O'Shaughnessy in mid-October before the Indians board meeting to say, "In my opinion St. Paul has sincerely been endeavoring to procure only the Cleveland Indians, and I am certain without reservation that if at the meeting next week a decision to move the franchise from Cleveland to St. Paul could be forthcoming, one of the greatest promotions for the 1959 season would begin immediately in St. Paul."[11]

The Indians decided to remain in Cleveland. An October 17 *New York Times* story quoted board chairman Daley as saying, "We're here to stay." Daley consulted with O'Shaughnessy by telephone and wrote to him the same day. "The announcement received great and favorable publicity, both in the news columns and editorially, with promises that the entire city would get behind the Indians," Daley wrote. "We are going to try to take advantage of the present enthusiasm to build a real season seat sale for the coming year."[12]

The Houston group wouldn't give up. In a three-page letter on

October 23, 1958, Craig Cullinan Jr., chairman of the Houston Sports Association, told Daley that the association still believed "that one of two things will happen at some unpredictable time in the future: (1) the Cleveland club will be sold or (2) it will be moved elsewhere. . . . From a sound business standpoint, the Cleveland club is worth what we offered for it but only if it were moved to Houston. We doubt that it's worth half that figure in Cleveland, unless someone wants to own it as an expensive hobby."[13]

Kelly wrote to O'Shaughnessy on the same day and asked that Houston remain an option because "we feel we have a great deal to offer," and he wanted O'Shaughnessy to stay with the organization. "Let me again state that if we are successful in our bid, we hope you will remain with us."[14]

The Indians did stay in Cleveland (and remain there today). As the 1959 season moved into its final month, they trailed the Chicago White Sox, and a newspaper photo showed O'Shaughnessy smiling at a newspaper cartoon showing the struggling team trying to hold back the clock in the pennant race.

O'Shaughnessy noted that his twenty-six grandchildren were not united in rooting for the Indians. "Some of them live in Chicago," he said, "and they've been giving me a rough time. They're all for the White Sox. My view is that the White Sox can help out our team by dropping dead." The White Sox would go on to win the pennant, finishing ahead of the second-place Indians and their 89–65 record by five games. The story ends with O'Shaughnessy saying that while he was satisfied with second place, "We want a pennant next year. . . . I'll show those grandchildren in Chicago yet!"[15]

It never was clear how much money O'Shaughnessy and his co-owners made—or lost—during his involvement with the team. Minnesota History Center files included copies of audited financial statements for several seasons. The 1956 statement, for example, showed operating income of $2.7 million, with net profit of $2,295.19. In 1961, operating income was $2.78 million, but operating expenses totaled $2.84 million for a year-end loss of $257,086.52.[16]

O'Shaughnessy largely remained out of the limelight, although on occasion he would contact the club for a favor. In July 1961 he sent a letter to the Indians' publicity director saying he had not received two autographed baseballs promised five days earlier; he intended to give them to the young sons of his secretary. "I thought that I would notify you," O'Shaughnessy wrote. "Perhaps you had better send them up with a policeman."[17]

The board and its shareholders met on November 28, 1962, to adopt a liquidation plan and approve a sale of assets to Cleveland Indians Inc., led by Gabe Paul. O'Shaughnessy did not attend the meeting. He remained a stockholder, but the value of his stake in the club was not publicized. Daley remained chairman of the board, and Paul became president and general manager.

A copy of the 1966 Indians yearbook includes O'Shaughnessy's photo as a director. He agreed that year to sell his Indians stock at a price of $320 per share, but it is unclear how many shares he held. On September 16, 1966, eleven seasons after purchasing the team, he wrote a one-sentence letter to the club on Indians stationery: "I hereby resign as a director of Cleveland Indians, Inc., effective this date."[18]

~~~~~~

Despite his exit from Cleveland, O'Shaughnessy wasn't entirely done with baseball, thanks to Daley.

His old friend informed him in November 1968 that he would receive two hundred shares of stock in Pacific Northwest Sports, which owned the Seattle Pilots baseball team. Globe Oil & Refining paid the $80,000 tab.[19]

The Pilots moved to Milwaukee in 1970 and were renamed the Brewers, and O'Shaughnessy somehow became a limited partner in that club—perhaps, again, because of his relationship with Daley. The club lost $4.4 million in 1971, and O'Shaughnessy's share of the loss was $88,000. His son John inquired on his behalf for a copy of the original partnership agreement, and an attorney for the Brewers responded that Daley had "assigned part of his interest in the Brewers to three other persons, but this action did not make them become a substitute limited partner."[20]

As it turned out, interest in the club was owned by Globe Oil & Refining of Illinois, which also had owned the stock in Pacific Northwest Sports. An April 1972 document showed Globe as a limited partner in the Brewers, with investments totaling $120,000 in 1970 and 1971, and an apparent $470,000 investment in 1972. It is not known how long Globe held its limited partnership in the Brewers.[21]

As involved, financially and professionally, as O'Shaughnessy became with Major League Baseball over the last two decades of his life, he also helped the sport flourish among the youth of St. Paul.

The Highland Little League was formed in 1952, and ten years later its president, William Bick, asked O'Shaughnessy for funds to construct two additional baseball diamonds, a concession stand, and a restroom on land owned by the Ford Motor Company adjacent to its Highland Park production plant. Bick estimated the project could be done for $5,000 using volunteer labor, and he added, "We have in the past through our program produced some excellent ball players and students for St. Thomas College." O'Shaughnessy mailed a $5,000 check.[22]

He made several contributions to the Hi-Tower Babe Ruth League in Highland Park, including $2,000 in 1957 toward the cost of a new field, $250 in 1966 for field improvements, and $500 in 1968 to help cover traveling expenses to a tournament in Indiana. He also donated $100 in 1961, 1963, 1964, and 1965 to the Hilltopper Little League.[23]

12

Ambassador O'Shaughnessy?

It was very pleasant meeting the President [Eisenhower], but I must say that I enjoyed your group even more. I hope that I will have the pleasure of meeting you again. Probably at that time we will not be bothered with the Minneapolis politicians.

—I.A. O'SHAUGHNESSY TO ST. PAUL MAYOR GEORGE VAVOULIS

As a businessman, I.A. O'Shaughnessy knew that dealing with the government and politics was an inevitable duty of his job, and he did so in a carefully measured and mostly quiet manner. He ran his oil businesses during uncertain and trying times, including the Great Depression and World War II, when the federal government was heavily involved in the politics of oil and the industry's impact on the economy, and he became an influential figure in the nation's capital as a representative of independent refiners.

As a millionaire, he knew he would be regular prey for political candidates seeking campaign contributions. He supported candidates on both sides of the aisle—perhaps more Republicans than Democrats—and gave sporadically and usually in the low four figures. Elected officials often amused him, and he wasn't shy about saying how he felt about them. J. Michael O'Shaughnessy recalled that he "spent many hours with Granddad watching the political conventions [on television]. His basic theory was that they were all crooks but you had to work with them."[1]

As a true patriot, O'Shaughnessy always put the interests of the country ahead of any personal concerns. During the Great Depression, he answered President Roosevelt's appeal to business and industry to put people back to work by immediately increasing the number of daily shifts in his refineries from three to four. Workers consequently had their shifts reduced from eight to six hours, but he did not dock their pay, and the *Wichita Beacon* heralded his action with the headline, "Globe is First to Adopt New Recovery Plan."[2]

Roosevelt subsequently appointed O'Shaughnessy to a Petroleum Administration Board committee, and he remained active on other federal government committees that dealt with fuel shortages during World War II.

Despite his work with the Roosevelt administration, O'Shaughnessy made a contribution (amount unknown) to Republican Alfred Landon's presidential campaign in 1936, perhaps because Landon was from Kansas. Roosevelt trounced Landon at the polls and invited O'Shaughnessy to the White House on January 20, 1937, the day of the president's second inauguration, likely for a reception. O'Shaughnessy later found himself under consideration for an appointment to an ambassadorship, first by Roosevelt and then by President Harry Truman, according to letters written by Robert Hannegan, chairman of the Democratic National Committee. In one, he wrote:

> I have been giving some thought to those who were so helpful to us in the past campaign, and therefore it follows that I thought about you. I am hopeful that from time to time in the near future I shall be given an opportunity to make suggestions to the President for appointments to positions of dignity, trust and importance, and there should be a number of such places

coming along, with the possible early termination of the war, together with the post-war problems that will follow.[3]

Roosevelt died two months after O'Shaughnessy received the letter, but Hannegan followed up with another letter that fall saying that Truman "would like very much to have you visit with him on Friday, October 26, at 11:45 a.m."[4] There is no record of what occurred during the visit, but John Hastings, a political ally of Hannegan, wrote to O'Shaughnessy the following January:

> Bob asked me to talk with you confidentially about your willingness to accept in the immediate future the post of United States Minister to Australia. He has not changed his mind about Ireland or Mexico but thinks the Australian post is particularly attractive and one intensively [sought] after by people in the diplomatic "know." If you are seriously interested in this appointment I am to advise him as soon as possible. I made some confidential inquiries among my friends in the diplomatic corps and they regard very highly the Australian post.[5]

Again, there is no record of how O'Shaughnessy responded to the Truman administration's query, but he declined, perhaps because he had no desire to leave his family and move to Australia.

O'Shaughnessy continued to make political contributions in the 1950s, including $2,000 in 1952 to Citizens for Eisenhower-Nixon[6] and $2,000 in December 1958 to the Eisenhower Presidential Library.[7] He crossed the aisle that same month to contribute to the successful US Senate campaign of Democrat Eugene McCarthy, a Minnesota native who had served in the House since 1948. McCarthy thanked O'Shaughnessy for his "generous support," having acknowledged in an earlier letter, "I know that my position on a number of issues is not wholly acceptable to you."[8]

O'Shaughnessy later wrote McCarthy to request a favor. He asked the senator to support the appointment of Harry Blackmun, then legal counsel to the Mayo Clinic in Rochester, Minnesota, to the Eighth US

Circuit Court of Appeals. "Believe he is very competent," O'Shaughnessy said. Blackmun later wrote to thank O'Shaughnessy for the letter to McCarthy, "and I only hope now that I can do creditable work on this federal bench," he said. He clearly made his mark, and in a nonpartisan manner, because ten years later President Richard Nixon appointed him to the US Supreme Court.[9]

O'Shaughnessy's support of McCarthy didn't dissuade him from continuing to support Republican candidates and causes. He sent $1,000 to the Republican National Finance Committee in 1960 and was enrolled as a National Republican Associate, and the following year he contributed $5,000 to the Minnesota gubernatorial campaign of Elmer L. Andersen.[10]

An Eisenhower visit to St. Paul shortly before the 1960 presidential election between Nixon and John Kennedy elicited a note from O'Shaughnessy to Mayor George Vavoulis, thanking him for photos taken with Eisenhower. "It was very pleasant meeting the President," O'Shaughnessy wrote, "but I must say that I enjoyed your group even more. I hope that I will have the pleasure of meeting you again in the not too distant future. Probably at that time we will not be bothered with the Minneapolis politicians."[11]

Nixon's presidential campaign received an apparent $3,000 contribution from O'Shaughnessy in 1960, and he also sent two $3,000 checks to the National Republican Committee and the National Television Committee GOP to underwrite television and radio programs featuring Nixon and other Republican candidates. O'Shaughnessy reportedly was perturbed that he never received a thank-you note from Nixon, who finally wrote to him the following September to apologize for the "inexplicable" oversight:

> I am sure you will understand how concerned I was to learn
> in the last few days, almost ten months after the election, that
> you had not received a personal letter from me expressing
> my appreciation for your generous contribution to my 1960
> campaign. . . . I can assure you that nothing could be more
> distressing than the fact that you, who should have been
> among the first to have been written, are among the last to hear

from me. . . . I hope that on some future occasion I will have a chance to express my appreciation personally to you.[12]

Vice President Hubert Humphrey wrote to O'Shaughnessy in 1966 after an event at the new St. Paul Hilton, which O'Shaughnessy had helped to finance. "It was good to see you and particularly to see you looking so chipper," Humphrey said. "A box of cigars is on the way from Washington."[13]

O'Shaughnessy contributed $1,000 to Barry Goldwater's presidential campaign in 1964 and $2,000 to the Minnesota Republican Finance Committee and its Nixon-Agnew Victory '68 Dinner. Contributions of $1,000 went to the Republican National Finance Committee in 1970 and the National Republican Congressional Committee in 1972 with the note, "I am sure you can put it to good use. Keep up the good work."[14]

Even at the age of eighty-seven, O'Shaughnessy was writing to members of Congress expressing concerns about tax reform proposals that might discourage charitable giving. He received replies from Representative Joe Karth and Senator Walter Mondale, both Minnesota Democrats.[15]

13

Honorary Citizen of Killarney

He said he found it hard to believe that a hardheaded businessman was buying an Irish castle because of its beauty. "Is there oil under the lakes of Killarney?" he asked me. I told him to be on his way.

—I.A. O'SHAUGHNESSY

On June 24, 1957, the *New York Times* published a story about eight Irish Americans and a Scotsman from Florida who had freed the Lakes of Killarney in Ireland from British control for the first time since the reign of Queen Elizabeth I.

A daring military maneuver? A brilliant diplomatic coup? A clever business transaction?

No . . . it was just a straightforward purchase of an 8,320-acre parcel of land known as Kenmare Estate, and one of the Irishmen was seventy-one-year-old I.A. O'Shaughnessy of St. Paul. He bought it for a very simple reason, he told the St. *Paul Dispatch*: "Everybody asks me why we bought a castle in Ireland—and they are skeptical when I tell them," he said. "I bought it because the lakes of Killarney—just the sound of

99

the name means something wonderful to me. I have a feeling that there are Irish all over the world who know nothing about Ireland except that name and that they share my feeling."[1]

The purpose of the lengthy *Dispatch* story, headlined "Pair Give Away Millions; O'Shaughnessys Wed Half-century," was to celebrate their golden wedding anniversary the following day. But more than half the story focused on O'Shaughnessy joining forces with other Irish Americans to purchase the estate in County Kerry and save it from the clutches of redevelopers. "I had heard that a real estate man had control of the estate and planned to commercialize the lakes of Killarney," O'Shaughnessy said. "I did not like the idea."[2]

So O'Shaughnessy bought the property: 5,000 acres of water (with eleven islands), 3,000 acres of land, the fourteenth-century Ross Castle, St. Finian's and Muckross Abbeys, and part of the town of Killarney itself. Queen Elizabeth I had given the estate to the Earl of Kenmare four hundred years earlier, the *New York Times* story stated, but the last family member died in 1952 and the property was put up for sale to pay inheritance taxes totaling $196,000. Reports indicated the sale price was $240,000 or $249,900 and that O'Shaughnessy's share was $10,000.[3]

The O'Shaughnessys spent five weeks in the summer of 1958 in Ross Castle, a manor house with fourteen bedrooms, an entrance hall, living room, dining hall, library, and chapel. The estate was staffed by twenty employees and included a golf course that wound around lakes and through forests and hills. O'Shaughnessy told the *Dispatch*, "It's a restful place, and a grand place for company. We sat down with 20 people at the table often. One of my grandsons, who went to Europe this summer with his parents, stopped at the place on the way home. He's only a lad but he told me that this was the one place he had seen all summer that he really wanted to come back to. That pleased me."[4]

It was the first trip to Ireland for the O'Shaughnessys. One of their guests was Archbishop William O. Brady of St. Paul, and they entertained the American ambassador to Ireland and the Belgian ambassador to the United States as well. The entourage also visited County Galway and found one of two castles where O'Shaughnessy's ancestors reportedly had lived centuries earlier, about twenty-five miles north of

Gannon; the other castle was in County Clare.

In his *Dispatch* interview, O'Shaughnessy recalled a visit he had received from another newspaper reporter about the Kenmare Estate:

> He asked me rather bluntly what I intended to do with the place. I told him I could not possibly improve on it—that it was perfectly beautiful as it stood. That stopped him for a minute. Then he said he found it hard to believe that a hardheaded businessman was buying an Irish castle because of its beauty. "Is there oil under the lakes of Killarney?" he asked me. I told him to be on his way. [5]

O'Shaughnessy did serve as chairman of the Killarney Real Estate Company, which may have included the other owners of Kenmare Estate, and a proposal surfaced to build twenty houses for millionaires on Ross Island. It's not clear who developed the proposal or if it had been in the works before the O'Shaughnessy group purchased the property, but the *London Times* reported in August 1958 that the proposal had been "abandoned." When asked if the company had any long-term development intentions, O'Shaughnessy told the *Times,* "What improvements could anybody possibly make in Killarney?"[6]

A number of O'Shaughnessy friends visited Killarney, and he always wrote to estate manager Michael Casey about the arrivals of Americans. One visitor was Father (later Archbishop) John Roach, who brought his parents to Killarney in July 1959. "Be sure to take good care of them," O'Shaughnessy told Casey in a letter.[7]

Killarney made O'Shaughnessy an honorary citizen in 1958. He was delighted, he told town clerk John Ashe in a letter. "Will you express to the council my deep appreciation for this fine recognition? It was a very kind gesture indeed and one I appreciate very much."[8]

The O'Shaughnessy group held on to Kenmare Estate for only three years before selling it to a Philadelphia man in 1960. No explanation was given for the sale, and the only clear reference in Minnesota History Center files was a 1966 letter from Gertrude Mathews, O'Shaughnessy's secretary, stating that he "sold the castle in Ireland some time ago."[9]

14

The Silver Link, the Silken Tie

True love's the gift which God has given

To Man alone beneath the heaven;

It is the secret sympathy,

The silver link, the silken tie,

Which heart to heart, and mind to mind,

In body and in soul can bind.

—Niece Kathleen Penny (and Sir Walter Scott)

The year 1958 was a special one for Ignatius and Lillian O'Shaughnessy.

They spent five weeks at Kenmare Estate in Ireland.

They received honors in Rome from Pope Pius XII. He made Ignatius a Knight Commander of the Order of St. Gregory the Great (with a silver star), the highest papal decoration for a layman not head of a state. Lillian was given the decoration *Pro Ecclesia et Pontifice* ("For Church and Pontiff").

And they observed their fiftieth wedding anniversary, made special when their oldest son, John, had family members and friends write congratulatory letters bound into two volumes with photos.

John wrote two letters, the second in longhand:

> I have been fortunate to have shared, as your oldest child and son, practically all of these fifty golden years. You have been abundantly blessed by God with health, happiness and security and have cooperated with Him in all things and so, He loves you as you love each other. As a young boy, I took your love for granted, then later appreciated it, and now realize it to be the cornerstone of your lives, and the strong foundation on which you have built for your children and grandchildren. . . . Thanks for the great heritage you have given us. May we use this treasure chest well and make an accounting of our stewardship as beautifully as you have done."[1]

Lucille, John's wife, wrote the words *Golden Wedding Day* in the left margin and then added a line for each letter:

G for the goals you sought together
O for the order of your lives
L for the laughter that was with you on your way
D for the dreams that were yours
E for the endorsements you made each passing year
N for the number of children that blessed your marriage

W for the wonder of two lives so closely knit
E for the effort you made for all things fine
D for your dreams that came true
D for your deeds of generosity
I for the inspiration you have given others
N for the now you have so deservedly reached
G for the goodness you have shared these golden years

D for the lucky day I began to share your dreams
A for all of the best I wish you today
Y for years of happiness ahead.[2]

Middle son Larry told his parents that the achievement of fifty years of marriage "is its own congratulations" and said that he and his siblings were fortunate to have observed "an image of matrimony in its peerless state," continuing:

> Having caused the hazards, frustrations and pains incidental to your marriage . . . we feel in a special way implicated in the mystery of your love as spies, agents and lucky learners. We have spied on the secret of love and, though no longer fraught with innocence, we have seen a small cure at least for the soul's terrible, unassailable isolation. We have been agents, even double agents, in your marital drama—angels and devils both. And, unlike poor Adam, who never had a mother or father, we have learned that in marriage we must be the guardians of one another's happiness.[3]

Don, the youngest son, emphasized the importance of the entire family celebrating the anniversary and expressed hope that he had lived up to the standards they had set as parents: "To me, this is the epitome of your nature. It signifies what is best of your character, that of love for your offspring. . . . As we grew in age, you molded our character through your example of every day living with others. You showed us that no person is too high or too low in his station in life that he should not be treated as we ourselves would like to be treated."[4]

Grandson Patrick also reflected on the standards that his grandparents had set "for anyone to try and follow." He mentioned standards of religion (papal honors) and education (buildings funded for Catholic schools), as well as "a mark for a good moral life. This mark you have shown by your daily lives cannot be beaten—just like the Irish."[5]

Patrick's brother, John Jr., now president of the O'Shaughnessy Foundation, recalled how he would laugh at his grandfather's stories, such as "spreading jellyfish on toast for breakfast." He wrote that he hoped that he would make "full use of the example you have given me personally and vicariously. I know that I cannot go wrong by following it."[6]

Don's wife, Barbara, shared her own favorite story, recalling how clothes were stolen from their car during their honeymoon in New York. She called her father-in-law to inform him of their plight. "Dad was not nearly as upset as [we] were," she said, "and immediately took command of the situation. 'What about my case of Scotch in the trunk of the car?' he asked. 'Oh, that is safe. Only the clothes we had moved from the trunk to inside the car to make room for the Scotch were stolen,' Don replied. 'Then what are you calling me for so early in the morning?' Dad asked. He then proceeded to tell us with whom to get in touch and what to do about our loss."[7]

Lillian also had a great sense of humor—and needed one to "still be celebrating fifty years of wedded bliss to Dad!" Barbara wrote. "Though he teases her, she always comes up smiling." Barbara also recalled Lillian's wise words when she asked her "what she had done to instill the truthfulness and trustworthiness in her children that she had. Her answer, which I have never forgotten, was, 'Why, I didn't *do* anything. I just always told them the truth.'"[8]

Granddaughter Michele wrote a poem:

I regret my tender age—
Else I might write you as a sage.
My years are few
My wishes great—
To write in rhyme I hesitate
But I know you'll have patience with this small fry
And that gives me needed courage to try.
A basket full of love
And wishes well
Come to you this day[9]

Kathleen Penny, a niece from Atlanta, quoted a favorite Sir Walter Scott verse:

True love's the gift which God has given
To Man alone beneath the heaven;
It is the secret sympathy,
The silver link, the silken tie,

Which heart to heart, and mind to mind,
In body and in soul can bind.

"Truly," Kathleen wrote, "your life together these past fifty years has been 'the silver link, the silken tie.' Your love for each other, your devotion to your family and your many kindnesses to all who seek your wise counsel stand as an example of a full and fruitful life of labor and love of God and fellow man."[10]

~~~~~

Friends also showered the O'Shaughnessys with congratulatory letters.

Father Theodore Hesburgh, president of Notre Dame, thanked them for their hospitality and for sharing their home with him. "Humility, goodness, and a true Christ-like spirit have been the hallmarks of your lives," he wrote, "and on this day I wish for you the complete realization that your labors have been pleasing to God . . . not only your friends, but countless unknown others have been enriched by the blessings which have come from God's hands through your noble hearts."[11]

Bob McDowell, once an employee at Globe's refinery in Blackwell, Oklahoma, said he never had known anyone who had lived with his wealth "more modestly, nor who has distributed it more generously," than O'Shaughnessy. He also said his old boss was blessed to have a "great 'running mate' in Mrs. O'Shaughnessy to keep him on the straight and narrow." He concluded:

Your philanthropies over the years will leave your name
indelibly enrolled in the archives and on the cornerstones of
a lot of physical edifices around the country. But in the final
analysis I would like to suggest that your greatest contribution
to your country and to a great industry . . . is the accumulation
of thousands of friends whose respect and admiration for you
have grown through the years, and whose personal lives have
been benefitted by knowing that great, jovial Irish character—
Ignatius Aloysius O'Shaughnessy."[12]

Two other anniversary gifts are worth noting. The College of St. Thomas dedicated its *Aquinas* yearbook to the couple, and the students, faculty, and staff of St. Thomas Academy sent the O'Shaughnessys the following spiritual bouquet:

> Receptions of the Holy Eucharist: 1,827
>
> Masses heard: 2,216
>
> Rosaries: 1,598
>
> Visits to the Blessed Sacrament: 1,737 [13]

~~~~~

On April 14, 1959—just six months after their fiftieth wedding anniversary—Lillian O'Shaughnessy died in a Miami Beach hospital. She was seventy-four, and she had suffered from a heart condition.

"A good and gracious lady has died after a long illness," said Archbishop William O. Brady, who had traveled to Rome with the O'Shaughnessys the previous year and would say her funeral Mass at St. Mark's Catholic Church in St. Paul. "The clergy of the Archdiocese of St. Paul express their sympathy to Mr. O'Shaughnessy and his family."[14]

PART III

15

Here's Your Christmas Present

*When you line up a shot on the billiards table in
O'Shaughnessy Hall and say to the fellow next to you,
"Gimme room, chum," look twice, because that "chum" may be
Ignatius O'Shaughnessy, donor of the building.*
—1939 STORY IN THE ST. THOMAS AQUIN

After I.A. O'Shaughnessy graduated from the College of St. Thomas in St. Paul in 1907, he more or less disappeared from campus for three decades. Records do not indicate that he was an active alumnus even though he purchased a Summit Avenue home a mile east of St. Thomas in the early 1920s and enrolled sons John, Larry, and Don in St. Thomas Military Academy, which shared the campus with the college.

But for some reason, O'Shaughnessy chose to get involved with his alma mater in the late 1930s, and his influence was felt almost immediately. It was an influence that would penetrate to the very core of the college and reverberate for the next thirty-five years as he quickly established—and then burnished—a record as St. Thomas's most generous

111

benefactor and "a constant and sagacious counselor to four presidents," as one story noted after his death in 1973.[1] In all, his gifts to St. Thomas totaled $8.5 million (or more than $100 million in inflation-adjusted 2014 dollars).

In some ways, the splash that O'Shaughnessy made at St. Thomas was similar to the marks he had made on the oil industry two decades earlier and would make at Notre Dame beginning in the 1940s. In each case, he almost seemed to come out of nowhere. He had no experience in the oil business when he opened his first refinery in 1917, but he quickly achieved success and became the largest independent refiner in the United States. After graduating, he initially spent little time at St. Thomas (and, later, Notre Dame) beyond that he needed to enroll his sons and he became not only their lead donor, but also one of their wisest and most thoughtful trustees.

At St. Thomas, the O'Shaughnessy Era seems to have begun with his October 1937 letter to Archbishop John Gregory Murray, who in addition to leading the Archdiocese of St. Paul also served as chairman of the college's board of trustees:

> I have been trying to contact you for the past several
> months with the thought in mind of discussing with you the
> possibilities of improving the financial structure of St. Thomas
> College, at least in a small way. Will you please accept the
> enclosed checks as a gift to St. Thomas College, and at some
> later date we can get together and decide for what purpose it
> should be applied? I had in mind that it might be possible to
> use this sum to get a larger amount from other sources.[2]

Archival records at St. Thomas and the Minnesota History Center do not indicate the size of those gifts, but O'Shaughnessy sent another check to Murray on December 9, 1937, joined the college's board in 1938, and sent a final check on February 27, 1940, with the note, "I believe that the enclosed check will take care of the balance due on the new building at St. Thomas."[3]

"The new building" was O'Shaughnessy Hall, an athletics venue and the first of five campus buildings that would carry the

O'Shaughnessy name.

There had been talk for years of the need for an athletics building that would provide more opportunities than the existing Armory. A 1932 memo written by Father William Cunningham, dean of studies, lamented the lack of a swimming pool and how students had to travel to the YMCA, Macalester College, or the College of St. Catherine to swim.

"But the problem is much larger this," Cunningham said, emphasizing "the importance of recreation in shaping the life ideals of young men. Those of us in college work see this in the fact that the development of a wholesome and vigorous 'school spirit,' i.e., a loyalty to the ideals for which the college stands, is conditioned by the degree to which the recreational life of the student body is centered upon the college campus."[4]

Cunningham proposed a two-story wing on the west end of the Armory, duplicating a wing on the east end. Ultimately, Ellerbe and Company architects developed plans for a separate, adjacent building clad in the same Mankato Kasota limestone featured on Aquinas Hall, the administration building. (Most buildings constructed at St. Thomas since Aquinas in 1929 also have Mankato Kasota stone cladding.)

O'Shaughnessy became interested in the project. He and Murray agreed "on an arrangement under which Mr. O'Shaughnessy would put up a building if Archbishop Murray would do likewise," recalled Leonard Rogge, a 1931 alumnus who held administrative positions at St. Thomas for four decades, in a 1977 oral history. "The building undertaken by Mr. O'Shaughnessy was O'Shaughnessy Hall."[5]

"Here's Your Christmas Present," stated the *Aquin,* the St. Thomas student newspaper, in a December 1939 headline referring to the $400,000 athletics building. "All but wrapped up in cellophane and ribbon," the story said, "the new O'Shaughnessy Hall will be open to students on their return from Christmas vacations."[6] The three-story building would include a gymnasium, swimming pool, squash and handball courts, locker rooms, four bowling lanes, a game room, classrooms, offices, and a women's lounge.

"One Pair of Wings for Mr. O'Shaughnessy!" headlined a *Minneapolis Times-Tribune* story the following month, and the lead paragraph stated, "This is about an angel." The story explained O'Shaughnessy's involvement in planning the building and inspecting every square inch of it throughout the construction process, including the women's lounge:

> Full-length mirrors [are] all around. Upper part of the walls and ceiling are done in a beautiful rose and the floors—well, they were green, but when Mr. O'Shaughnessy inspected the place, he ordered the green tile-like floor changed to another color—just like that . . . so they're ripping up the floor. The point about the ladies powder room is that the place was designed with infinite detail by O'Shaughnessy. And that's true of the entire building. He saw to it the furniture in the huge clubroom was just the thing. Leather-cushioned chairs, "round-table" davenports, chintz-covered. Special lighting effects (upside-down lighting, as Father Moynihan describes it) all were hand-picked by O'Shaughnessy. After all, he's footing the bill.[7]

"Make Room for Mr. O'Shaughnessy," read another *Aquin* headline. The lead paragraph of the story advised, "When you line up a shot on the billiards table in O'Shaughnessy Hall and say to the fellow next to you, 'Gimme room, chum,' look twice, because that 'chum' may be Ignatius O'Shaughnessy, donor of the building." He looked forward "to a dip in the pool and a workout on the handball courts," the story said, and "he has already scheduled a bowling match, with Father [James] Moynihan as his partner against Father [Vincent] Flynn and Father [James] Moran." Moynihan was president, Flynn would succeed him in 1944, and Moran was an administrator.[8]

O'Shaughnessy told a dedication ceremony audience that he had long believed St. Thomas needed new recreational facilities and a place where students could just hang out. He became more aware of those needs through his three sons, who attended the academy:

> Recognizing the importance of small private colleges in our American life and recognizing the many needs of these institutions, I have had in mind for some time to do something in that direction. It was only natural that I should turn to the

institution which gave me so much in my youth. What I have done, I did in appreciation of what I have received, what my sons are receiving now . . . and what I hope their children will receive.[9]

The *Aquin* reported that O'Shaughnessy turned to Murray and said, "Your Excellency, I am giving this building to you without any expectation of reward in this life. It is a gift from my heart. May others follow my example!"[10]

In an interview with the *Aquin,* O'Shaughnessy recalled his time nearly forty years earlier as a student and a football player and how everyone celebrated when a school holiday was declared after enrollment had reached "the magnificent sum of 200." He extolled the advantages of a small college, including closer contact with the faculty and more individual attention, before stopping to say, "Enough of the serious side of education, though. The real idea is for everybody to get in that building and have a good time. . . . Tell them to leave room for me."[11]

Leave room, indeed, the story concluded: "So if you are lining up a billiard shot, look twice before shouting, 'Gimme room,' because there's nobody deserving of more room, both in our building and in our hearts, than Mr. Ignatius O'Shaughnessy."[12]

Seventy years later, O'Shaughnessy Hall fell to the wrecking ball to make way for the new Anderson Student Center. In preparation for the demolition, St. Thomas removed and opened the time capsule that had been placed behind the cornerstone near the entrance of O'Shaughnessy Hall during its construction in 1939. The tin box contained newspapers, invitations and programs for college and academy graduation ceremonies, and a 1939 Canadian silver dollar. At the time the capsule was opened, no one was quite sure why a Canadian silver dollar was in the box, but it later was determined that silver dollars were not minted in the United States in 1939.

~~~~~~

O'Shaughnessy's challenge for others to "follow my example" certainly came to fruition during his lifetime and beyond. In the 1990s and

2000s, St. Thomas raised $765 million during two capital campaigns. But for three decades—the 1940s, 1950s, and 1960s—it always was O'Shaughnessy who primed the pump, whether the project was large or small.

The Chapel of St. Thomas Aquinas, constructed in 1918, was one of O'Shaughnessy's favored projects. He sent Moynihan a $20,000 check for chapel decorations in 1942. The president later shared with him a financial statement indicating the cost of improvements had totaled $63,297.36 against a $60,000 budget, meaning a deficit of $3,297.36 plus anticipated additional expenses of nearly $6,200. The deficit ended up at $9,481.36. O'Shaughnessy approved payment of $9,500.[13]

In 1945, O'Shaughnessy agreed to serve as general chairman of In the Light of Tomorrow, an expansion program for St. Thomas. He made an initial gift of $100,000 toward a goal of $3.8 million and worked with college officials to develop a 55-page list of 550 potential donors. There is no record of how many individuals made contributions and how much money was raised, but the effort presaged the capital campaigns that would follow.

The campus master plan at the heart of In the Light of Tomorrow envisioned the development of two quadrangles. The lower quadrangle would consist of a new science building (the number-one priority at $920,000), an auditorium, art, and music hall ($400,000), and a library and student union ($520,000) as well as the existing Aquinas Hall, O'Shaughnessy Hall, and Armory. The upper quadrangle would include a new academy classroom building ($500,000), an academy residence hall ($840,000), and a faculty residence ($250,000). (While not all of those buildings were constructed, the quadrangles were developed over the next twenty-five years largely along the lines of the 1945 blueprints.)

The expansion plan also called for $180,000 in improvements to outdoor athletic facilities, including concrete bleachers for the football field. O'Shaughnessy took the first step with this project by funding the expansion of the field into what would become O'Shaughnessy Stadium. A 1947 letter from Rogge to O'Shaughnessy indicated a project cost of nearly $593,000, up from 1946 estimates of $378,000, and Rogge identified potential cuts of $73,000. O'Shaughnessy chose to defer construction of the east stands but installed lights for night football, and the stadium was completed in 1949.[14]

Before construction of the stadium began, O'Shaughnessy learned that a friend (identified in Rogge's oral history only as "Mr. Ames") was in dire financial straits because he had a seriously ill son. "Mr. O'Shaughnessy chose not to make a direct gift to Mr. Ames," Rogge said, "but he did advise me to have plans drawn for a south wall of what now is O'Shaughnessy Stadium. . . . Mr. Ames thereafter was made the job superintendent and was paid for his services."[15]

The new president, Father Vincent Flynn, wrote to O'Shaughnessy on Christmas Eve of 1946 to thank him for the O'Shaughnessy Stadium donation ("a truly great gift"). He offered thanks as well for "the great and imponderable gift of the support you have given me in our whole program—in the meetings of the committees [that] are raising funds, in the trustees' meetings, and in the general influence of your name and support. There is no way of measuring the value of this support, but I know that it is very great, and I wish you to know how deeply I appreciate it."[16]

Flynn and Murray made good on the deal reached in 1938 by Murray and O'Shaughnessy. The archbishop had promised he would lead funding for one building if his trustee covered the costs of O'Shaughnessy Hall. Using the expansion program blueprint as a guide, funds were raised for a science hall, and Albertus Magnus Hall opened in September 1947. O'Shaughnessy contributed $100,000 toward the $1.5 million building.

The president wanted to honor O'Shaughnessy in a special way and wrote to him with a suggestion that he accept an honorary degree in the spring of 1949:

> Years ago, Father Moynihan told me that he had wished to give
> you the doctorate after you had put up O'Shaughnessy Hall,
> and that you had refused. That discouraged me, or I should
> have asked you long before this. However, since you accepted
> a degree from Notre Dame last year, it occurs to me that you
> might be willing to accept one from St. Thomas this year—the
> year in which Donald [O'Shaughnessy] graduates, and the

year in which Father [John] Cavanaugh of Notre Dame will be giving the commencement address.[17]

O'Shaughnessy accepted the honorary degree, and his philanthropy continued into the new decade with a gift of $8,500 for repairs in O'Shaughnessy Hall and the chapel, $100,000 toward the retirement of the college's debt, and $7,500 for chapel roof repairs. Wrote Flynn in 1951:

> I hope you will not think me presumptuous when I say that
> I am sure that Almighty God will reward you for your many
> generous and thoughtful deeds in behalf of St. Thomas. There
> is no way that I can adequately thank you; however, I wish you
> to know that it is my hope to give whatever is left of my life to
> St. Thomas. I want St. Thomas to be the model for Catholic
> colleges in America, and I know that with your help and advice
> and encouragement, St. Thomas will thrive and prosper.[18]

Flynn wrote again in 1953, saying "it is superfluous to say anything about your generosity to Catholic education in America. But I think it should be a matter of supreme satisfaction to you to be able to reflect that you have contributed more of your wealth to Catholic education than any other man, living or dead—and that by doing so you have given an example which others are beginning to follow."[19]

Knowing that Flynn received a modest salary as president, O'Shaughnessy remembered him every Christmas by sending him $500 and bottles of liquor. "I shall serve their contents to contributors only!" the president remarked one year in a thank-you note.[20]

O'Shaughnessy sent another $100,000 gift—this one conditional on a match from Archbishop Murray—to reduce the college's $525,000 debt in 1954 and received this reply from Flynn: "I saw the boss [Murray] the other day and he agreed to raise same."[21]

Flynn worried about the college's finances and mused in a four-page letter to O'Shaughnessy about how to persuade the archdiocese to provide an annual subsidy:

I think that the archdiocese must soon decide whether we wish to keep the present status of the institution, or whether we wish to lower our standards, as we shall have to do—for the present, at least—without a subsidy. No doubt we can balance the budget by ruthlessly cutting our budget in all directions. However, if we so act, I doubt very much whether any of us would like what we should be left with.

In a postscript, Flynn noted that since the letter had been typed, he had discussed with Murray the issue of archdiocesan support for St. Thomas. "We agreed to postpone any action until we can both talk with you when you come home," he said.[22]

16

The Bond of Loyalty

In the long pull of a man's mature, adult years,
he will look with increasing appreciation and admiration on the
school, the priests, and the professors who put before him in his
youth a shining and attractive image of the great things to be
accomplished for his soul, his family, and his society by hard work,
discipline, and sustained effort.

—I.A. O'SHAUGHNESSY

Father Vincent Flynn died in July 1956, and Murray appointed Father James Shannon, a thirty-five-year-old English professor, as the twelfth president of St. Thomas.

Deferring to the 1945 expansion plan, Shannon immediately identified what he perceived to be St. Thomas' greatest needs. He wrote to O'Shaughnessy twice in December 1956 with details on plans for three new buildings, all of which were constructed within four years: O'Shaughnessy Library (1959), Dowling Residence Hall (1959), and Murray Hall, the student union (1960).

Shannon later recalled that after his first meeting with trustees in November 1956, he walked around the campus with O'Shaughnessy, who asked him about the college's greatest need. A new library, Shannon replied, to which O'Shaughnessy said, "I'm glad to see you're thinking along these lines. The library is the heart of any campus. You get an architect, and I'll build the building."[1]

Eight days after his inauguration as president in May 1957, Shannon sent O'Shaughnessy some newspaper clippings and thank-you notes that had followed Archbishop William O. Brady's announcement at the ceremony that O'Shaughnessy had agreed to fund a library. "No letter would be adequate to tell you the extent of joy and gratitude occasioned by the announcement of the new library for St. Thomas," Shannon wrote to O'Shaughnessy. "In quite another vein, I should like to tell you of my personal gratitude for your action in giving this graphic and public endorsement of our school and of my administration. I shall do all in my power to be worthy of your endorsement."[2]

In his oral history, Rogge said when he informed O'Shaughnessy that early plans for the library projected a cost of $2 million, O'Shaughnessy requested that they cut it to $1 million. "We did," Rogge said, "but we indicated what the omissions would have to be. From then on it became a matter of additions." At one point, Rogge told Shannon "that we could build a much less expensive building if we were to forego the Gothic architecture. When we presented the idea to Mr. O'Shaughnessy, he addressed [Shannon] something to this effect: 'How much money are you putting into this building?' So it was that we had a Gothic library."[3]

An April 28, 1958, letter from general contractor M.J. McGough to O'Shaughnessy stated the library would exceed the $1.25 million price tag that he had set by as little as $90,000 and as much as $350,000. McGough's bid the following month came in at $1,529,045.60. A March 1959 financial spreadsheet projected expenses at $1,577,820.73, and they increased to $1,613,573.79 in December 1959, with an unpaid balance of $44,286.96. On February 1, 1960, after the library had opened, O'Shaughnessy wrote to Shannon, "I am enclosing a check for $44,286.96 which, apparently, is the balance due on the new library." Rogge sent O'Shaughnessy a seven-page itemized list of expenses—

down to the last penny—and a one-page summary of twelve cash gifts from O'Shaughnessy, starting with $100,000 on December 2, 1957, and concluding with the final check. The total of $1,613,573.79 included $286.83 in interest on funds, bringing O'Shaughnessy's contribution to $1,613,286.96 for the project.[4]

As costly as the building was, O'Shaughnessy wanted to make a statement about his fondness for the liberal arts with special elements such as stained glass medallions in the library windows to depict writers, philosophers, and church leaders. "He was saying, 'We need a library that will embody the ideals of scholarship and church,'" historian John Lindley said. "These things are extras, luxuries even, in the construction of a building, but I.A. was willing to pay because they were important to him. It was more than four walls and a roof."[5]

In his oral history, Rogge expressed amazement about—and admiration for—O'Shaughnessy's level of interest in the library and his ability to keep track of so many elements of the project:

> He was possessed of a fine mind; he was able to make
> quick judgments; he was able to admit error and seek to do
> something about it. He delighted in telling stories about
> himself. I recalled one story that revolved around his insistence
> that his staff not drink before five o'clock. On the occasion of a
> certain recognition party for Mr. O'Shaughnessy, he was given
> a watch by his employees with all the numbers on the watch
> shown as fives.[6]

Shannon kept O'Shaughnessy up to date on library construction throughout the project. "You would be pleased to see the hole in the ground tonight on the site of the new library," Shannon wrote in a June 1958 letter. "It warms my heart to realize that this great and necessary building is finally underway. Generations of St. Thomas men as yet unborn will have reason to speak your name with praise and to murmur an earnest prayer in your behalf."[7]

At the library dedication ceremony luncheon on October 29, 1959, Shannon introduced O'Shaughnessy as a "Catholic gentleman" who is "proud of his Catholic faith." But "beyond the limits of the Catholic community," Shannon said, "the O'Shaughnessy family has demonstrated to the American public that a good and faithful Catholic is by definition a citizen who is vitally interested in civic, social, and cultural affairs affecting the whole community. Their religion is not a kind of isolated personal piety separate [from] society and unaware of its obligation to promote the common good." The O'Shaughnessys would never be forgotten, Shannon added, "and the name of O'Shaughnessy will be held in benediction and revered with gratitude."[8]

The crowd of six hundred people greeted O'Shaughnessy with a standing ovation. He spoke about St. Thomas with fondness, eloquence, and passion and recalled Father John Dolphin's kindness more than a half-century earlier in accepting him as a student after he had been kicked out of St. John's. He said he never would forget Dolphin's example "of priestly virtue and gentlemanly conduct." Furthermore, he continued:

> It is my sincere personal opinion that the bond of loyalty
> between any alumnus and his alma mater depends primarily
> on whether the school did for him in his youth what it
> promised to do. If in his mature years, he finds by experience
> and competition that his early instruction was sound and his
> youthful formation was complete, his appreciation for the
> school in which he was trained, and shaped, and made aware,
> will grow . . . . In the long pull of a man's mature, adult years,
> he will look with increasing appreciation and admiration on
> the school, the priests, and the professors who put before him
> in his youth a shining and attractive image of the great things
> to be accomplished for his soul, his family, and his society
> by hard work, discipline, and sustained effort. On this happy
> occasion, I can say with pride that in my youth on this campus,
> this vision of what was possible, for a man to attain by means
> of effort and grace, was put before my youthful imagination.
> And I shall always be grateful for the spiritual formation,
> intellectual discipline and the manly example that was offered
> to me and to my generation at St. Thomas as the means
> available for turning such visions into reality.[9]

O'Shaughnessy also reminisced about his discussions with the Moynihan brothers, Fathers Humphrey and James, who had served with distinction as presidents of St. Thomas. They had longed for an "adequate" library and not just shared spaces in Ireland Residence Hall and Aquinas Hall, O'Shaughnessy said, adding, "I can still recall the graphic remark of Father James: 'Once a man has learned to read carefully and with discrimination, all he needs is a bibliography and a quiet place.' . . . The heart of the campus, the college library, is at long last adequate."[10]

Even so, O'Shaughnessy warned, the knowledge that students would attain in a library—and at the college, for that matter—would not guarantee that they would be truly "educated" because they would learn "that study is always difficult and that knowledge is hard to come by. But that it is in the end a reward of great price and a treasure which never can be taken away by thieves or rust or moths."[11] He added:

> I would also remind you young scholars that extensive and
> intensive knowledge, necessary though it is for your success
> in business, will never make you an educated man. Nor will it
> suffice to answer for you in your later years the basic questions of
> life. Knowledge is necessary for wisdom, but wisdom is necessary
> if one is to secure for himself the rewards of eternal life. This
> college is committed to the task of teaching you to use the means
> for attaining this salutary wisdom. I am proud that I have been
> able in some ways to assist you in this search for wisdom.[12]

Letters and telegrams of congratulations poured into St. Thomas after the library opened. Nicholas Coleman, the 1949 Mr. Tommy Award winner who would go on to a distinguished political career as majority leader of the Minnesota Senate, told O'Shaughnessy that the library was "unbelievably wonderful. . . . St. Thomas will [become] the sort of center of learning that I would have had trouble getting into (particularly if I remained insistent on ending sentences with prepositions). . . . But! The better the school, the more for me to brag about in the future."[13]

The year after O'Shaughnessy Library opened, a new professor, Eoin (John) McKiernan, joined the St. Thomas English Department as its chairman. He launched *Ireland Revisited* and *Irish Diary,* two public television series that earned a nationwide audience, and their success prompted him to establish the Irish American Cultural Institute in 1964, with its headquarters on the St. Thomas campus. McKiernan showed great foresight and ingenuity in creating these programs, but he might never have had the opportunity were it not for a chance introduction to O'Shaughnessy. Their relationship showed the extent to which O'Shaughnessy was willing to go to help someone.

McKiernan was brought to O'Shaughnessy's attention in a 1953 letter from C. Agnes Rigney, chair of the Speech and Dramatic Art Department at the State University Teachers College in Geneseo, New York. It's not clear how Rigney knew O'Shaughnessy, but she wondered if he would sponsor McKiernan in his pursuit of a doctorate. He had received a fellowship offer, but it would not cover family expenses (he and his wife had five children, with a sixth on the way).[14]

O'Shaughnessy and Rigney spoke by phone on April 30, and McKiernan subsequently wrote to O'Shaughnessy to express a desire to enroll at the University of Minnesota. He would need at least $3,000 and perhaps $4,500 for a year's full-time study. O'Shaughnessy responded five days later that he "might be able to make arrangements for a loan of $3,000" and added, "I could possibly arrange to get you a part-time job at St. Thomas College."[15] McKiernan shared the news with Rigney, who wrote immediately to O'Shaughnessy:

> In all the more than thirty years during which I have been in education work, I never have been so thrilled, so overwhelmed as I was on April 30 when a gentleman in your position responded so graciously, so generously to an appeal for financial help for an exemplary Catholic, a perfect husband and father, a splendid scholar, and a master teacher, John McKiernan. When I told Mr. McKiernan about my letter to you and your response by phone, I thought, although he is in his early thirties, that he might have a heart attack. I think I never have seen such genuine appreciation on the part of any

individual as that shown by Mr. McKiernan. He could scarcely believe that a gentleman of your stature was so genuinely interested in his educational progress.[16]

McKiernan wrote to O'Shaughnessy on May 7 that he was encouraged "beyond the ability of words to express. . . . It is unique to find a man like you who is ready not only to help but also to trust a fellow human. . . . The key to all is faith and trust."[17]

McKiernan did not hear from the University of Minnesota that month, so O'Shaughnessy wrote to Flynn, then president of St. Thomas, asking that he intercede at the university on McKiernan's behalf. As it turned out, McKiernan enrolled at Pennsylvania State University, thanks to a $1,000 loan from O'Shaughnessy. McKiernan finished his studies in the summer of 1954, returned to the faculty at Geneseo, and received his doctorate from Penn State in 1957. He again wrote to thank O'Shaughnessy, who responded, "Unquestionably, you are the only man in America with eight children who has accomplished this feat. You certainly deserve a lot of credit for your persistency."[18]

McKiernan attended a conference in Minneapolis in November 1957. O'Shaughnessy was out of town but asked him to get in touch with Shannon. The two men met and Shannon resolved to bring McKiernan to St. Thomas, telling the young professor that he would find excellent opportunities in St. Paul to cultivate Irish studies. He joined the St. Thomas faculty three years later.

~~~~~

With the library opening behind him, O'Shaughnessy turned his attention to other tasks at the college.

He contributed $345,000 toward the cost of Murray Hall, the new student union that opened in 1960.[19] The original plans did not include a basement, but one was made possible "through the good offices of Mr. O'Shaughnessy, to say nothing of the good dollars of Mr. O'Shaughnessy," Rogge said in his oral history.[20]

O'Shaughnessy offered to pay for the 1964 reconstruction of the stadium's east wall, originally poured concrete, so it would match the

Mankato Kasota limestone on the south entrance and the main (west) side of the stadium. "Mr. O'Shaughnessy was sitting in the stands," Rogge said, "looking across and finally he said, 'We've got to get rid of that old wall.'"[21] The cost was $39,000. That summer, O'Shaughnessy also paid $30,700 for painting and electrical work in the chapel.[22]

Another big O'Shaughnessy project during Shannon's term as president was to provide assistance in the college's first formal capital campaign, A Program for Great Teaching. Buoyed by a $1.5 million matching challenge grant from the Ford Foundation, Shannon announced the campaign in April 1963 after smoothing out a disagreement with O'Shaughnessy over the timing of the news. Shannon sent an eleven-page handwritten letter to O'Shaughnessy in response to the trustee's "disappointment" over their disagreement and conceded, "I can only say that my error was made in good faith, and possibly under the influence of too much zeal for the success of our current efforts to match the Ford gift."[23] Shannon went on to thank O'Shaughnessy for his own personal pledge of $1 million to the campaign:

> At this time allow me to say that St. Thomas does not have and
> has never had a better or more indulgent friend than you. Your
> willingness to give further support to the St. Thomas program
> at this time is only the most recent in an endless series of acts
> of favor and courtesy and generosity. . . . There is no friend
> of St. Thomas whose good judgment and favor I esteem more
> than yours. It troubles me to think that in my zeal I have done
> anything to injure that bond.[24]

O'Shaughnessy's personal pledge would be split in two, with $500,000 going to the college for its endowment and $500,000 to the academy for construction of its new campus in the St. Paul suburb of Mendota Heights. Half the money came in the form of two checks for $250,000 each and half in the form of Lario Oil & Gas stock. In accepting the gift, Archbishop Leo Binz issued a statement saying that O'Shaughnessy's latest act of philanthropy "is one of vision; it looks to the future of St. Thomas. It is more than a gift; it is an investment in Catholic liberal arts education, an investment for which we are most grateful."[25]

Shannon formally thanked O'Shaughnessy for his contribution in a June 1964 letter and the president attempted to assess the impact of O'Shaughnessy's gifts in the past quarter century:

Each of your gifts over the years has had a specific objective.
Their effects, however, cannot be adequately measured
by merely adding up the buildings and projects they have
supported or made possible. They have had an influence
that transcends their immediate objectives in that they have
stimulated every phase of institutional life. In so doing they
have contributed immensely to the development of that
intangible asset, sometimes called morale, which is necessary
for any successful group undertaking. They have made possible
in the St. Thomas family a spirit of confidence and pride, a
sense of purpose and of accomplishment, a group identity and
commitment.[26]

St. Thomas concluded the capital campaign in 1965, having raised $6.3 million. Shannon was named a bishop of the archdiocese but remained as president of St. Thomas until 1966, when his executive vice president, Monsignor Terrence Murphy, succeeded him. Shannon continued to correspond with O'Shaughnessy on matters large and small, mostly those having to do with the board and planning issues, and Larry O'Shaughnessy joined his father on the board in 1966. (I.A.'s commitment to the board would become part of his legacy. Don O'Shaughnessy, Larry's younger brother, served on the St. Thomas board from 1980 to 1990, and grandson John O'Shaughnessy Jr. has been a trustee since 1991, bringing the family's years of continuous board service to seventy-six and counting.)

Murphy began to correspond with O'Shaughnessy and other trustees in 1966 about the need for another classroom building. The federal government had approved a $951,524 grant for the $3.6 million building, and Murphy told trustees that the college would apply for federal loans totaling $1,346,000. The college itself would need to provide 25 percent of the costs, or $800,000.

O'Shaughnessy had given St. Thomas $832,492 to cover its share of the construction costs, Murphy told trustees at their October 4, 1968, meeting, and the following spring he agreed to cover $280,000 in cost overruns.[27] Rogge said in his oral history that O'Shaughnessy also provided endowment funds equal to the debt to meet payments on the building, "a final gesture on his part, if you will, an echo of the wisdom that had come to him."[28]

"Your easy, ready, and almost casual assumption of the added burden doesn't mislead me into a failure to recognize the great generosity on your part and the inconvenience this may well cost you," Murphy wrote to O'Shaughnessy on April 29, 1969, the day after a groundbreaking ceremony for what became O'Shaughnessy Educational Center. It opened in January 1971.[29]

In an oral history interview, Murphy reflected on his relationship with O'Shaughnessy and offered an interesting theory on the benefactor's willingness to give money to his alma mater. The many projects he funded over thirty-five years—from entire buildings to repairs and renovations to reducing the college's debt—suggest that presidents and gift officers must have spent a large amount of time preparing requests for their largest benefactor. That wasn't the case, Murphy said:

> He never wanted to be asked for money. . . . He said there
> were two institutions he never wanted to ask him for
> money. . . . Notre Dame and St. Thomas. Other institutions,
> other people would, but he never wanted our institutions to
> do so. I don't know why that was, except that he may have felt
> that he knew them well enough to know what they needed,
> to know what he wanted to do. . . . So, on the O'Shaughnessy
> Educational Center, when that was suggested, he was the one
> who came forth. I got a telephone call, and he told me that he
> would make the contribution, a major contribution; really do
> the thing himself or see that it got done.[30]

O'Shaughnessy's final gift to St. Thomas was his largest—40,000 shares of Globe Oil & Refining stock, valued at $2.2 million after his death and later redeemed for $2.75 million. The bequest was added to the college's endowment fund.

17

A Bet on Notre Dame

*The underlying importance of the liberal arts derives from the
point that, properly taught, they show a man how to think. Now, I
can't help believing that it is much better for a man to know how
to think than how to do. . . . The man who has been taught how to
think is never going to allow anybody to teach him what to think.*

—I.A. O'SHAUGHNESSY

It isn't clear exactly when, how, or why I.A. O'Shaughnessy became
interested in the University of Notre Dame. But as soon as their relationship began, it flourished quickly, and it endured for more than three
decades until his death. His youngest son may have lit the first spark.

O'Shaughnessy's interest in the College of St. Thomas in St. Paul
made eminent sense. He was a 1907 graduate, and his three sons had
attended St. Thomas Military Academy, then located on the college's
campus, for their high school studies. John went on to enroll at Georgetown University, and Larry, the middle son, attended St. Thomas for
two years before transferring to Yale University in 1941.

131

Don O'Shaughnessy, the youngest of I.A. and Lillian's five children, enrolled that same year at Notre Dame, and upon that occasion
his father wrote to Arthur Haley, director of public relations, with
a concern. "Mrs. O'Shaughnessy and myself are really not looking
forward to this with a great deal of pleasure as both Donald and Larry
will be leaving us," he told Haley. "We have always had the children
with us so the house will feel quite empty. Perhaps we had better go
back to school ourselves and find out what it is all about."[1]

They did visit, and after spending a day at Notre Dame,
O'Shaughnessy remarked years later that he found "a fine comradeship"
in the student body and came to appreciate the "wonderful spirit of
friendship" that existed between students and faculty.[2]

O'Shaughnessy corresponded regularly with Haley and relied
on him for certain favors. In October 1941, for example, Haley sent
O'Shaughnessy a note confirming that eight tickets for the Notre
Dame–Navy football game had been reserved at a cost of $3.33 each,
plus 20 cents postage. Several days later, O'Shaughnessy sent Haley a
thank-you note and a check for $26.84.[3]

The old football player in O'Shaughnessy reveled in Notre Dame's
successes on the gridiron, and he exulted to Haley in a December 1941
letter that the past fall "was probably the most successful football season
I have had in some years," with Minnesota winning the national championship and Notre Dame finishing second. "I don't know why anyone
could expect anything greater," he said. "The only trouble was that it
looked, on several occasions, as though I was going to find it necessary
to take myself out of some of the games during the last quarter; but, with
great fortitude, I stayed right in there and waited until the last whistle."[4]
O'Shaughnessy's letter must have included a gift, likely of liquor,
because Haley followed up with a note: "What a generous Santa Claus!
Never has the Haley 'cupboard' contained such a fine assortment."[5]

Upon his return to Notre Dame in 1942 for his sophomore year,
Don O'Shaughnessy wanted to live in Dillon Hall. His father interced-
ed for him on two occasions that summer, and Haley came through in
August, telling O'Shaughnessy that his son would live in Dillon with
roommate Richard Ames, a family friend whose tuition O'Shaughnessy

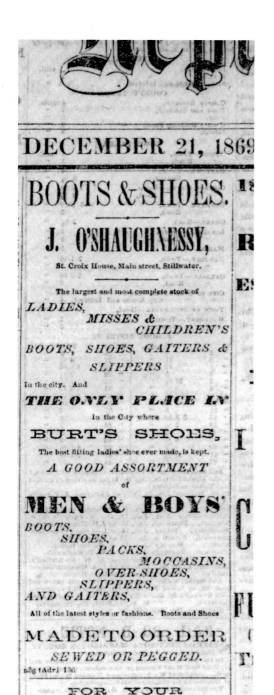

John O'Shaughnessy, I.A.'s father, advertised his boot and shoe shop in the *Stillwater Republican* in 1869.

The O'Shaughnessy family crest

Father John Dolphin, president of St. Thomas, admitted O'Shaughnessy as a student in 1902 after St. John's University expelled him.

O'Shaughnessy wore his College of St. Thomas football letter sweater in 1905.

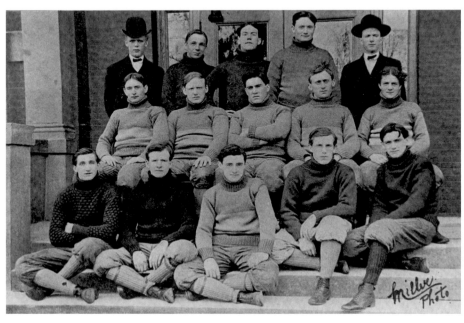

The St. Thomas football team won the state championsip in 1905. Captain O'Shaughnessy is in the middle of the back row.

O'Shaughnessy met Lillian Smith aboard the Capitol, a Mississippi River boat, in 1903. They married in 1908.

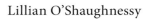

Lillian O'Shaughnessy

The O'Shaughnessys bought this home at 1705 Summit Avenue in St. Paul in the early 1920s, and he lived there (and in Florida) until his death in 1973.

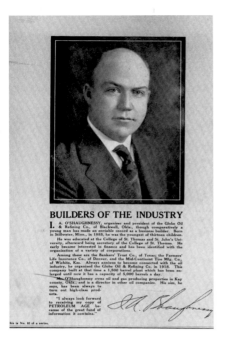

Petroleum Age magazine featured O'Shaughnessy in a "Builders of the Industry" series in the early 1920s.

John O'Shaughnessy, I.A.'s oldest son (left), and Francis Jehle worked for Globe and Lario their entire careers.

O'Shaughnessy built the Globe Oil refinery in McPherson, Kansas, in 1933.

Globe transported its products throughout the Midwest.

Globe employees got around Lemont, Illinois, in a 1946 Mercury station wagon.

O'Shaughnessy owned the Marileen, a 65-foot yacht,
from 1948 until his death in 1973.

The O'Shaughnessys gather in Miami for the christening of the
Marileen in 1948. From left are Father Vincent Flynn, president of St.
Thomas; daughters Eileen and Marian; Lillian; and I.A.

Lillian O'Shaughnessy christens the Marileen with a bottle of champagne as her husband and daughter Marian looked on.

The Skipper

O'Shaughnessy, right, loved to go fishing.

O'Shaughnessy jokingly
prepares to portage
while on a hunting trip
in northern Minnesota.

The O'Shaughnessy family in the 1940s. Behind I.A. and Lillian are Don, Marian, Larry, Eileen and John.

O'Shaughnessy loved to shoot home movies.

The O'Shaughnessys celebrate grandson Brian's birthday with grandson Patrick.

O'Shaughnessy paid for the entire construction ($2.2 million)
of O'Shaughnessy Hall of Liberal and Fine Arts, which opened
at Notre Dame in 1953.

O'Shaughnessy and Father John Cavanaugh,
president of Notre Dame from 1946 to 1952.

Father Theodore Hesburgh, who served as president of Notre Dame from 1952 to 1987, and O'Shaughnessy at the entrance of O'Shaughnessy Hall.

Photo credit: University of Notre Dame

O'Shaughnessy Hall, the first St. Thomas building that he funded, opened in 1940. It cost $400,000.

Father Vincent Flynn, president of St. Thomas, reviews long-term expansion plans with Archbishop John Gregory Murray and O'Shaughnessy in 1945.

O'Shaughnessy family members, with I.A. and Lillian seated at the piano, gather for opening day of the Cleveland Indians' season in 1956. He became a part owner of the team that year. *Sports Illustrated* published the photo in its May 14, 1956 issue. Standing from left to right are son Larry and his wife Betty; grandson Ched Lyman and his mother Marian; grandsons Tim and J. Michael O'Shaughnessy and Gary Lyman; son Don O'Shaughnessy; daughter Eileen and her husband John J. O'Shaughnessy; and Barbara O'Shaughnessy (Don's wife).

The O'Shaughnessys meet with sisters at the Convent of the Visitation in St. Paul.

O'Shaughnessy applies mortar during construction of O'Shaughnessy Library at St. Thomas in 1959.

Father James Shannon, president of St. Thomas, and O'Shaughnessy enjoy lunch during the O'Shaughnessy Library dedication in 1959.

O'Shaughnessy funded the entire cost ($1.6 million) of the St. Thomas library.

O'Shaughnessy waits in the O'Shaughnessy Library auditorium at St. Thomas.

O'Shaughnessy and Hesburgh meet with Pope Paul VI in 1964 to discuss his vision of an ecumenical institute for religious scholars near Jerusalem.

Mary Rea, a family friend, shares a light moment with O'Shaughnessy.
Even in his 80s he loved a good cigar!

O'Shaughnessy outside O'Shaughnessy Educational Center,
which opened in 1971 at St. Thomas.

Blanche and I.A. O'Shaughnessy attend an opening ceremony for O'Shaughnessy Auditorium. Photo credit: St. Catherine University

O'Shaughnessy Auditorium opened in 1971 at the College of St. Catherine in St. Paul. Photo credit: St. Catherine University

Hesburgh and O'Shaughnessy share a laugh in 1971.

O'Shaughnessy's funeral was held November 26, 1973,
in the Cathedral of St. Paul.

would cover.

A notice to parents that year announced the cost to attend Notre Dame would increase in 1943 by $50, to $434.50 for tuition, room, and board, "because the war crisis has greatly increased the operating costs of the university. Such an increase by no means offsets the constantly mounting expenses incurred in the education of each student, but the adjustment is made considerately, so that the burden upon the student or his parent will be as light as possible during the present emergency."[6]

Less than fifteen months after Don matriculated at Notre Dame, his father made the first of many gifts to the university. He sent a $100,000 check to Haley in December 1942 with the note, "I am in hopes that this will stimulate the interest you are so desirous of attaining." Haley sent O'Shaughnessy a telegram that said, "Just returned to office and found letter and magnificent enclosure." A more formal thank-you followed by mail: "Your magnificent gift of one hundred thousand dollars made this Christmas at Notre Dame a very, very happy one," he said. "Your gift gave great and sincere joy to Father [and President Hugh] O'Donnell and all here at the university. . . . May the good Lord be good to you and yours always. I am happy to say that we have had a number of contributions, but nothing near in size to your gift."[7]

A Notre Dame news release announced that the $100,000 would establish the O'Shaughnessy Fine Arts Foundation in the College of Arts and Letters, with a goal of strengthening the college "in the face of a growing tendency toward the purely technical and vocational aspects of higher education."[8]

In the midst of this flourishing relationship, Don left Notre Dame in the middle of his sophomore year to enlist in the Army. By early 1946, according to his correspondence, he had advanced to the rank of captain and was serving in the Philippines. After finishing in the service, he enrolled at St. Thomas and graduated in 1949. Nonetheless, his father's commitment to Notre Dame continued to grow.

In October 1943, O'Shaughnessy wrote to Haley about his interest in attending the Notre Dame–Navy game in Cleveland. "With everybody playing on everybody's else's football team this year, it really has destroyed certain interests that they formerly had," he said. "For instance, this year we will find some of Minnesota's best players of last year playing with Michigan and Northwestern, our two arch enemies. I suppose you have the same condition at Notre Dame."[9]

One might think that football tickets for a benefactor of O'Shaughnessy's stature would be free, but he always insisted on paying for them. On one occasion, he wrote to Haley and asked how much he owed for tickets for the Army game, and Haley responded $67.20 for fourteen tickets at $4.80 each. Within days, O'Shaughnessy sent the check.[10]

O'Shaughnessy was elected to Notre Dame's board of lay trustees in November 1943. The Notre Dame news release announcing his election quoted a *Chicago Journal of Commerce* story calling O'Shaughnessy "a rugged individualist, a man who never has hesitated to go the limit in standing for his principles. His acquaintances often have called him a fighting Irishman—his close friends a fighting American, a man of many accomplishments and interests in business, civic, philanthropic and religious fields, which his material success has permitted him to expand and serve generously."[11]

He made another $100,000 contribution to Notre Dame and its I.A. O'Shaughnessy Fine Arts Foundation in December 1945 with the notation, "Additional contribution . . . an ANONYMOUS contribution." In response, Haley wrote:

> It is a rare privilege for me to acknowledge such a large
> benefaction, and I do want you to know, I.A., how very
> grateful we are to you for your very generous gift. The need
> of the nation, indeed the need of the world, for well-balanced
> Christian leadership cannot be overemphasized. Through
> contributions such as yours the University will continue to send
> forth each year hundreds of men who will carry with them
> wherever they may go, these qualities of Christian leadership so
> necessary in statecraft, in the professions, and in industry.[12]

Father John Cavanaugh succeeded O'Donnell as president of Notre Dame in 1946, and Cavanaugh wrote O'Shaughnessy in August to thank him for a "heartening message" that he had sent. "To have your endorsement and best wishes, as I take up the new duties, is a blessing for which I am most grateful."[13] Notre Dame conferred an honorary degree, Doctor of Laws, upon O'Shaughnessy in June 1947, and the two men corresponded regularly. Cavanaugh visited O'Shaughnessy in St. Paul in July 1948 and toured St. Thomas, after which he concluded a thank-you letter with a promise: "Daily in my Mass and breviary and in other ways, I shall continue to ask upon you, Mrs. O'Shaughnessy and the family God's choicest blessings and rich satisfaction in the great good that you do."[14]

O'Shaughnessy made another $100,000 gift to his Notre Dame foundation in November 1949, and Haley was quick to respond with a telegram: "My theme song of today is 'Oh, What a Beautiful Morning,' and you know why. To say thanks a million is putting it lightly." In a subsequent letter Haley noted that, including investment interest, O'Shaughnessy's donations were valued at $539,094.74—"certainly a most handsome amount"—and that O'Shaughnessy had been elected the new president of the board of lay trustees.[15]

~~~~~~

In the seven years after O'Shaughnessy's first major gift established the foundation, there was no public hint of what the funds, now valued at more than half a million dollars, might be used for other than to "strengthen" the College of Arts and Letters.

But Cavanaugh had a clear sense of what interested O'Shaughnessy, who had noticed buildings for the physical sciences, commerce, engineering, and law. While walking on campus with Cavanaugh one day, O'Shaughnessy recalled, "I asked him where the liberal and fine arts building was. He told me that was one of the weak points in the building program, (that) they had no building of their own and were scattered on various parts of the campus."[16]

The president's response bothered O'Shaughnessy, and he suggested he might assist with unifying the College of Arts and Letters by helping to fund a new building. Cavanaugh wrote to him in 1950 to outline Notre Dame's building needs—thirty classrooms, an art gallery, offices for department heads, and fine arts space—and to offer a suggestion:

After we get this preliminary work shaped into some tangible and intangible form, I think we should then sit down with you and communicate fully to you what we are thinking about. . . . Whenever I seem to be invading too much your time or attention, I know you will be frank in telling me to desist; on the other hand, all of us will be gratified as we can come to you and keep you in touch with the steps as we contemplate them. This letter is already beyond the length of reason. You told me you usually threw in the ash can anything you couldn't see on one page. Please break a rule in this case, and I shall be much more brief in the future.[17]

It didn't take long for Notre Dame to get its "preliminary" work into "tangible" form. Less than two weeks after the Cavanaugh letter, Father Theodore Hesburgh, executive vice president, sent O'Shaughnessy preliminary sketches drafted by Ellerbe and Company of St. Paul and an eighteen-page description of what could be in a new liberal and fine arts building. "I know that you will understand when I say that it is impossible to convey adequately the depth of our gratitude to you for making all of this possible," wrote Hesburgh, who would chair the building committee. "We can only say, may God bless you for it."[18]

Haley sent similar platitudes just days later. "Your gift of a Fine Arts Building to Notre Dame is a fitting tribute to your own personal success in life and an everlasting inspiration to your family," he wrote. "I hope that down through the years there will be many O'Shaughnessy grand-children who will come here for a Notre Dame education."[19]

A Notre Dame news release in May announced an O'Shaughnessy gift of $1.5 million—a new $1 million gift on top of earlier gifts—for a liberal and fine arts building.[20] Six months later O'Shaughnessy sent the money, along with an impish idea on how it could be spent. It was the largest gift in Notre Dame history, and Haley immediately responded:

On Saturday morning, the unearthly check for one million enormous dollars came to my desk from your good self for the University of Notre Dame. In itself this is an historical event; and surely the single sentence which you penned, "Suggest

136

you place the enclosed on Notre Dame Saturday," makes
the event altogether unique. Only a man who has found, in
communication with his Lord, a profound understanding of
his stewardship could write such a wonderful sentence under
the circumstances.[21]

Hesburgh kept O'Shaughnessy up to date throughout 1951 on planning progress for the building. "The architects have been pressing us
about a title for the building," Hesburgh wrote to O'Shaughnessy in the
spring. "We have been referring to it as the I.A. O'Shaughnessy Liberal
and Fine Arts Building. But they seem to think that O'Shaughnessy
Hall of Liberal and Fine Arts would be a better title in stone. If you have
any preference in the matter, we would be delighted to hear from you."[22]

As Hesburgh's committee, along with the St. Paul team of Ellerbe
architects and McGough Construction Company continued their
work, they came to the realization that Notre Dame would be unable
to construct the hall for the proposed cost of $1.5 million and main-
tain its original design. One option was to build only the liberal arts
main section and postpone the fine arts and art gallery wings, but
O'Shaughnessy would hear nothing of it. He offered to contribute
another $673,533 to complete the project and bring his gift to nearly
$2.2 million.

"You really had me floored," Cavanaugh later wrote to
O'Shaughnessy. "I was afraid for awhile that you might be kidding." He
wasn't alone:

> What this will mean to the courses and departments scattered
> around the campus, what it will mean to the morale of the
> professors and to the effectiveness of the work of the students,
> is beyond anyone's estimation. Last evening, we had a dinner
> and dance for the lay faculty, and I cannot tell you how many
> of them took time out to come and tell me how happy they are
> made by what you have done and how optimistically they look
> forward to the days to come. Words from me are altogether
> cheap and inadequate, but God knows and you can be sure Our
> Lady is grateful for what you have done for her University. I am

having another one hundred Masses offered for you and Mrs. O'Shaughnessy and the family.[23]

Hesburgh wrote O'Shaughnessy several days later to add his own thanks for the "wonderful" gift:

As we added up the bids here in the office, I did not even allow myself to hope that we could go beyond Section A of the building, as even that was over the original gift. When you said that we could proceed with the whole building, I must say that it was one of the greatest thrills of my life . . . . We realize that fundamentally the only way we can really say thanks is to keep you in our daily Masses, and I know I can assure you that that is being done for you and all your family. We feel that you have a stake in this University as no other man has had since its founding, and that whatever good is accomplished here in the years to come will redound in large measure to you and your family because of this magnificent gift. I know that as long as the rugged tower of the I.A. O'Shaughnessy Hall of Liberal and Fine Arts raises itself into the sky here at Notre Dame, your name will be both legend and deeply honored by all our priests and students here.[24]

Cavanaugh later expressed similar sentiments, saying he hoped O'Shaughnessy would receive "constant prayers of gratitude" from future generations of students, faculty, and staff:

No human being, trying his best, can properly estimate these factors, and they must be left in the judgment of a bountiful God. I, for one, coming to the end of my term in this office, feel every day more gratitude for having had the privilege of being near to you and to your wonderful family. Your benefaction to Notre Dame is far greater than any that has ever been made, and your friendship and advice and loyalty mean, as you know, something that no person can express. If you ever need a family chaplain, I wish now to make application.[25]

As construction continued, Hesburgh filed progress reports with

O'Shaughnessy. "I have spent some delightful hours climbing around your Liberal and Fine Arts Building here," he wrote in February 1952. "We finally obtained all of the steel we need, although, for a while, it looked like we would have to perjure ourselves to get the priority from the government. I am beginning to think that NPA [National Production Authority] stands for 'Nobody Produces Anything.'"[26]

A significant milestone during construction projects is the laying of the cornerstone, and Notre Dame held a ceremony on May 24, 1952, to mark the occasion. O'Shaughnessy gave a fifteen-minute speech during which he spoke eloquently of how the liberal arts at Notre Dame now would have "a fitting temple," representing what he called "the most practical, useful—indeed, indispensable—field of learning in the world":

> Now, I don't propose in this distinguished company to attempt to define with precision the exact scope of the liberal arts. I would be on controversial if not shaky ground if I were to try to specify exactly those academic subjects which are "liberal" and those which are not. It is always easier to say what the liberal arts are *not* than to state concretely what they are. Yet I think that few of my auditors will take violent exception if, in speaking of "liberal" education, I mean that kind of education which regards that knowledge that man has accumulated throughout the ages as essentially *one*, which regards the apparently different fields of study as mere facets of one universal truth. Such an attitude permits a man to regard facts in a perspective broad enough to develop sound judgment, a sense of values and above all, a moral sense.[27]

O'Shaughnessy said the business of the liberal arts "is to liberate" and that "the greatest prison is always ignorance." An American can enjoy the most extensive political freedom in the world, he said, "yet be carrying manacles if he is unable to see the truth when it is presented to him." He went on to say:

> The study of the liberal arts does teach men facts. Indeed, it teaches them the great and important facts of the universe. Yet the underlying importance of the liberal arts derives from

the point that, properly taught, they show a man *how to think.* Now, I can't help believing that it is much better for a man to know how to think than *how to do,* especially where political freedom is concerned. The man who has been taught how to think is never going to allow anybody to teach him *what* to think.[28]

O'Shaughnessy said he believed the liberal arts "find their most wholesome environment" in Catholic colleges and universities such as Notre Dame, Fordham, Marquette, "and my own alma mater, the College of St. Thomas." He challenged alumni of these schools "to give not only of our means, but of our time, our voice, and our effort toward the cause of liberal education."[29]

18

Spark and Torch

Grace and wisdom: these I equate with the Catholic Church and liberal education. These are our twin pillars. These are the sine qua nons of science and of modern life. These are our faith, in these are our hope, on these are built our charity.

—I.A. O'SHAUGHNESSY

Midway through the construction of O'Shaughnessy Hall of Liberal and Fine Arts there was a change in the president's office at Notre Dame. At the age of thirty-five, Father Theodore Hesburgh succeeded Father John Cavanaugh as president and would go on to serve thirty-five years and become the longest-tenured university president in the United States.

Hesburgh knew his success would depend, to a certain extent, on cultivating relationships with I.A. O'Shaughnessy and other trustees and benefactors who could help him fulfill his vision of creating a truly great Catholic university.

"This, of course, is a well deserved promotion," O'Shaughnessy wrote to Hesburgh. "The work you have been doing at the university for the past several years has meant a great deal to the school. I know that you will carry on in the same spirit, for as you know we are expecting great things from you." Hesburgh responded five days later, "I can tell you in all honesty and sincerity that, if it were not for men like you, who have continuously sought to aid everyone and everything that affects Notre Dame, I would feel hopelessly lost and bewildered. . . . I will count upon you always to feel perfectly free in giving me your judgment and advice."[1]

Judgment, advice and, of course, money. It didn't hurt that O'Shaughnessy continued to surprise Hesburgh with occasional gifts. "It just occurred to me that I still owe the University some money," O'Shaughnessy wrote to the president before Christmas in 1952. "I am not sure of the exact amount so I am enclosing a check for $150,000 which I believe is in the neighborhood of the total owing."[2]

Hesburgh also found a good friend, and almost a father figure, in O'Shaughnessy. The two usually got together every March in Florida aboard O'Shaughnessy's yacht, the *Marileen,* along with Father Edmund (Ned) Joyce, who had succeeded Hesburgh as executive vice president of Notre Dame and served in that position until the two of them retired in 1987. After one such trip, in March 1953, Hesburgh thanked O'Shaughnessy, beginning his letter, per his custom, with the salutation, "My Dear I.A." He wrote:

The companionship, the food, the joy of visiting with dear friends, the rest and uninterrupted peace afforded by the cruise—each experience seemed more perfect than the one before, and constituted a series of kindnesses, considerations, and attentions which I shall never forget. Our private conversations were, of course, the greatest sources of pleasure and happiness for me, and I shall always hold very dear to my heart the intimate talk we had on the boat in the early hours of the morning.[3]

Five days later, Notre Dame named O'Shaughnessy the recipient of the Laetare Medal, awarded annually since 1883 to an outstanding American Catholic layman. "In an age in which material prosperity has often been misused, Mr. O'Shaughnessy has particularly distinguished himself as one who understands and practices the Christian steward-ship of wealth," Hesburgh said in a statement quoted in newspaper stories published around the country. "His benefactions appear to be the largest made by any single person in the history of Catholic higher education in the United States."[4]

<hr />

O'Shaughnessy Hall of Liberal and Fine Arts was dedicated on May 16, 1953. The Tudor Gothic–style building, covering 700,000 square feet over three wings, featured thirty-five classrooms; seminar rooms; offices for department heads and faculty; studios for music, painting, and sculpture; and five art galleries. The Great Hall windows, created by St. Paul artist Pete Dohmen, depicted the seven liberal arts of the first universities in the Middle Ages—arithmetic, astronomy, dialec-tic, geometry, grammar, music, and rhetoric—and symbolized "the heart of education as the building itself stands at the academic heart of Notre Dame."[5]

George Kennan, former US ambassador to Russia, was the principal speaker at a program the evening before the dedication ceremony and would receive wide coverage for his remarks about Communism. But it was O'Shaughnessy who drew the greatest applause when he spoke with eloquence the next day—as he had a year earlier when the corner-stone was laid—about the value of a liberal arts education in a Catholic university. He told a luncheon audience of 1,200 people:

> Grace and wisdom: these I equate with the Catholic Church and liberal education. These are our twin pillars. These are the *sine qua nons* of science and of modern life. These are our faith, in these are our hope, on these are built our charity. What I admire about Catholic education, and Notre Dame education in particular, is that it is not afraid to talk about wisdom and grace. Catholic education tackles them directly; it proclaims them as its main aims; it applies them incessantly, to every situation, to every human problem.[6]

While both wisdom and grace were necessary to the mission of Notre Dame, O'Shaughnessy continued, he believed wisdom to be the rarer quality, and "it is to the acquisition of wisdom that I give this building. . . . I feel that it must come by the old hard ways—by the mastery of language, by the analysis of philosophical truths, by a knowledge of history, by understanding and loving the human arts. The old human studies and skills, lovingly pursued, will result in humility of spirit, rightness of judgment, good taste and good sense. Surely this is the lesson of the Christian centuries."[7]

O'Shaughnessy concluded his remarks by acknowledging that the new building itself would be only a "shell" to house those who work in it. But he had faith, he added, that Notre Dame would continue to attract as faculty and students people "whose decent human spirits and high ideals will hallow these walls . . . and make, in good time, this building no shell but a very temple, in which wisdom and grace, to the glory of God, shall be ever served."[8]

Three days after the ceremony, Cavanaugh, then director of the Notre Dame Foundation, thanked O'Shaughnessy for an excellent speech that "was simple, sincere, moving, truthful, and should be influential in bringing others to do in their own measure what you have done so generously."[9] Five years later, writing to the O'Shaughnessys on the occasion of their fiftieth wedding anniversary, Cavanaugh reported that the building already was having a remarkable impact:

> In giving to Notre Dame the finest building of its kind in the
> world of Catholic education, you have made a continuing
> contribution of inestimable value, in its external influence,
> in what it does internally towards unifying, organizing and
> increasing the morale of teachers and students, and of helping
> them to highest excellence. . . . Because of you, young and old
> people, in many walks of life, are daily being changed for the
> better.[10]

144

Other O'Shaughnessy gifts to Notre Dame followed, although none of the size and impact of his contributions to the construction of O'Shaughnessy Hall.

Football remained near and dear to O'Shaughnessy's heart, and he agreed in 1954 to pay for the addition of an elevator to the football press box. As he had with gifts to other causes, and would continue to do in the years ahead, he agreed to fund half of the $26,100 project as long as his gift was matched, and he ended up writing a check for $13,050. "This new addition will surely please the many writers who cover our games," Athletic Director Edward "Moose" Krause wrote to O'Shaughnessy. "For years we have had a number of complaints about our cardiac staircase." Added Hesburgh, "It appears to me that the price of your admission to the Old Timers Game last year was pretty steep. So was the climb up to the press box, but now that is all taken care of."[11]

In October 1955, a new studio in the O'Shaughnessy Hall galleries was dedicated in the name of sculptor Ivan Mestrovic, who at age seventy-two was joining the Notre Dame faculty. O'Shaughnessy made an $86,000 gift for the studio.

There were other gifts, as well—gifts of spirits. O'Shaughnessy enjoyed sending bottles of liquor—many bottles, it appeared—to friends at Christmas, and Hesburgh and Cavanaugh always were among the recipients. "The latest evidence of your unfailing thoughtfulness and kindness came in the form of a hand-picked variety of most palatable liquids," Hesburgh wrote in January 1956. Two years later, in thanking O'Shaughnessy for his Christmas gift, Hesburgh wrote, "The cupboard was just about depleted when your new supply arrived. We will be thinking of you gratefully whenever we have visitors in the office, thirsty visitors, that is."[12] Cavanaugh was even more gracious—and loquacious—in his tongue-in-cheek gratitude:

> Now that I am sober, after having just received the box of every
> kind of liquor to delight the human taste, I wish to thank you.
> Having such exquisite temptation in proximity to my poor,
> weak Celtic frame is a constant drain upon my determination
> to live soberly and justly. As soon as this box came to me
> from you, I began to notice sweeter looking faces all about

me. Everyone seemed considerate. Everyone has wanted to
help. But I am resisting in the hope that I shall put myself
under obligation to no one and therefore can with a more free
conscience retain for my own pleasure . . . rather than yield to
the temptation of sharing this extraordinary experience with
others.[13]

The Cavanaugh note was similar to many that he wrote to
O'Shaughnessy, for many reasons. "Many, many times, I have told
others that I had an 88 on *the* finest course in the country with *the* finest
gentleman I have ever known," he wrote O'Shaughnessy after a round of
golf in Florida in 1955.[14]

Hesburgh didn't hesitate to call on O'Shaughnessy to flex his
muscles in dealing with board issues. He received a letter from the president in 1956 about a number of issues, including difficulty in placing
an O'Shaughnessy acquaintance on the board:

I wouldn't write these things to anyone but yourself, but I know
you'll be able to read between the lines and give me a helping
hand without my raising a diplomatic incident. I tried to prime
a couple of the other members before the meeting, but no one
said anything to the chairman's objections, so I kept quiet,
too. The men I talked to privately seemed very much in favor
of (X). When I discussed it after the meeting with (Y), he said
just put it in I.A.'s hands and he'll slide it through like nobody's
business. So there you are, I.A.[15]

As influential as O'Shaughnessy was with fellow trustees—and,
truth be told, with Hesburgh—he also respected boundaries and didn't
try to push the president around if they disagreed on an issue . . . even
football. One such occasion occurred in 1964, when the Orange Bowl
made a concerted effort to persuade Notre Dame to change its policy of
not accepting postseason bowl bids in order to play in the New Year's
Day 1965 game. It was to be the first game televised in color, with an
estimated audience of 18.5 million homes and a minimum payment of
$205,000.

"To facilitate the arrangements, I or authorized representatives of the Orange Bowl Committee will be willing to meet with you and the officials of Notre Dame at any time and place," a committee official wrote to O'Shaughnessy. He responded that if the university changed its policy, "naturally I would be interested in having them accept a bid." Several days later, a Florida judge wrote to O'Shaughnessy asking him to help the committee "in its effort to prevail upon Notre Dame to change their policy on bowl participation and to have Miami the choice of their bowls."[16]

Joyce, as executive vice president of Notre Dame, had been copied on O'Shaughnessy's note to the Orange Bowl Committee official and wrote to O'Shaughnessy, "I don't think there is too much chance of deviating from the past policy. Father Ted is pretty strongly against it." O'Shaughnessy then wrote to the Orange Bowl several days later, having spoken with Hesburgh at trustee meetings the previous week: "He [Hesburgh] told me that the administration had not and would not change its position or policy about accepting bids. I am afraid that I am very much in sympathy with its plans."[17]

As busy as O'Shaughnessy was dealing with high-profile issues, he always had time for family. His grandson J. Michael, then a student at Notre Dame, once wrote him about a two-month trip that he and three friends planned to Europe in the summer of 1960. "Do you think that we should have a flexible itinerary or should we follow a definite time schedule?" he asked his grandfather. "How does renting motor scooters or a small car sound?" O'Shaughnessy's response: "I think this [trip] is an excellent idea. As I will be in Winnetka [Illinois] at Thanksgiving, we can discuss the various places and means of transportation at that time."[18]

～～～

A new library was among the top priorities for Hesburgh as Notre Dame moved into the 1960s, and O'Shaughnessy helped to make it a reality.

On March 26, 1962, Notre Dame announced a $1 million gift from O'Shaughnessy to help finance a thirteen-story library on campus. In a press release, Hesburgh described the gift as "magnificent" and reiterated that O'Shaughnessy's benefactions "have been the greatest of any individual private donor in the university's history."[19] The gift qualified Notre Dame for an additional matching grant of $500,000 from the Ford Foundation.

The following day, Arthur Haley wrote to O'Shaughnessy and reminded him of the comment that he made twenty years earlier in donating his first $100,000 to Notre Dame: "I am in hopes that this will stimulate the interest you are so desirous of attaining." Haley continued:

> Well, since then there [have] been about fifteen new buildings
> constructed; numerous fellowships and scholarships
> established; research grants and other contributions resulting
> in millions of dollars. In all of this it took someone to light the
> spark—others "have been stimulated"—and you through the
> years have continued to add fuel to the torch. So, I.A., a great
> amount of the above benefactions are indeed due to you in
> starting the grand parade of accomplishment.[20]

Hesburgh also wrote with his thanks for "an absolutely tremendous gift," but he conceded he was at a loss as to "how you go about thanking someone for such monumental contributions." His solution: "I offered a Mass for You and the family this week, and keep you in my Mass daily. I feel sure that our dreams are your dreams, too, and certainly Our Lady will repay you for the very special help you are giving to make them come true."[21]

O'Shaughnessy contributed another $100,000 to the library fund the following year. "Haven't seen so many ciphers following the figure '1' on a report that I have received from the Notre Dame Foundation office for quite a long time," Haley wrote in thanking O'Shaughnessy for the gift.[22]

Another O'Shaughnessy gift went to the International Federation of Catholic Universities, of which Hesburgh was a leader, and it came as a surprise to the president after they had a casual conversation about some difficulties that he was having with the federation. "You never cease to amaze me by your constant thoughtfulness and world-shaking generosity," Hesburgh wrote after receiving the $15,000 contribution in 1964. "Now you anticipate all that by sending this magnificent check."[23]

As casual as O'Shaughnessy could be about six- and seven-figure gifts, he was overly attentive when it came to paying for an event that he attended. "I am enclosing a check for seven dollars for the Ella Morris Testimonial Dinner," he wrote to Haley in 1963.[24]

As O'Shaughnessy moved into his eighties, his role with Notre Dame and Hesburgh changed, developing a focus on helping the president fulfill Pope Paul VI's dream of establishing an ecumenical institute in the Holy Land (see Chapter 26). Beyond those considerable duties, however, O'Shaughnessy still entertained Hesburgh and Joyce on the *Marileen* every spring and attended board meetings. Notre Dame changed its bylaws in 1967 to replace the board of lay trustees with a newly constituted board of trustees of thirty to forty individuals, in addition to designated Fellows of the University. O'Shaughnessy became a fellow and remained a trustee.

He also retained a soft spot for financial requests that appealed to the athlete in him. In February 1968 he received a request from the Notre Dame Rugby Football Club for a contribution to defray cost overruns of $5,000 during an Easter tour of Ireland. He sent $1,000.

His final gift to Notre Dame—matching his final contribution to the College of St. Thomas—came after his death. In his will, he left Notre Dame with 40,000 shares of Globe Oil & Refining stock, then valued at $2.2 million.

19

Steady Hand and Cool Head

*You have exemplified the good steward in the gospel. It is certainly
true that to whom much is given, much is expected. May I say,
in my humble opinion, that you certainly have fulfilled your
responsibility to God and your fellow men.*

—FATHER JOHN LEE

The growth of the College of St. Thomas after World War II led to
cramped conditions on the campus, which the college had shared with
St. Thomas Military Academy since Archbishop John Ireland founded
the institutions as St. Thomas Aquinas Seminary in 1885.

The academy became a separate school in 1922 but remained on
the same campus as the college and, under the leadership of the same
administration, shared buildings, services, and some teachers with the
college. The In the Light of Tomorrow expansion plan adopted in 1945
called for a new academy classroom building and residence hall to be
constructed on the upper quadrangle. But Father James Shannon, after
becoming president in 1956, came to realize that would not be feasible.

151

"When the trustees were establishing priorities for new buildings, it was apparent that the continuing growth of both the college and the academy would make it difficult to accommodate both student bodies on one campus," Joseph B. Connors wrote in his centennial history of the college, *Journey Toward Fulfillment*. "In addition, Shannon had come to realize within the first year of his presidency that the equitable distribution of the resources . . . would be an increasingly complex problem."[1]

Shannon reviewed the issue with Archbishop William O. Brady, and they planned to discuss it with the board of trustees at a March 1, 1957, meeting. O'Shaughnessy would not be at the meeting, but Shannon wanted his assistance. "If I had a letter from you," he wrote to O'Shaughnessy, "I am sure the other trustees would be prone to give your advice considerable attention. There are serious problems to be faced whether we move or stay. My present feeling, however, is that the certain future growth of the college will eventually put an intolerable pressure on the academy. It seems wise to me to plan now for a transfer."[2]

O'Shaughnessy agreed with Shannon, and several days later Brady suggested to the trustees that the academy staff should look for a new campus. Some academy alumni opposed the idea, but "again the steady hand and cool head of I.A. O'Shaughnessy guided the discussion," Shannon wrote in his autobiography, *Reluctant Dissenter*.[3]

Shannon and Father John Roach, headmaster of the academy, found a site on the south shore of Rogers Lake in Mendota Heights, a suburb of St. Paul, and launched a fund drive to raise $2.8 million. They believed that O'Shaughnessy, whose three sons were academy graduates, would be both a significant donor and key influencer, and their faith was borne out in November 1960 when Brady told Shannon that Patrick Butler would increase his pledge from $50,000 to $250,000. Shannon relayed the news to O'Shaughnessy in a letter:

> In his conversation with the archbishop, Mr. Butler indicated
> that this increase was at least occasioned, if not caused directly,
> by a recent conversation with you in which you apparently
> recapitulated some of the arguments and lamentations which
> I advanced at the last meeting of the Board of Trustees in

STEADY HAND AND COOL HEAD

the absence of Mr. Butler. I have on more occasions than one remarked that you are a born "quarterback." No one else could have presented our case and our need as well as you have done in this instance . . . I should like to thank you for this most recent evidence of your abiding loyalty to St. Thomas and of your habitual concern for the success and the progress and the growth of the academy and the college. Without your interest and endorsement we would be today just one more marginal institution. With your support and friendship we can proudly say that our academy and college deserve comparison with the best in their class across the nation. God bless you.[4]

O'Shaughnessy ultimately donated $728,000 to the project, with the first $500,000 coming in 1963 as part of a $1 million gift shared equally by the college and the academy. As construction continued, costs ran higher than budgeted, and O'Shaughnessy agreed in July 1964 to cover $245,000 in projected overruns. The actual overrun amounted to $251,387.05, Roach informed O'Shaughnessy in May 1965, less than four months before the academy would open its new home. "Once again, let me tell you how deeply grateful I am to you," Roach said. "I will be most anxious to have you see the completed buildings. Your generosity has made them possible."[5]

Perhaps the most touching letter of thanks came from Father John Lee, an academy instructor, who wrote to O'Shaughnessy in March 1964:

I confess that I have lived in amazement at the way you have exemplified the good steward in the gospel. It is certainly true that to whom much is given, much is expected. May I say, in my humble opinion, that you certainly have fulfilled your responsibility to God and your fellow men. The countless institutions both parochial and educational across this country, especially on this campus, will certainly be forever indebted to you.[6]

In 1972, the academy dedicated the fiftieth edition of its *Kaydet* yearbook to O'Shaughnessy and paid tribute to his fifty-year association with the school, dating back to his son John's days as a student. "The expanse of Mr. O'Shaughnessy's generosity both in gift and time is greater than steel beam or concrete," the tribute stated. "It has been a service to generations of academy students."[7]

O'Shaughnessy died the following year, but his foundation continued to be generous to St. Thomas Academy. Grants after his death have totaled more than $2.2 million, including gifts of $1 million in 1996 and $600,000 in 2006.[8]

20

The Hand of Aid

It was going to be quite a speech, Mr. O'Shaughnessy,
but I never gave it. I did pray though and hope you'd remember us
in more than just your prayers. And you have.

—Kate Moorman

Kate Moorman never got a chance to give her big speech to
I.A. O'Shaughnessy about how he should make a gift to the College of
St. Catherine, but she did pray that he would remember the school. He
did, and in a big way.

The young woman arrived on campus as a freshman in the fall of
1963, when the St. Paul women's college was involved in efforts to match
a $1 million challenge grant from the Ford Foundation. She knew that
O'Shaughnessy was a generous benefactor of the nearby College of
St. Thomas, his alma mater, and she thought it was time for a significant
gift to St. Catherine:

> Somewhere I heard you didn't believe in higher education
> for women and that's why we hadn't benefited from your

155

generosity. I always wanted to walk right over to your home and say, "Mr. O'Shaughnessy, it's important for women to have a higher education. Then they can assist and complement the men of our society. Women need further education to be good nurses, social workers, teachers, etc." Then I was going to tell you that their education wouldn't be wasted if they got married. It would give a woman so much more to share with her husband, and after raising children she could go back to her profession if she wanted to. It was going to be quite a speech, Mr. O'Shaughnessy, but I never gave it. I did pray though and hope you'd remember us in more than just your prayers. And you have.[1]

Moorman wrote her letter the same day—January 17, 1965—that the *Minneapolis Tribune* reported O'Shaughnessy's $500,000 gift to St. Catherine, the largest single gift in the college's history. The funds would be used for two purposes—$300,000 for an endowed chair in education and $200,000 for the general capital fund program—and would bring St. Catherine close to the $2 million mark in its $3 million capital fund drive. St. Catherine also used income from the endowment to hold the I.A. O'Shaughnessy Education Symposium, a series of lectures studying the potential influence of Vatican II on Christian education in the modern world.

The *Tribune* story pointed out that a $500,000 gift normally "would be a major feather in the cap of the chairman of the college's St. Paul area campaign." But the chairman just happened to be Larry O'Shaughnessy, the benefactor's son and a St. Catherine trustee, and in this case "both men agreed the initiative came from father to son," the *Tribune* reported. O'Shaughnessy went on to tell the newspaper, likely tongue in cheek, "I don't take orders from my children—I give 'em."[2]

The gift emboldened St. Catherine to seek another contribution from O'Shaughnessy in 1968. Sister Alberta Huber, the college president, asked him for $500,000 for a fine arts building, and she promised to name the auditorium after him. He responded with a pledge and ultimately contributed up to $1 million for the project. The $5.4-

million Mother Antonia McHugh Fine Arts Center—and its 1,800-seat O'Shaughnessy Auditorium—opened October 1, 1970.

~~~~~

Contrary to Moorman's concerns, O'Shaughnessy had made a series of gifts—albeit relatively modest donations—to St. Catherine over nearly twenty years.

The earliest record of a contribution was in October 1946, when Sister Antonius Kennelly, president of St. Catherine, thanked him for underwriting a concert series. Seven years later, her successor, Sister Antonine O'Brien, received a $25,000 gift that arrived on Christmas Eve to help pay for construction of St. Joseph's Hall. "As you know," she wrote to O'Shaughnessy, "I have personally been trying to get an appointment with you to seek your help. Perhaps it is just as well that I did not. I am not a good beggar, nor a good salesman; and I probably [would] have talked Saint Catherine's out of $25,000." She later wrote the following words at the top of her copy of the letter: "Solicitation made by telephone. Asked for interview—which he did not have time for! Was going to Florida—sent check from Florida."[3]

On occasion, O'Shaughnessy would surprise St. Catherine with an unexpected contribution. He wrote to Sister Mary William Brady, president, in September 1960, saying that he had been contacted by a construction company executive about an effort to raise money for scholarships for private college students, including $1,500 for six St. Catherine students. "I told him I would be happy to help him," O'Shaughnessy told Brady, "so I am enclosing a check for $1,500."[4]

He also touched the life of a St. Catherine history professor with a 1962 offer of a $2,000 loan to pay for another year of graduate school. James Cunningham recalled in a 1965 letter to O'Shaughnessy how he was completing his master's degree at the University of Iowa and wanted to pursue a Ph.D.:

> I had no money with which to do so, so I wrote to you asking
> if you would lend $2,000 to see me through the first year of
> Ph.D. work. The spring of 1962 and the summer were rather

a low morale period for me and I was flabbergasted when I
got a letter from you with the loan. During the course of the
summer I decided that I would have a more elevated view of
life if I did not go straight on for the Ph.D., but taught a year or
two instead. I sent the money back. So, why am I writing now?
Simply to say thanks. Thanks for having extended the hand
of aid at a moment when life appeared singularly bleak. The
morale lift was enormous. I do not exaggerate when I say that
I probably would not be a college teacher today, nor would I be
working on my Ph.D., had I not received an offer of help at a
low moment."[5]

A few months after O'Shaughnessy's death in 1973, Cunningham
wrote a letter to the president of St. Catherine and recalled the philanthropist's generosity. "Even though I returned the money unused,"
Cunningham told Huber, "I have always been grateful to O'Shaughnessy
for the morale lift he gave me then. I was completely unknown to him
and never did meet him, but have had a warm spot in my heart for him
ever since."[6]

When O'Shaughnessy died, he left 20,000 shares of Globe Oil
& Refining stock, then valued at $1.1 million, to St. Catherine. It was
the largest bequest in the college's history, and the shares later were
redeemed for $1,380,000. His intention, Huber said, was for the bequest
to provide income for operation and maintenance of O'Shaughnessy
Auditorium.[7] She thanked his widow, Blanche, for his gifts and the
opportunity to have known him:

> His wit, and his directness, impressed me almost as much as
> his generosity and the real joy he took in giving his money
> to causes in which he was interested and watching them
> prosper as a result of his benevolence. Many, many people
> have said fine things about him since his death—all the praise
> well deserved. Many praised him also while he was alive and
> although he deserved that also and, I think, enjoyed it, he
> accepted it with great good sense.[8]

In all, St. Catherine estimates that O'Shaughnessy's gifts to the school totaled $2,606,000—an impressive number to disprove one undergraduate student's fears that he "didn't believe in higher education for women."

21

Opening the Doors to Knowledge

*I know of no other person beside yourself
who will send a $25,000 check . . . by simply filling out a
personal check and without further ado, enclose it in a
plain envelope and without a formal letter.*

—FATHER ALPHONSE SCHWITALLA, ST. LOUIS UNIVERSITY

I.A. O'Shaughnessy's highly publicized involvement with St. Thomas and Notre Dame from the late 1930s until his death in 1973 sent a clear signal to the education community that those institutions would benefit the most from his time (as a trustee and advisor) and his money (as their largest benefactor).

But that didn't stop other schools from asking him for assistance. They were forthright in their requests and he was generous, especially to schools with which he had even a slight connection. He favored proposals from Catholic institutions, always remembering the impact that they had on him and on the lives of his own children and grandchildren; such gifts were his way of saying thank you.

O'Shaughnessy also found himself the recipient of awards, honorary degrees, and other honors. To be fair, they were conferred in the spirit of recognizing his lifelong commitment to advancing education, but they also might have been seen as attempts to curry favor with a donor with deep pockets. Fred Hughes, a St. John's University trustee, carefully and eloquently addressed that issue when he wrote to O'Shaughnessy to inform him that he would receive the university's Pax Christi Award in 1963:

> It may be difficult for you to believe that our motives were free of selfish thoughts of a future participation in your generosity. It may also be that this letter does not persuade you of the truth of this assertion, but I say in all candor and honesty, our suggestion that you be the first lay man to receive the [award] springs from the desire to honor a man whose conduct and example in the vital area of stewardship merit for him, in an eminent degree, what we who love and revere St. John's consider to be a distinct honor [and comes from] a desire to recognize and reward an exemplary Catholic life.[1]

In these careful exchanges of support and accolades, O'Shaughnessy continued to give where he thought it best. Aside from St. Thomas, Notre Dame, and St. Catherine, the Catholic institution with which O'Shaughnessy had the closest ties may have been St. Louis University.

It is not clear why he contributed to St. Louis, but some of his earliest recorded gifts went there. He made regular contributions, $50 twice a month, in the late 1920s and early 1930s, with the first funds earmarked for a dental clinic. Beginning in 1932, his $1,200 annual contributions went to provide care for poor patients in Firmin Desloge Hospital at the university, and he pledged $100,000 in 1945 for the School of Medicine. Upon receiving a $25,000 payment in 1946, Father Alphonse Schwitalla, dean of the school, wrote to him, "I know of no other person beside yourself who will send a $25,000 check . . . by simply filling out a personal check and without further ado, enclose it in a plain envelope and without a formal letter. But that is your way of doing things and that way has on more than one occasion merited my unstinted admiration."[2]

The School of Medicine at the university named its library for him in 1947, and he also became a founder of the Pius XII Memorial Library, which opened in 1959. He contributed $118,000 in Globe stock to the university in 1965.[3]

Loyola University of Chicago asked O'Shaughnessy for scholarship funds in 1953, and he agreed to cover two two-year, full-tuition scholarships at a cost of $1,050 each. One recipient, Raquel Murphy, wrote to tell him of her plans to become a social worker and said she would try to make her career "a continuous expression of gratitude. Without your generosity, it is doubtful that I could have completed my studies in the foreseeable future."[4] Loyola followed up in 1957 with another scholarship request. He said no, but the university still conferred a Doctor of Laws degree upon him in June 1959.

In 1966, O'Shaughnessy helped to endow the Walter and Mary Tuohy Chair of Ecumenical Studies at John Carroll University in Cleveland.[5] Other notable contributions over the years were $5,000 to the University of St. Thomas in Houston in 1948; $5,000 to Loretto Heights College in Colorado in 1957; and $1,000 to assist with the founding of the Catholic University of Korea in 1961.[6]

He turned down several well-known Catholic universities, usually citing his involvement with philanthropic causes in the Twin Cities area or, in later years, his age. "Nothing would give me a greater pleasure than to be able to erect a building at Fordham University but, unfortunately, that will be impossible," O'Shaughnessy wrote in 1956 to the school, which had asked for assistance in developing its Manhattan campus in New York City. "We have so many calls upon us here in the Archdiocese of Saint Paul that it is really becoming a burden to all of us."[7] He gave a similar reason two years later in a letter to the president of Rockhurst College in Kansas City. "I am always glad to see you," O'Shaughnessy wrote. "Rather than waste your time I must warn you that I will be unable to contribute anything to Rockhurst College. We are overburdened here in the Twin Cities with a program for the erection of ten high schools to say nothing of other projects. Naturally, I am more interested here than elsewhere. I am quite sure you will understand my situation."[8]

DePaul University in Chicago conferred an honorary Doctor of Laws degree on O'Shaughnessy in 1966, even though he had declined to become a member of its newly formed board of advisors two years earlier, saying, "I believe that this is work for younger men."[9]

<hr/>

O'Shaughnessy had a softer heart for Catholic elementary and high schools, likely because he had seen firsthand the impact they had on his own children.

He honored a 1939 request from Cretin High School in St. Paul to help boys with their financial needs, and two years later he sent unsolicited another $500, saying, "You apparently are doing very good work with the small amount of funds at your command. It occurred to me that you could use a little more money." The school asked him to cover the cost of new wrestling mats in 1964, and he sent a check for $719.60, for which he received a thank-you letter signed by team members.[10]

He gave $1,000 to Regina High School in Minneapolis the day after he received a starkly candid request in 1969 from Sister M. Kateri:

> This is a begging letter. I thought I might as well tell you before you read it. I am the moderator of the alumnae at Regina High School. . . . We need to outfit an office and I could easily do this with $1,000. If you would be so inclined to help us we would give the alumnae office your name. Another thing—our principal, Sister Mary Eileen, is "hounding" me for money all the time because at the end of this year our school will be in debt $45,000. This makes me nervous, because we don't have any money to give away. That's why I thought of you. I've seen the buildings that God and you have brought about, but I'll bet you've never had a room named after you. Would you please help us?[11]

O'Shaughnessy also made large contributions to Loyola Academy in the Chicago suburb of Wilmette, where his grandsons were enrolled. He agreed to pay for the construction of a swimming pool in 1956; the cost estimate was $180,000 and he ultimately gave $200,000.[12] He contributed $20,000 in 1965 toward construction of a new theater, and the following year the academy gave him an award for his assistance to young people in pursuing an education.[13]

He donated sets of *World Book* encyclopedias to St. Mary's, St. Louis, and St. Vincent Catholic elementary schools in St. Paul in 1959. "The doors to knowledge that you have opened, the propulsion to interest in areas of learning that might never have been discovered except for you, may lead many of these youngsters to significant accomplishment in the colleges and libraries you have endowed," parent Bernice Roberts wrote him.[14] He also assisted St. Mary's with bus transportation in 1963 because of congestion issues related to the construction of Interstate 94 in downtown St. Paul. The school asked him for $400 a month; he sent $800.[15]

Over the years, O'Shaughnessy also contributed $2,500 to De La Salle High School in Minneapolis to pay for furnishings for the Christian Brothers' new residence,[16] an unknown amount for construction of an auditorium at the new Murray High School in Maplewood in 1956,[17] and $100,000 toward a new building at Our Lady of Peace High School in St. Paul in 1962.[18]

Always interested in sports, he was an early benefactor of the Catholic Athletic Association, a new organization for elementary schools in St. Paul. He made a $1,000 loan in 1949 to the association, which made regular payments as small as $20 and as large as $100 in 1949 and 1950, when he forgave the entire loan. "The money in itself was a lifesaver to our program," the association said in a thank-you note. "The realization that a man of your standing has taken a personal interest in this undertaking has been a tremendous morale stimulant for us."[19]

And, as always, O'Shaughnessy couldn't say no to someone interested in a religious vocation. He received a 1957 letter from St. Patrick's School in Waukon, Iowa, asking if he would help a poor young woman who wanted to become a member of the Sisters of Presentation order. "She will be eternally grateful to you for being her financial guardian angel," the letter said. He sent $300.[20]

O'Shaughnessy also gave on occasion to non-Catholic colleges and universities. Most of his University of Minnesota contributions went to support medical school projects (see Chapter 23), and he was generous to Carleton College in Northfield and Macalester College in St. Paul.

Carleton received gifts of $5,000 in 1952, $10,000 in 1956 (intended for an endowed professorship in philosophy), and $100,000 in 1962. The professorship gift may have been motivated by his son Larry's ongoing studies in philosophy. "I remember well a remark you made to me once to the effect that if you had your life to live over again, you thought you would like to be a college professor," wrote Louis Headley, chairman of the Carleton Board of Trustees, in thanking him for the gift. "You should take special satisfaction therefore in Larry's advanced studies in philosophy in preparation for such a career."[21]

O'Shaughnessy gave money to Macalester for building projects, including $5,000 in 1946 for Bigelow Hall and $5,000 in 1951 for a student union, but the college's timing was off with its 1957 request for a contribution to its $10 million long-range development fund. "You have caught me at a very inopportune time as I plan on building a library at St. Thomas that will cost more than one million," he wrote. "Perhaps sometime in the future I can be of assistance." And he was, giving $25,000 to Macalester's building program in 1965.[22]

Other schools benefited from annual contributions by O'Shaughnessy or his foundation to the Minnesota Private College Fund in the 1950s and 1960s, including $6,000 in 1955, when Carleton President Laurence Gould joined a chorus of thank-you notes by writing, "I think of you as a great pillar of strength." His annual contributions to the fund jumped to $12,000 in 1958 and $15,000 in 1960 and later.[23]

Outside of Minnesota, O'Shaughnessy favored universities such as Yale and Lehigh, as well as the United States Naval Academy, because of personal connections. Larry O'Shaughnessy was a 1944 Yale graduate, and his father remembered the school with a $100,000 contribution for a Catholic studies endowed chair in Larry's name in 1962 and a $75,000 gift for the T. Lawrason Riggs Professorship of Religion Fund in 1965.[24]

He established a $50,000 endowed scholarship in the name of J. Porter Langfitt, a friend and Lehigh trustee, in 1957 at the Pennsylvania school. "This has been well thought out," O'Shaughnessy wrote in response to President M.D. Whitaker's proposal, "and it is my intention to use this same form on other scholarships that I am anticipating sponsoring for some of my other friends."[25]

The Naval Academy received a $20,000 contribution toward a new football stadium in 1957, and O'Shaughnessy thanked Rear Admiral W.R. Smedberg for joining him at that fall's Navy–Notre Dame game. "As the old saying is at Notre Dame, 'If we have to lose a game, let's lose it to Navy,' so you undoubtedly felt the sense of how they felt while you were there," O'Shaughnessy wrote.[26] He made another gift to the stadium in 1958, but the amount was not publicized; a thank-you letter acknowledged that he was the largest individual contributor to the $2.9 million project.[27]

Other schools were not as fortunate with their requests, often because O'Shaughnessy said he had other priorities. Sioux Falls College asked him in 1970 for a gift "in the low four figures or modest five figures" to help with construction of a $2.5 million fine arts center. "I am afraid that I cannot be of any help," he replied. "At the present time I am building a building at St. Thomas College, an auditorium at St. Catherine's College and an Ecumenical Institute in Jerusalem. Three buildings in one year takes a lot money."[28]

22

The Last Vigil Light

My dying father, who counted it an honor to meet you on the
occasion of the dedication of the Blackwell church, said to you then,
"You have done the greatest thing a human being can do: You have
used for God's glory the gifts He showered upon you." God bless you.
—Bishop Stephen Leven, San Antonio

If I.A. O'Shaughnessy had a soft spot in his heart for anyone other
than members of his family, it was for priests and sisters, and their
causes in religious organizations.

That made sense. A genuinely devout man, O'Shaughnessy identified with their commitment to service and appreciated their selflessness
in making the world a better place. Consequently, he sought to help
them financially whenever possible. He found it hard to say no to them,
and he honored scores of requests for assistance during his lifetime,
ranging from $500 for a piano at a Catholic school in a small North
Dakota town to $4.5 million for a Jerusalem ecumenical institute that
was the dream of Pope Paul VI. He frequently enclosed notes with his

checks, encouraging the beneficiaries "to keep up the good work."

O'Shaughnessy often reflected on the kindnesses that priests and nuns had shown him throughout his life, including that of Father John Dolphin. O'Shaughnessy never forgot how the College of St. Thomas president had befriended him in 1902, and nearly six decades later at the dedication of O'Shaughnessy Library, he recalled the priest's actions as a turning point in his life.

O'Shaughnessy came to count priests among his closest friends. He was particularly close to Father Theodore Hesburgh, president of the University of Notre Dame from 1952 to 1987, and the two men spent many days each spring on the *Marileen*, O'Shaughnessy's yacht, in Florida. Hesburgh and other priests, including Father Edward Joyce of Notre Dame and Father James Shannon of St. Thomas, said Mass on the *Marileen*, and O'Shaughnessy served as their altar boy. He also played that role at the Chapel of St. Thomas Aquinas on the St. Thomas campus, assisting Monsignor James Lavin at early-morning Masses.

"Mr. O'Shaughnessy was a man of very deep faith," said Monsignor Terrence Murphy, president of St. Thomas from 1966 to 1991. "You would not call him an intellectual in the sense of a lot of theological considerations, but [he had] a very strong and deep faith; a very deeply committed Catholic." Murphy also praised O'Shaughnessy's ecumenical views, which he developed "long before that became the 'in' thing to do. He helped a black Baptist church in St. Paul . . . paid off their mortgage and bought an organ for them, and a bus to take the old folks to church on Sunday."[1]

Friends and strangers alike recognized O'Shaughnessy's brand of faith as special and even rare. Bishop Stephen Leven of San Antonio wrote to the O'Shaughnessys in 1958 on the occasion of their golden wedding anniversary and recalled I.A.'s generosity twenty years earlier after making the difficult decision to close his first refinery in Blackwell, Oklahoma. It would have been easy for O'Shaughnessy to have simply walked away from the town, said Leven, who at that time was pastor of the Catholic church in Blackwell. But he didn't walk away. He made large gifts to a new church, a Catholic hospital, and a Catholic school, and "your generosity in paying the final costs of construction gave me the privilege of offering Holy Mass for you in a debt-free church," Leven said. He continued:

> My dying father, who counted it an honor to meet you on the
> occasion of the dedication of the Blackwell church, said to you
> then, "You have done the greatest thing a human being can
> do: You have used for God's glory the gifts He showered upon
> you." God bless you and your family always. Many times over
> the years I have repeated my father's prayer for you. When
> your plane brought me as a newly consecrated bishop to my
> new post, I repeated it. I repeat it now: "May God bless you for
> yesterday and today and all the tomorrows. May you continue
> to bless Him in all that you do."[2]

That soft spot in the O'Shaughnessys' hearts—Lillian's as well as Ignatius'—may have been most pronounced in their interactions with several orders of sisters.

The couple befriended the Sisters of the Good Shepherd in St. Paul beginning in the early 1930s. Bernard H. Ridder Sr., publisher of the St. *Paul Dispatch* and *Pioneer Press*, wrote to O'Shaughnessy in 1952 about a visit Ridder had from two nuns soliciting funds for a building project, and he poked a little fun at his friend:

> I hope your sense of humor as an Irishman will overcome
> your indignation at having the Sisters of the Good Shepherd
> approach you through somebody other than yourself, but the
> real story is a fantastic one. . . . Two very sweet and lovely sisters
> from Sioux City arrived yesterday and started their proceedings
> by calling on me. They did not know a single soul in St. Paul,
> which, of course, I didn't know. They were flabbergasted when
> I contributed $1,000 to their building fund and then they asked
> whether I would call up Mr. O'Shaughnessy or some name like
> that, who might be very generous.[3]

O'Shaughnessy replied to Ridder that the two sisters had found him, and he had "promised that I would pay them a visit and do what I could to help them. As you know, this is a very old institution here in St. Paul and has done a tremendous lot of good."[4]

After one visit in 1955, O'Shaughnessy wrote to thank the sisters for their good work with youth and enclosed a $1,000 check, "which I hope you will use to give the girls an enjoyable Christmas." He went on to say that when he got into his car after his visit, "I looked down and found a dollar bill, which I am enclosing as perhaps whoever lost it has been looking for it and perhaps notified the office." Mother Mary of St. Francis Xavier replied to O'Shaughnessy two days later that nobody had claimed the money and added, "if they do not, we shall have a Mass said."[5]

The following year, the O'Shaughnessys contributed $120,000 to the order to pay for construction of a transition home for troubled girls and young women. The St. Paul home opened in 1958 at 931 Blair Avenue as the Lillian G. O'Shaughnessy Residence. Mother Mary Paul, provincial of the order in Portland, Oregon, wrote to thank the O'Shaughnessys for the "magnificent gift" and said she hoped to hold down expenses "so that there will be something to return to you when all the bills are paid. Only the O'Shaughnessys would be so magnanimous as to take a chance on 'overpaying in advance.' We assure you we will not betray your trust."[6]

The home proved to not be large enough, and in 1965 O'Shaughnessy agreed to serve as advisory chairman of a $2 million drive to build a school and home on land once owned by railroad baron James J. Hill in North Oaks, a northern suburb of St. Paul. O'Shaughnessy lauded the sisters for supplying "what has been lacking in the lives of these young girls. . . . Once the people in the community know the story of the Good Shepherd, I think they will want to help the Sisters provide the desperately needed new facilities for their girls—their girls and *our* girls too—for they are the future wives and mothers of America."[7] He contributed $100,000 toward the project in 1969, and Sister Mary Louis sent him her thanks. "Monday's mail sack is always fat and full but never before has it contained a gift of $100,000," she wrote. "God love you! You can never know the joy you bring us. . . . We can only say that God is so good in giving us your friendship."[8]

O'Shaughnessy also was fond of the Little Sisters of the Poor, whose St. Paul quarters were on the west edge of downtown St. Paul, and they remembered the smallest of details when it came to maintaining his friendship. One year on the feast of St. Ignatius, they sent him the saint's picture in a frame that a resident had carved out of a cigar box. "As July 31 also happens to be my birthday," O'Shaughnessy wrote in a thank-you note that day, "you can see that I am more than pleased with this gift."[9]

The Little Sisters began efforts began in 1947 to raise $350,000 to make improvements to a residence that housed the elderly, and O'Shaughnessy contributed $25,000. "You are being repaid a thousand-fold in the earnest prayers of the Little Sisters and in the knowledge that the old people under their care again are safe and comfortable," wrote Charles Ward, president of Brown & Bigelow and chairman of the building fund committee for the project, to O'Shaughnessy. "We planned this project at my home in November of 1947, and today it is a reality. You helped to make it come true."[10]

In 1960, O'Shaughnessy considered purchasing a nearby house for use by the Little Sisters, but he was advised that the structure was in "deplorable" condition and that a greater need was a new elevator at their primary facility. The cost would be $25,114, and he was asked to pay half. The seventy-five-year-old man sent a check for $12,557 with the note, "I am sure that the erection of this elevator will be of great help to the old people."[11]

O'Shaughnessy became involved in the 1955 construction of a new Christ Child School in St. Paul for children with physical disabilities. The school had opened several years earlier in a house on St. Paul's East Side, but growth made a new facility necessary. O'Shaughnessy and the College of St. Thomas owned property across Summit Avenue from the campus, and he arranged to have St. Thomas deed to him four lots so he could transfer them to Sister Anna Marie, director of the school.[12]

He came to the aid of his boyhood parish in Stillwater in 1959. He earmarked his $100,000 contribution for construction of a new convent for the Sisters of St. Joseph of Carondelet, who staffed St. Michael's School. "The sisters are very happy," parishioner Francis Miller wrote to O'Shaughnessy, "and maybe we presumed a great deal, but it was suggested with your approval to dedicate the convent in memory of your father John and mother Mary. It is our ardent wish that you shall watch our progress and visit the old home parish often, because we feel that you always have been a part of it."[13]

Another religious order, the Ursuline Sisters, involved him in Villa Maria Academy, a girls' residential high school in Frontenac, Minnesota, on the Mississippi River southeast of St. Paul. The academy wanted to refinance debt that exceeded $400,000 in 1957, and he agreed to guarantee a $125,000 loan for ninety days at 4 percent interest. Mother Mary Jerome wrote him a thank-you letter, and he responded three months later: "I have taken up your note of $125,000 from the First National Bank, which I am enclosing marked paid," he wrote. "I also paid the interest."[14]

During a visit in October 1963, O'Shaughnessy and Mother Mary Jerome again discussed the academy's debt and ongoing financial struggles. It isn't clear what he offered to do, but she wrote to him two days later, "We will never be able to tell you how much we appreciate the experience to transfer [the] magnanimous amount from the column of liabilities to the column of assets. God loves you for it and so do the Ursulines! . . . Rest assured, Mr. O'Shaughnessy, we shall be mindful of your wonderful, generous contribution and dedicate the nicest part of the structure to your name."[15]

Another Ursuline, Mother Mary Catherine, also wrote to him the same day. "A complete entry has been made in the Villa's annals," she said, "so that future Ursulines may also call you 'Prince.'"[16]

Nuns often sent him personal requests. Sister M. Leocreta, a Franciscan whom he never had met, asked him in 1953 for a favor after "reading the papers of your kindness." Her brother was ill in Spokane, and she and a friend wanted to visit him by train. "Would you know of some person who would issue a trip pass?" she asked. O'Shaughnessy wrote to Philip Ray, executive committee chairman of the First National Bank of St. Paul and a board director of the Northern Pacific Railroad, also based in St. Paul. Ray passed along the request to Robert MacFarlane, president of the Northern Pacific. He wrote to Sister Leocreta that while "ordinarily, we clear requests for such passes through the bishop of the diocese in which the applicant resides," he would make an exception and grant two passes for round-trip fares between St. Paul and Spokane.[17]

Sister Jane Marie of the College of St. Elizabeth in Convent Station, New Jersey, wrote to thank O'Shaughnessy for his hospitality in 1955. She was among the 150 nuns who attended the St. Paul convention of the International Federation of Catholic Alumnae, and O'Shaughnessy paid for their lunches and a tour of the city.[18]

As word got around religious communities about O'Shaughnessy's generosity, requests for assistance flowed into his office on a regular basis from around the country. They usually sought the smallest of gifts or loans, and he usually responded in the affirmative.

One plea for funds came in 1938 from the Reverend William Gelsdorf of St. Elizabeth Church in downtown Minneapolis. He enumerated a number of bills, and O'Shaughnessy sent him a check for $100 and wrote, "Sometime in the future if I get time, I will be glad to visit you and discuss your problems with you." Gelsdorf thanked him for the donation and wrote again that November to ask if he "would be kind enough to give me a lift over the rough spots at this time. I shall be very glad to pay you back in a year." O'Shaughnessy mailed him a $200 check, and eight days later Gelsdorf's thank-you note promised "that we will consider you as our greatest benefactor for whom we will pray every day and whom I personally will remember at the altar every day." He repaid the $200 three months later.[19]

O'Shaughnessy received a thank-you note in 1957 from Sister Mary Samuel, academic dean of Dominican College in Racine, Wisconsin, for a contribution (no amount or purpose for the funds was noted in correspondence). She gave equal credit to St. Jude:

After I had written I feared that some one or other of your faithful staff might see the letter and decide to spare you the necessity of answering another request. So I asked one of our sisters in the kitchen, one who is a great friend of St. Jude, to ask him for some help. She asked me what I wanted, and I told her I wanted a letter from Mr. O'Shaughnessy. She said she would burn some vigil lights—if I would give her the lights! So I scared up as many lights as I could and she kept them burning. One morning when I checked on the lights she said, "When these are used up you will get your letter." So I stopped there again a few mornings later and she said, "This is the last one. You'll get your letter today." She always seems to be half-teasing, so I thought I'd see how much weight she had with St. Jude. But it really *was* that day that your letter came. So you see, both you and St. Jude came through.[20]

An executive at City National Bank and Trust in Chicago sent O'Shaughnessy a letter in 1957, asking if he would contribute to a fund to raise $17,500 to purchase a Cessna airplane for two Chicago-area priests who had established a mission in Nigeria. Nine days later, O'Shaughnessy sent a check for $1,000.[21]

Bishop R.O. Geroz of the Diocese of Natchez-Jackson asked O'Shaughnessy in 1957 for funds that would allow him to establish more Catholic parishes in Mississippi, where twenty-four counties did not have a church. O'Shaughnessy made a contribution, and a year later he heard from Geroz again:

When you see this letter I can imagine your saying: "Here comes that beggar from Mississippi again." Well, Christ Himself warned you about that a long time ago when He said that the poor we would have with us always. You just can't get rid of them. Like the man in the Gospel: "To dig I am not able," but unlike him, to beg I am not ashamed when I know that I am not begging for myself nor for my own needs, but rather, for the needs of Christ Himself and His Church.[22]

O'Shaughnessy sent him $100.

He became a donor to King's House, a retreat facility that opened in 1952 in Buffalo, Minnesota, west of Minneapolis, and Father A. Simon followed up in 1958 when he wanted to build a chapel. "For two years prayers have been said every day that such a gift to God might appeal to your magnanimous heart," Simon wrote. "May the Lord of the Altar guide and direct you when you consider your answer to my humble, fervent prayer." O'Shaughnessy wrote to Simon, promising a visit, and he picked up half the cost ($3,000) of an annual sponsors' dinner at the retreat house in 1961. Simon persisted in seeking funds to defray the chapel construction expenses. "You are the key to $300,000," Simon said in his request for a gift of $30,000 to $35,000. "Will you, please, if you please? I should never bother you again." O'Shaughnessy responded, "I am willing to give, as suggested in your letter, $30,000 providing you can get four other persons to give a like amount. This should put you in good shape."[23]

O'Shaughnessy liked to use such matching gifts on projects. Thomas McCann, an alumnus of both the academy and college at St. Thomas, asked him in 1961 for assistance in building a $15,000 rectory at a tiny mission church in Culbertson, Montana. "If you can succeed in raising $14,000 of the $15,000 necessary," O'Shaughnessy said, "I would be glad to furnish the last $1,000."[24]

In other cases, he simply gave. The music minister of Wesley Methodist Church in downtown Minneapolis wrote to him on behalf of St. Benedict's School in Strasburg, North Dakota, in 1961. The minister had met a Benedictine sister who taught there, and he asked O'Shaughnessy to pay for a piano for the school. "I know in your life-time you have received many unusual and sometimes strange requests for money. This may top them all," the minister wrote. "I think that I can put yours in the top category," O'Shaughnessy replied. "It will be a pleasure for me to have you purchase a piano if you can secure one in the neighborhood of $500. Keep on praying to St. Joseph as he, in turn, might do you a good favor."[25]

Closer to home, he contributed $25,000 in 1963 toward construction of Dunrovin, a Christian Brothers retreat house north of Stillwater.[26]

Miami clergy also leaned on O'Shaughnessy, who typically spent more than half of his time in Florida. He gave $25,000 in 1968 and again in 1969 to the Annual Bishop's Charities Drive.[27] In 1972, Monsignor Joseph O'Shea of St. Joseph's Church in Miami Beach asked him for a $100 donation for an advertisement in an event publication. "I have received your insulting letter and I hesitate to make any more donations to your second-rate church," O'Shaughnessy said, sarcasm still in fine form at age eighty-seven. "However, on second thought, I like to see my name in print, so you can put it in the Journal for $100."[28]

Other requests to O'Shaughnessy involved projects overseas. He sent $100 each year in the 1950s and 1960s to the Columban Fathers in St. Paul for their annual fundraising teas in support of their missionary work. "I would have liked very much to have attended your tea as I am quite a hand at pouring," he wrote in 1957 when he made his contribution. "I know that you would appreciate having me there to carry on that function."[29]

O'Shaughnessy made a series of contributions in the 1950s—including $5,000 in 1952 and 1953—to the Family Rosary Crusade, a global effort founded in 1941 by Father Patrick Peyton of the University of Notre Dame. It was estimated in 1963 that Peyton's crusades had involved 20 million people in thirty-two countries, and three years later Pope Paul VI agreed to participate in a televised rosary program at Christmas. O'Shaughnessy came through with the necessary funding, reminding Peyton, "Last spring in Miami, I indicated that I would be willing to help in the financing of this program. We did not discuss the amount because at that time we had no knowledge of the cost of producing the film. Apparently, the time has now come when it will be necessary to do some work toward raising the necessary funds. I am willing to start off this program with a promise of $25,000."[30]

To the Missionary Sisters of St. Peter Claver, a St. Paul order, he contributed $100 in 1956 and gifts of $100 and $1,000 in 1961 for a project in Rhodesia.[31] When Father R. Martin asked him in 1959 for help with installing lights in a monastery in South Africa, he gave $500.[32] And Father Edward Duff received $2,000 in 1961 for his expenses, as editor of the Institute of Social Order in St. Louis, to travel to India to cover the Third Assembly of the World Council of Churches.[33]

At times, however, O'Shaughnessy said no—even to a bishop. He received a request in November 1951 from Bishop John Treacy of La Crosse, Wisconsin, for $250,000 to pay for an auditorium-gymnasium at the Holy Cross Seminary there. "I can quite understand the necessity of having this building and only wish it were possible for me to comply with your request," O'Shaughnessy wrote. "Unfortunately, I have exhausted what funds I had available for such purpose."[34]

He also turned down the Franciscan Sisters of the Sacred Heart in Mokena, Illinois, who wrote to him in 1963 asking for a contribution to help build a new high school. "There is hardly a day goes by but that I receive requests for assistance for very worthwhile projects such as yours," he replied. "Naturally it is impossible for me to be of help to all these various projects. Here in Minnesota, there are also very many projects that need help and find it difficult to secure aid. Naturally, I am more interested in these local needs. I am quite sure you will understand my situation."[35]

O'Shaughnessy also cited "local needs" in declining a 1964 request from the Sisters of Christian Charity in Wilmette, Illinois, who asked for assistance in reducing the order's $700,000 building debt. "I have been trying to figure out some way to give you a donation for the building debt on your school," he wrote, "but so far I have not been able to come up with anything. There are so many worthwhile things that need assistance here in the Archdiocese of St. Paul that one really does not have to look further."[36]

~~~

Not all of O'Shaughnessy's dealings with priests and sisters involved requests for money, thankfully, and he treasured his interactions with priests in the Twin Cities area.

Father Terrence Moore had been one of his professors at St. Thomas. In 1942, O'Shaughnessy attended Moore's golden jubilee celebration as a priest and wrote to him the following day:

> I attended the services at your very beautiful church and heard the archbishop tell what a great fellow you are. As a matter of

fact, after he got through, I started looking for the halo over your head; but, knowing you to be a very modest man, I knew you must have brushed it aside. . . . My only hope is that I will be here when you celebrate your diamond jubilee, so that I can join you on that occasion.[37]

O'Shaughnessy also was friends with Father George Garrelts, director of the Newman Center at the University of Minnesota. They occasionally golfed together, and Garrelts once offered to spot him a stroke a hole on all but the par 3s. O'Shaughnessy's response:

It certainly took you a long time to make up your mind whether or not you had the courage to carry out my challenge for a golf game. The idea of offering me a stroke a hole is very repugnant. You perhaps are not aware that I have been the champ of my golf club for many years. After thinking this over very carefully, you will perhaps want to ask me for strokes. Regarding the date of November 15, I think this would work out very well as no doubt that time we will have about a foot of snow so that we can use a red ball.

Garrelts, thinking the match might be played on grass in a more favorable climate, politely demurred. "If the golf game looks shaky I would settle for 18 minutes of conversation at your convenience," he said. "I am indifferent but my caddies are disappointed about losing out on the Florida trip."[38]

Lavin, who spent his career as a professor and counselor at St. Thomas, considered O'Shaughnessy a good friend and recalled how, in the 1940s, he would show up for Mass in the Chapel of St. Thomas Aquinas, followed by breakfast in the priests' dining room in Ireland Hall. Lavin had a special interest in the chapel's architecture, especially its stained glass windows, and appreciated O'Shaughnessy's many gifts over several decades for restoration and decorations.

Lavin also marveled at O'Shaughnessy's ability to use joking and teasing to set strangers at ease. Lavin recalled a day when he gave two nuns, in St. Paul for a historians' conference, a tour of Stillwater. They visited St. Michael's, O'Shaughnessy's boyhood parish, and the Lowell

Inn, where they bumped into O'Shaughnessy himself. Lavin said:

> He invited us to have a drink with him. The nun history
> teacher refused politely but firmly. I had promised to get her
> back for the evening history speech. She was holding me
> to that promise. I.A. liked her firmness. His drink arrived.
> He said, "You won't let me get a drink for you, but you can't
> refuse taking a sip from mine. When you get back to your
> community, just tell your superiors that you had a drink with
> Mr. I.A. O'Shaughnessy in the historic Lowell Inn." The two
> nuns each took the tiniest sip.[39]

One of O'Shaughnessy's closest priest friends was Monsignor
Francis Gilligan of St. Paul, the longtime pastor of St. Mark's Cath-
olic Church near the St. Thomas campus. It was at St. Mark's that
O'Shaughnessy had met Lillian, and they were married there in 1908.
St. Mark's also became the O'Shaughnessys' parish when they moved
back to St. Paul from Oklahoma.

Gilligan and O'Shaughnessy loved to tease each other. In April
1961, the priest sent O'Shaughnessy a cleverly written letter chiding him
for failing to live up to his promise that he would have himself ordained
in time to help with confessions during Holy Week:

> We kept one confessional with the confessor's section vacant
> for you. And we had a sign on the outside of the confessional
> which stated that it was reserved for penitents that were
> Bulgarians, Romanians, and Turks since the confessor had
> great skill in handling that type of penitent. Yet you deserted
> us. I did not get a chance during the rush to look out to see
> how many Bulgarians were standing in line waiting for you to
> arrive. . . . If a confessor fails to take his place in the box during
> such busy times, you are aware that there is a penalty—namely
> that he is not eligible for clerical Social Security.[40]

O'Shaughnessy typically sent $500 to St. Mark's at Christmas, and
Gilligan used the funds for special projects. He always wrote to explain
how he spent the money, as in this 1962 missive:

You wrote, "Use it wisely." I did, or at least I hope that I did. How? The beautiful reredos [a screen depicting religious iconography] in back of the main altar in the church was covered with much dust. For four years I have been looking at the dust and wondering how we could clean it, since the janitors could not reach it. So with your money I brought in some professionals who put up much scaffolding and thus were able to both clean it and repair a few spots. And while they were here I had them do some work on the side altars and also on the shrine to the Sacred Heart which Mrs. O'Shaughnessy some years ago donated to the church."[41]

Another year, Gilligan purchased an organ for the lower level of the church. He procrastinated in sending a thank-you note before finally writing, "The Irish element in my blood must be atrophying since for some days I have been trying to conjure up some Gaelic phrases which would adequately express my appreciation." A phrase that would "fully give expression to my gratitude did not come," he added, "so in simple language I am writing to tell you that we are grateful."[42]

23

Public Need and Public Gain

There are times in a man's life when something occurs that makes him feel something wonderful and worthwhile has happened. When you told me that the good people of Stillwater had rallied to the needs of their community and raised one million dollars to build a new hospital, that was most gratifying news.

—I.A. O'SHAUGHNESSY, WHO ADDED $100,000 TO THE STAKE

When it came to philanthropy, I.A. O'Shaughnessy primarily was known for his support of Catholic higher education. But he was nearly as interested in health care issues and bankrolled projects ranging from fundraiser expenses at hospitals to research laboratories at the University of Minnesota.

His motivation was pure and simple. He wanted to improve the quality of life in the community and to create a more humane society, especially for the less fortunate and those who could not afford to pay for the care of a good doctor.

Near the end of his life, in 1973, St. Joseph's Hospital in St. Paul took time at its 120th anniversary celebration to thank him. Sister Alice Smith read a beautiful tribute, saying that "our debt of gratitude to him is boundless, and there is nothing we can do but look for words to express it." She recalled how Irish poet William Butler Yeats had said of his contemporary John Taylor Shaw, "He caught up into his imagination the public gain as other men their private gain," and that, for her, summed up the twentieth-century Irishman whose friendship she treasured. "Ignatius O'Shaughnessy has consistently exercised the power to see the public need and to translate that need into public gain," she said.[1]

O'Shaughnessy was too ill to attend the St. Joseph's celebration, but if he had he surely would have shrugged off the praise and attention. He would have said that he gave because he thought it was the right thing to do, and he would have spoken the same words of encouragement with which he often concluded letters:

"Keep up the good work."

O'Shaughnessy's involvement with hospitals in the Twin Cities area extended over three decades. He served on numerous boards and was retained as a director on many of them, even though he seldom attended meetings, because they knew he would provide financial support and open the doors to other benefactors.

Miller Hospital, located near the site of what is now the Minnesota History Center in St. Paul, was a good example. O'Shaughnessy was on the hospital's board, and he contributed $5,000 in 1944 toward an $115,000 effort to meet a training program requirement and $25,000 in 1948 toward a $2 million expansion. Twenty-two years later, he wrote to the hospital's administrator and conceded that because he was "of very little, if any, use to the Miller Hospital, I feel that I should resign from the Board of Governors so that someone could be appointed in my place who could be of more value." The hospital accepted his resignation but also appointed him an emeritus member of the board.[2]

His most significant contributions may have been to University of Minnesota health care entities. The governor appointed him in 1944 to serve on the Committee of Founders of the Mayo Memorial to plan a suitable way to honor Drs. William and Charles Mayo, founders of the Mayo Clinic in Rochester, in the form of a University of Minnesota building for medical education and research. The Minnesota Legislature approved a $750,000 appropriation for the $2.1 million project, and O'Shaughnessy gave $15,000 in 1945.[3]

During those postwar years, O'Shaughnessy developed an enduring friendship with Dr. Owen Wangensteen of the University of Minnesota Medical School, and what happened to them over the course of several projects illustrates the lengthy cat-and-mouse games often played by donors and recipients.

Wangensteen approached O'Shaughnessy to seek funding for a surgical research laboratory at Ancker Hospital, a predecessor to today's Regions Hospital in St. Paul, and solicited a $10,000 pledge in December 1949. O'Shaughnessy typically was prompt, if not early, in paying pledges, so when he had not made a payment by August 1950 Wangensteen wrote to him. O'Shaughnessy replied that he thought the project had fallen through and agreed to send the check—but forgot to sign it. By the time the check was cashed the project was running short of funds, and this time Dr. Ivan Baronofsky, associate professor of surgery and laboratory director, took up the chase. "I need your help," he said in a 1951 letter to O'Shaughnessy. "I know that you have contributed magnificently and again I repeat, I am reluctant to ask again; but my feeling is that this project must not fail." O'Shaughnessy finally came through with a second contribution—this one for $5,000—and the project moved forward. The following month, the Minnesota Medical Foundation elected O'Shaughnessy a trustee.[4]

Wangensteen had O'Shaughnessy in his sights five years later for a surgery research center at the university and received a $150,000 contribution to match other private funds and federal funds. "Your cheering message gave us all a wonderful Thanksgiving," Wangensteen wrote.[5]

A $1 million library was the next project on Wangensteen's list, and he knew where to turn for funding in 1959. "An Ignatius and Lillian O'Shaughnessy Medical Library will pay homage for untold years to two wonderful citizens," he wrote the day after O'Shaughnessy visited a university hospital to witness a heart operation. "No name amongst

Minnesota's citizens would add greater luster to this important edifice than that of O'Shaughnessy, and what pride the faculty of the medical school would take in that glorious name—not alone now, but forever."[6] Wangensteen asked O'Shaughnessy for $600,000 over three years and was turned down, but in July 1960 he landed a $225,000 pledge, which O'Shaughnessy paid within three years.[7]

<hr />

In 1955, O'Shaughnessy joined a new lay advisory board for St. Joseph's Hospital in St. Paul, and none other than Archbishop John Gregory Murray forewarned him about a $5 million expansion project: "I personally would prefer to keep you immune from solicitation so that your own spontaneous generosity might have free play in the edifying stewardship you have demonstrated in disposing of the gifts God has given so abundantly to you."[8]

O'Shaughnessy made a $250,000 contribution within a month and received a quick reply from Sister Antonius Kennelly, the hospital administrator. "Of course," she wrote, "all the Sisters of St. Joseph were quick to point out that St. Joseph must have inspired your generosity because it was on a Wednesday—St. Joseph's day of the week—that you called to give us the grand news."[9]

Dr. Samuel Hunter asked him to help fund a new cardiac research laboratory the following year, but O'Shaughnessy replied, "At the present time I am afraid that I would be unable to be any help." A month later, however, he came through with a $25,000 donation.[10]

Five years later, Hunter wrote to him about the need for a cardiovascular diagnostic laboratory; $48,000 of the required $70,000 had been raised. "I know only too well how you are badgered for money from all sides, so I send this letter with sincere trepidation," Hunter wrote. "I honestly hope that you may see your way clear to help us, but on the other hand, I in no way wish to infringe on my friendship with you in order to gain monetarily, for in the long run this would be a very great loss to me." O'Shaughnessy offered an $11,000 challenge match. "Let's say your gift has been most timely—we'll do the rest," Hunter wrote the following month.[11]

O'Shaughnessy also made a matching gift challenge—a favorite ploy in dealing with medical organizations—in 1961, when the Marian Medical Research Foundation in Minneapolis asked him to help fund a $100,000 laboratory at St. Mary's Hospital. The National Institutes of Health would provide $50,000 in matching funds, he was told, but he chose not to cover the other half. "I would be willing to contribute $5,000 if you could find nine others who would be willing to meet the same amount," he said.[12]

Two of his largest hospital gifts came in September 1958. The first gift, for $100,000, went to the United Hospital Fund of Minneapolis and Hennepin County as part of a $17 million fund drive, but the drive fell $750,000 short of its goal. The hospital asked him the following January if he would increase his gift by $25,000; he did.[13] The second gift, also for $100,000, went to the new Lakeview Memorial Hospital in Stillwater. His pledge letter to project director Robert Slaughter showed some emotion for his hometown and was reprinted in the *Stillwater Evening Gazette*:

> There are times in a man's life when something occurs that
> makes him feel something wonderful and worthwhile has
> happened. When you told me that the good people of Stillwater
> had rallied to the needs of their community and have raised
> one million dollars to build a new hospital, that was most
> gratifying news. It shows the caliber of the people who live in
> Stillwater and the surrounding country. After all, a million
> dollars is a lot of money to raise. To say that they ought to be
> congratulated is putting it mildly. I would feel derelict in my
> duty if I did not do something to add to what has already been
> pledged. I do not know when I enjoyed anything more than
> when I told you how delighted I would be to subscribe $100,000
> to this commendable project. Perhaps nothing is more
> important to any community than a well-equipped hospital.[14]

The hospital returned to O'Shaughnessy a decade later for support of an expansion project, and he contributed $25,000.[15]

Over a five-year period, from 1959 to 1964, O'Shaughnessy made gifts to five hospitals involved with expansion projects—$25,000 to Bethesda Hospital in St. Paul, $15,000 to Divine Redeemer Memorial Hospital in South St. Paul, $5,000 each to Mounds Park and Midway hospitals in St. Paul, and $25,000 to Eitel Hospital in Minneapolis. "As to announcing my gift to the hospital in the papers," he told Divine Redeemer in 1962, "I would prefer that you not do this as it just brings on an avalanche of requests."[16]

In addition to gifts to such direct funding requests, O'Shaughnessy also found himself agreeing to cover the costs of fundraising events. In 1957, he picked up the $1,500 tab for a St. Joseph's fundraising dinner attended by three hundred people at a cost of $5 per person, but he sent a check to the Minnesota Club for $1,600. "The extra $100," he wrote, "is to take care of the help who did such a fine job in serving us." He paid the costs ($3,827) of the St. Joseph's Auxiliary Ball in 1963 and the following year was asked for an appointment to discuss that year's event. "It will not be necessary to put you to that trouble as I shall be very glad to take care of the dinner arrangements as I have in recent years," he wrote. The cost: $3,473. Five years later, he paid for the ball again: $8,666.[17]

Other hospitals approached O'Shaughnessy seeking the same favor. Children's Hospital of St. Paul, beneficiary of $100 annual gifts throughout the 1940s and 1950s for its "free bed fund" and a $10,000 contribution to a building expansion in 1959, found in him a ready donor for its annual balls in the 1960s. "I do not know anything that I would rather do than to pick up the tab for the Children's Hospital Ball provided, of course, you have not already secured somebody else," he wrote to the event director in 1964. "I think balls are a lot of fun, especially when I can have the pleasure of dancing with you." He paid the $5,855 bill.[18]

O'Shaughnessy also was among the earliest donors to the Hazelden Foundation, which opened in 1949, giving $5,000 that year for a guesthouse to be used by alcoholics seeking rehabilitation. He served on the Hazelden board in the 1950s and 1960s and contributed $10,000 toward a $500,000 building expansion. "I am enclosing a check for $10,000," he wrote to fellow board member Patrick Butler, a close friend. Butler's son

Peter wrote a thank-you letter that explained how the funds actually would be used, and O'Shaughnessy responded two weeks later, "Had I known that you were going to put on this drive when I sent [the] check, I would have made it for $20,000. Hence, the enclosed $10,000 check."[19]

Hospitals in the Miami area also received O'Shaughnessy gifts. He agreed in 1956 to serve on the board of St. Francis Hospital in Miami Beach, made $5,000 annual contributions for several years, and gave $100,000 in 1965 to a building project. At Mercy, another Catholic hospital in Miami, he agreed to be the anonymous donor for door prizes at a 1965 charity dinner and paid $2,000 for ten pieces of Tiffany jewelry.[20]

~~~~~

As willing as O'Shaughnessy was to sit on hospital boards and make five- and six-figure contributions to building drives, he found just as much pleasure giving small contributions to organizations and individuals caring for the poor and those who had disabilities.

Dr. William Grey, a St. Paul dentist, asked O'Shaughnessy in 1948 to equip a dental office at Visitation Convent in St. Paul. When he came through with the $6,000, Grey was ecstatic:

> This is one of the happiest days of my life, as I have worked
> so hard and so long to accomplish in fact—the idea—you
> have made possible at last to carry out. Only wish Mr.
> O'Shaughnessy that you could have been with me this
> afternoon to share in the gladness shown when I took your
> check over to the Visitation Convent. [Sister Mary Teresa]
> called in two other sisters and then asked if she could have
> the letter to read to all of the sisters. . . . Mother said she never
> dreamed that such good fortune would come to them.[21]

O'Shaughnessy seemed to have an affinity for organizations that worked with the blind. He contributed to the Minnesota State Organization of the Blind, the Minnesota Society for the Prevention of Blindness, and the Institution for the Chinese Blind in New York. He once sent two checks in the same week, one for $60 and the other for $100, to the National Braille Press in 1942, and the Boston-based organization wrote to ask him if there was a mistake. "It was an error on my part in sending a second check; but inasmuch as you have it, I am sure you can put it to better work than if you return it to me," he responded. "So please keep it and do what good you can with it."[22]

He began giving to the St. Paul chapter of the Red Cross in 1937 ($100) and made donations almost every year, some as high as $7,500 in 1944.[23] He also gave regularly to groups such as the Arthritis and Rheumatism Foundation in St. Paul, the St. Paul Association for Retarded Children, and the Minnesota Heart Association. He funded Minnesota Society for Crippled Children and Adults "camperships" to cover fees for children to attend Camp Courage for two weeks and made contributions to Camp Friendship, operated by the Minnesota Association for Retarded Children near Annandale. He sent an unsolicited check for $1,000 to Our Lady of Good Counsel Cancer Home in St. Paul in 1953 "in appreciation of the very fine work you sisters are doing," and he promised to visit the home the following summer.[24]

Some organizations tested his patience, however, especially if he felt they were returning to him too often. He gave $5,000 in 1955 and again in 1956 to the St. Paul Rehabilitation Center, which worked with people who had physical disabilities, and the center sent him another solicitation in 1957. He responded that he was under the impression, after his 1956 donation, that "it would not be necessary to call upon me again. However, I am enclosing my check for $1,000, which I hope will be of some help."[25]

24

Making a 1 a 2

I search my lexicon and my heart for expressions of gratitude
to suit your wonderful gift, and confess that I still
do not know how to thank you.

—Arturo di Filippi, Opera Guild of Greater Miami

Carol Fiske may have come up with the perfect description in 1972
when, as president of the Saint Paul Opera Association, she wrote to
I.A. O'Shaughnessy to thank him for his "magnanimous and unques-
tioning support." She added that, without him, "the Saint Paul Opera is
a mere whisper."[1]

O'Shaughnessy had been generous—$5,000 to the association in
1969, as well as paying for opera fundraising dinners that year and
in 1966—but not overly so, especially in comparison to the six-figure
gifts that he gave other arts organizations. Yet her description accu-
rately depicted how many in the arts community came to feel about
O'Shaughnessy; without him, "our star in the north, *raison d'etat*, hope
forever," Fiske reasoned, they would be but shadows of themselves.

While he enjoyed music and theater and sought to improve conditions for musicians, actors, and their patrons, he also provided opportunities for younger people with little disposable income to enjoy a good concert or play. In 1960, for example, he bought ninety-four season tickets to Schubert Club concerts for College of St. Thomas students.[2]

O'Shaughnessy's first known support of the arts came in 1946, when he made a $1,000 contribution to the Minneapolis Symphony Orchestra (renamed the Minnesota Orchestra in 1970). He joined its board the following year and continued to make annual contributions of varying sizes, including $3,000 in 1964, when the orchestra struggled with operating deficits. He left the board that year but was succeeded by his middle son, Larry, and in 1967 pledged $100,000 to the orchestra.

Judson Bemis, president of the orchestra, asked him the following year to increase his gift and either endow an I.A. O'Shaughnessy Chair or underwrite the orchestra's St. Paul series as the I.A. O'Shaughnessy Concerts. O'Shaughnessy responded that he felt "quite flattered" to have the concert series named after him, but he subsequently told Bemis, "I would suggest that we go back to my original promise of $100,000 and forget about the rest. I have a couple of very large commitments; I am more interested in education than I am in music."[3]

Bemis would not give up and said he still hoped O'Shaughnessy would endow a chair at $250,000. It worked, although O'Shaughnessy got in a little dig in making his pledge: "As you have not been too successful in getting contributions to the New Dimensions Fund drive, I have decided to go ahead and endow a chair. Almost any instrument would be acceptable but I notice that the clarinet is open so I suggest that we take that. I plan to pay one-half of the $250,000 this year and the other half next year."[4]

The orchestra announced the gift with a profile of O'Shaughnessy in concert programs. "Each Man is Preferred For Some Special Excellence. To Endow Excellence is to Encourage Greatness," read one headline. Cloyde Williams, a Minneapolis native and Juilliard School of Music graduate who had played with the orchestra since 1955, would occupy the I.A. O'Shaughnessy Principal Clarinetist's Chair.

A large gift in 1959 helped to construct a new $2.2 million St. Paul

Arts and Science Center in downtown St. Paul, with the ground level to be named the O'Shaughnessy Floor in memory of Lillian, who had died earlier that year. "Over the years, you have done more for the people of St. Paul than has any other individual," wrote the center's president, P. W. Fitzpatrick. "St. Paul owes you unending gratification."[5]

O'Shaughnessy gave $6,000 in 1969 and 1970 to the center's Arts and Science Fund, and in a thank-you letter the woman who had solicited his gift recalled how hard he made her work for it. "I loved calling you up," Louise Otis said. "You did give me a very bad time of it. It is hard enough trying to tell when you are pulling my leg when I see you but when I only hear you, I'm pretty much at your mercy. But go ahead, because you are one of the great crashers-through in St. Paul."[6]

He liked flirting with fundraisers. "Your persuasiveness made me make a '1' a '2'," he told Thelma Hunter in a letter to the Schubert Club in St. Paul in 1964. At the bottom of the letter he scrawled, "Sent $2,000 to Schubert Club."[7]

O'Shaughnessy also contributed regularly to the St. Paul Philharmonic Society, which sought to establish the St. Paul Chamber Orchestra in the 1960s. His annual gifts ranged from $3,500 to $4,000 between 1966 and 1969.[8]

In Minneapolis, he contributed $25,000 in 1962 toward construction of the Guthrie Theater, $1,000 a year from 1956 through 1967 to the Minneapolis Society of Fine Arts, and $500 to Shakespeare in the Streets in 1967 and 1968.[9]

In Florida, he gave $6,000 to the Opera Guild of Greater Miami in 1969. Its artistic director and general manager, in thanking O'Shaughnessy for the gift, expressed the same concern that others often did when addressing their benefactor. "I search my lexicon and my heart for expressions of gratitude to suit your wonderful gift," wrote Arturo di Filippi, "and confess that I still do not know how to thank you."[10]

25

Just Saying Thank You

I want you to know that whenever or wherever your name is
brought up, you are spoken of as a friend and benefactor to us all. I
join with so many—I am sure from the top on down to me,
the common man, in saying God bless you, Mr. O'Shaughnessy.

—ANONYMOUS LETTER

When newspapers published stories about I.A. O'Shaughnessy's generosity to schools and organizations, one thing naturally and inevitably
occurred: he received inquiries from individuals who needed a helping hand.

He may have said no more often to requests from individuals than
organizations, and in some rejection letters he told people that he was
not in the loan business and suggested they needed to see a banker. It
surely must have been tempting for O'Shaughnessy to simply ignore the
requests and not respond to them, but he was a dutiful correspondent,
believing that if people took the time to write to him, they deserved
an answer.

Some requests came from college students. Leo Durbin, apparently a family friend because he addressed his recipient as "Dear Nashe," wrote to ask for a $5,000 loan in 1957 to finish his dental surgery education in Omaha. O'Shaughnessy responded that he would be happy to help but wanted to know how Durbin would repay the loan. He must have provided a satisfactory answer, because O'Shaughnessy sent two checks of $2,500 each in consecutive years. In 1960, Durbin, having resettled in Florida, began a dental practice and sent O'Shaughnessy the first payment.[1]

In 1961 and 1962, O'Shaughnessy engaged in correspondence with a St. John's University alumnus who was pursuing a master's degree in Russian history at Iowa State University and asked for a loan of $300. O'Shaughnessy agreed to provide the money, but then the student found funds elsewhere. The following April, the student wrote again to O'Shaughnessy and asked for $2,000 to fund the first year of his doctoral studies. O'Shaughnessy sent the student's letter to Father James Shannon, then president of St. Thomas, with a handwritten note asking his opinion. "I vote yes," replied Shannon. O'Shaughnessy subsequently sent the $2,000, although the student returned the money after choosing not to remain in school but to take a teaching position at the College of St. Benedict in St. Joseph, Minnesota.[2]

Leo Fecht was a graduate art student at Notre Dame in 1962 and received an offer of $6,200 to teach at Mount Saint Mary's in Los Angeles. He had no funds to pay for moving costs, which he estimated at $1,100, and wrote to O'Shaughnessy for a loan. "If not, I know it was a stupid and awkward approach and I hope you'll forgive it," he said. "God bless you." O'Shaughnessy replied with a check for $1,100, and Fecht paid off the 4 percent loan less than two years later. "We'll never forget your kindness," he told O'Shaughnessy.[3]

O'Shaughnessy always took care of relatives. In 1969, he offered to pay the college bills of Valparaiso University sophomore Maureen Kelly, a grandniece, after her father died. Before Maureen started her senior year, her mother sent O'Shaughnessy a sheet of estimated costs totaling $3,109. He wrote back five days later with a check for $3,109.[4]

Other requests for money seemed to come out of nowhere.

In 1941, Mrs. Vincent Doyle wrote to O'Shaughnessy about her unsuccessful efforts to sell forty acres of land near Minnetonka and wondered if he had any interest. It's not clear how they knew each other or if he responded, but six years later she wrote to him and asked for a $500 loan to cover miscellaneous expenses, as she had been ill. Another ten years went by before, in 1957, she sent him a $100 check to apply against the $500 loan and promised to pay him $100 a year: "I don't know what I would have done without your help with expenses at the time, but can only say, 'God bless you' and my prayers have always been for you and your family," she wrote. O'Shaughnessy responded that he was "very much surprised and pleased" by her letter. "I had quite forgotten the incident. I am sure that you are in more need of this money than I am so you can just forget about the balance of $400 and the interest you mentioned. I hope that everything will work out fine for you and from now on your troubles will have been in the past."[5]

A St. Paul man wrote to O'Shaughnessy in 1960 for funds. The man worked in a drugstore and said he and his wife had six children and had fallen behind in paying their bills. "I know, Mr. O'Shaughnessy, you are probably besieged every day by such requests and it certainly must be annoying, but I know of nowhere else to turn," he wrote. Responding ten days later, O'Shaughnessy wrote, "I am afraid that I cannot be of any help. Many people have approached me requesting loans of this character and I always refer them to the First National Bank. It would be impossible for me to carry on a loan business. I am quite sure that you understand."[6]

He also turned down a St. Paul woman who wrote to him in 1963 about how the small business that she and her husband owned for twenty years failed after two customers who owed $5,000 filed for bankruptcy. They sold their equipment to satisfy creditors, and each of them found work, but they still did not have enough money to pay off their debts:

> We've been proud people, Mr. O'Shaughnessy, and took such satisfaction that by working together we could raise our five children and give them the education neither of us were able

to have. Now, in our middle age, with our job a long way from being completed we find ourselves with breaking pride and a day to day struggle to keep each other's spirits from doing the same. . . . My husband doesn't know I have written you, and he might agree with you that I am naïve, [but] I pray for a miracle that would help to give him back his self-respect.

O'Shaughnessy said no: "I regret very much that I will be unable to give you any financial assistance. Hardly a day goes by but that I am asked to help many worthy causes and it is quite obvious that this is an impossibility."[7]

~~~~~

Helen O'Shaughnessy of Saratoga Springs, New York, once came across his name in a magazine and decided to write to him. They were not related, and she did not want money—just a chance to thank him. "I read all about you," she said. "Your goodness to churches, colleges, hospitals, etc.—it all seemed like a wonderful fairy story. How proud your Mrs. and five children must be. Please do not misunderstand me. I'm not seeking help or anything like that. I just wanted the thrill (even in my late years) of writing to an O'Shaughnessy, never dreaming that it would be a man as famous and as well known as you."[8]

He replied that it was "kind and thoughtful" for her to write to him. "If at any time you are out in this part of the country I would be glad to have you call upon me."[9]

Finally, there was the handwritten letter that he received in March 1959 from a man who, like Helen O'Shaughnessy, just wanted to say thank you:

I want you to know that whenever or wherever your name is brought up—whether among the boys having a cocktail at the Lex . . . or on the steps of the church after Mass—you are spoken of as a friend and benefactor of us all. I join with so many—I am sure from the top on down to me, the common man, in saying God bless you, Mr. O'Shaughnessy. To sign this letter would not add to its sincerity or heartfelt thanks.

Sincerely,

One of the many friends you don't know you have.[10]

26

Fulfilling a Papal Dream

With most people who give you a million, that's the price of doing something. To go back and say you need twice as much—that's not a good way to raise money. Not O'Shaughnessy. I'll quote his exact words, because I'll never forget them: "Oh well, Ted, it's just money. You need it. I got it. You can have $2 million."

—FATHER THEODORE HESBURGH

In 1964, Father Theodore Hesburgh, president of the University of Notre Dame, asked I.A. O'Shaughnessy one more time for assistance on a building—only this time the project would be not at Notre Dame but in Jerusalem, and the man with the dream was none other than Pope Paul VI.

The pope had long envisioned an institute where religious scholars of all faiths would explore the world's beliefs in a collaborative and cooperative manner. He created a special Vatican secretariat in 1963 to make contact with faiths beyond Christianity on matters of common interest, and the following January he met with Orthodox Patriarch

Athenagoras I of Constantinople (Istanbul) on the Mount of Olives in Jerusalem. It was the first face-to-face encounter between a Catholic pontiff and an Orthodox patriarch in five centuries.

Knowing it would take a leader of immense interpersonal skills and fundraising ability to direct the institute project, the pope turned to Hesburgh, who also was president of the International Federation of Catholic Universities at the time. And Hesburgh, knowing it would take significant private contributions to make the center become a reality if the political issues could be resolved, turned to O'Shaughnessy for advice . . . and funding.

Hesburgh had known the pope since his days as Cardinal Giovanni Montini and brought him to Notre Dame one year to give the sermon at a graduation Mass. "Whenever he had a project that was academic," Hesburgh recalled of the pope during an April 2011 interview with director Ali Selim for a video biography on O'Shaughnessy's life, "he used to call me up and say, 'Can you help me with this?' And I'd say, 'I will do the best I can.'"[1]

After he became pontiff, Paul VI described to Hesburgh a lifelong dream of bringing Christians together "to swap ideas and work on projects, to become more unified." The pope mentioned several sites— Assisi, "but that's too Italian"; Geneva, "but that's too Protestant"; and Oxford or Cambridge, "but they're too Anglican." He paused and told Hesburgh (in the American's words):

> I had the opportunity for first time in my life to visit the Holy
> Land where Jesus was born, preached, died and was raised
> from the dead some 2,000 years ago. I traveled there, and I
> knelt down and kissed the ground . . . and it occurred to me,
> that's where we ought to have a building that would welcome
> all Christians who could come together to study and pray and
> work to bring churches together in peace.[2]

The pope acknowledged that Hesburgh was "pretty busy" running Notre Dame, "but if you don't mind I am going to add more burden to your life. I'd like you to create in Jerusalem a center where scholars from all of the world's great Christian religions could live in peace and work on theology together. I guess we have to begin by getting some land."[3]

Hesburgh went to Jerusalem and found a thirty-six-acre site called Tantur, which he said the Knights of Malta had owned since they captured Jerusalem from the Turks during the Crusades. He returned to Rome to tell the pope, "I think I found the right place," and the pope agreed but expressed concern that the Knights of Malta could be "a pretty tough group to work with. I reminded him that he was the pope and they're a Catholic order . . . and I told him, 'Don't give them more than $300,000. It's all you can afford.'"[4]

After Paul VI acquired the land, Hesburgh assigned a Notre Dame architect to design the buildings and discussed the project with O'Shaughnessy. The two men planned to meet with the pope during a two-week trip to Europe in August and September 1964.

"Last Saturday morning in the basement chapel at St. Thomas, I offered Mass for you and for this project," Hesburgh wrote O'Shaughnessy on August 4, 1964. "I do believe it is most important in the present state of the church in the modern world. Also, I know you'll get a great thrill from seeing Paul VI, because he is a wonderful person and this one project seems to be uppermost in his mind at the moment."[5]

Hesburgh and O'Shaughnessy had a private audience with Paul VI on August 29 at Castel Gandolfo, his summer residence. Associated Press reports from Vatican City described O'Shaughnessy as a St. Paul "industrialist" interested in supporting the project, and Hesburgh later wrote a descriptive memo summarizing the audience:

> The Holy Father's welcome was most gracious, as His Holiness came from behind his desk and welcomed Mr. O'Shaughnessy with arms extended. He then led Mr. O'Shaughnessy to the chair next to him at the desk. I told the Holy Father that I had shared with Mr. O'Shaughnessy the ideas we had discussed on April 27 of this year regarding the Jerusalem Memorial, and that Mr. O'Shaughnessy had expressed great interest in this project. Mr. O'Shaughnessy then told the Holy Father directly that he thought the idea most important for promoting the union of Christians in our day and that he felt the project

should be realized soon, while the memory of the Holy Father's visit to the Holy Land was still fresh in the minds of the world's people.

The Holy Father then told how completely he agreed with Mr. O'Shaughnessy's thought of doing something soon. He told Mr. O'Shaughnessy that it was providential, and most pleasing to him personally, that someone of Mr. O'Shaughnessy's stature was concerned about this, as it was also one of his greatest concerns at the moment. Then, Mr. O'Shaughnessy, knowing all the problems facing the Holy Father daily, said that he did not want the Holy Father to worry about the means of realizing the idea once it was thought out. The Holy Father said that this was a great help in moving ahead and that on Mr. O'Shaughnessy's word he would not preoccupy himself about the means.

He then told Mr. O'Shaughnessy that God would bless him and his family for this interest, that this was not just a material thing, but a matter of deep spiritual profit now and in eternity . . . and that he hoped in the years to come, when all of this we discussed was a fruitful reality, it would continue to be a source of spiritual satisfaction and blessing for all of them . . . .

After a photograph, we knelt for his blessing. The Holy Father asked Mr. O'Shaughnessy not to bother kneeling, but that stubborn Irishman did so anyway. Then the Holy Father blessed us, and all the O'Shaughnessy family, and grasped Mr. O'Shaughnessy by both arms, helping him to his feet.

It was a very special hour, unusual in anyone's life, and long to be remembered in ours.[6]

O'Shaughnessy later thanked Hesburgh for the trip and the opportunity to meet the pope. "Our trip was not only enjoyable but educational and I think we accomplished something while we were in Rome," he wrote in a September 29 letter. "As you know, this was the first time that I ever had a personally conducted tour. I am always doing the conducting. This was an unusual experience."[7]

Eight years later, in a *Minneapolis Tribune* profile, O'Shaughnessy described the papal audience and the agreement to proceed with the project in more colorful terms than those used in Hesburgh's memo:

> Pope Paul is a fine person. When I was talking with him, he started in English. I don't speak Italian. But these linguists are fellas who can start a conversation and control it and make it work. But when you try to do it, it's not so good. Hesburgh was educated in Italy, speaks the language very well, so we went into English, the Pope into Italian. So, as quick as we decided on it, I told Hesburgh to tell His Holiness to get off his pants and get at it right away because people forget soon. Hesburgh had a rough time trying to say that, in Italian and in a different way, to the pope. But the deal was made.[8]

Planning for the center began in earnest in 1965, with an early working title of the Ecumenical Institute for the Study of the History of Salvation. Ultimately, it would be named the Ecumenical Institute for Advanced Theological Study, and today is known as the Tantur Ecumenical Institute.

An academic council of twenty-five Roman Catholic, Orthodox, Protestant, and Anglican theologians from around the world held a planning meeting in November at Lake Como, Italy, and announced details of the project the following month. "In recent ecumenical encounters, the desire has been expressed for a program of common theological research, with special emphasis on the theme of the redemptive acts of God in history and their meaning for the men of our day," a news release stated. The institute "will be concerned first and foremost to provide established scholars and post-graduate theological students with the means for common research" as well as involving clergy and the laity in study, seminars, and conferences.[9]

Hesburgh sent a copy of the news release to O'Shaughnessy and attached a handwritten note. "The Lake Como meeting was difficult but very successful," wrote Hesburgh, who would serve as chair of the council. "December 15 is the birthday of the Jerusalem Ecumenical Institute. So we are under way at last. Thanks again."[10]

Dr. Albert Outler of the Perkins School of Theology at Southern Methodist University in Dallas served on the council and gave a progress report titled "The Jerusalem Institute for Ecumenical Research" to the Catholic Press Association on September 30, 1966. Outler praised Hesburgh's leadership, calling him "a rare combination of vision and pragmatic know-how, of spirituality and sophistication. He'd be a visionary if he weren't so effective—or, alternately, an 'operator' if his zeal was less transparently idealistic." Outler went on to say of the project and Hesburgh, "No genius-idea struggling to be born ever had a better midwife!"[11]

While Hesburgh clearly was Catholic, Outler said, "the best way to make [the institute] both ecumenical and academic, in the best sense of those two terms, would be for the Catholics to get it started and then transfer it to the direction of a company of scholars in which they had neither majority nor veto. . . . If this project really comes off, it will presage a change for all the accustomed patterns of so-called ecumenical cooperation (where each party keeps at least one leading string in its clutch!)."[12]

The Edward W. Hazen and Danforth Foundations provided seed grants for travel and planning. Outler believed the Tantur site was "magnificent" because of its location. "From the top of the hill to the south you can see the Basilica of the Nativity in Bethlehem, to the north the Holy Sepulchre (and Jerusalem), to the east (toward the Dead Sea) the Judean Wilderness, to the west Israel. . . . At the bottom of the hill, on its west slope, runs the old Roman road to Bethlehem, the track of Joseph and Mary on their way to Bethlehem." He pointed out that the institute "is not yet financed on any adequate basis whatever" and said he hoped for independent funds from private or at least non-ecclesiastical sources—else we shall still be within the reach of partisan pressures."[13]

Oddly, there was no reference to O'Shaughnessy in Outler's report even though newspaper stories two years earlier had identified him as the "industrialist" interested in the project. Hesburgh may have chosen to keep O'Shaughnessy's name out of the press until plans had firmer footing. He had written to tell his benefactor the previous May that the pope had acquired the property but "is very worried about the cost of the buildings. I assured him that this is something he should not worry about since you have yourself assured the Holy Father on this point almost two years ago."[14]

Later in the letter, Hesburgh said early estimates were that the four buildings on the institute site would cost $500,000 to $1 million. "Everyone seems agreed that this is one of the greatest projects of our time," Hesburgh wrote to O'Shaughnessy, "and I am happier than I can say to know that you are involved in this. I don't want to be irreverent, but I must add that you always have had a good nose in determining where the real action is."[15]

In his interview with Selim, Hesburgh recalled a meeting with O'Shaughnessy to review the institute plans and budget: "We were out on his boat one night and I said, 'I.A., the pope has given me this job, and it's kind of rough. . . . He said, 'What do you need?' I said, 'I think I can probably do it for a million dollars.' Typical O'Shaughnessy, he said, 'OK, you got a million dollars.' It was that simple."[16]

The Six-Day War between Israel and Egypt, Jordan, and Syria in June 1967 led to rampant inflation, and construction costs for the institute escalated to $2 million. Hesburgh headed to Florida for another meeting with O'Shaughnessy, and later described it:

> We were on the boat again at 1 in the morning, nursing a
> Scotch and soda, and I was telling him about the progress
> on the land and the building: "But now comes the bad news,
> I.A. The building that I had contracted for $1 million is going
> to cost $2 million." With most people who give you a million,
> that's the price of doing something. To go back and say you
> need twice as much—that's not a good way to raise money. Not
> O'Shaughnessy. I'll quote his exact words, because I'll never
> forget them: "Oh well, Ted, it's just money. You need it. I got it.
> You can have $2 million." . . . That story more than anything
> else tells the story of I.A. O'Shaughnessy—of his generosity and
> his wonderful ability to see a worldwide church with worldwide
> needs to reach out to Catholics and Protestants and Anglicans
> and the Orthodox, and bring them all together where it all

began—in Jerusalem . . . . He made all of that possible. What I liked about I.A. is that he made it possible in a very simple way. No fuss about it. No grandstanding.[17]

As it turned out, the project cost $4.5 million—and O'Shaughnessy paid every penny. He also contributed to a $6 million endowment that would provide operating funds and he leaned on others for donations. "I don't know if anyone else has ever done it," he told the *Catholic Bulletin* newspaper, "but I told the Rockefeller Foundation that I would match any funds they would contribute."[18]

As a gesture of gratitude for O'Shaughnessy's support of the project, Pope Paul VI named him a papal count in January 1967. The apostolic letter that accompanied the honor cited "devotion and unfailing loyalty toward this holy apostolic see by splendid deeds" and said O'Shaughnessy would receive "all the privileges, prerogatives, honors, and indults which other men who possess the distinction of such a title use and enjoy."[19]

He had received several Vatican honors over the previous two decades, including Knight Commander in the Order of St. Gregory the Great (the highest honor granted a layman not a head of state), Knight of the Holy Sepulchre of Jerusalem, Knight of the Order of Malta, and Papal Chamberlain of the Sword and Cape. The designation as a papal count touched him deeply, and he expressed his feelings in an April 8 letter to the pope:

I was greatly moved and deeply humbled to receive from the hands of Your Holiness the nomination of Count. I accept this not only as a testimony of great goodness on the part of Your Holiness towards me, but I also want to accept it in a spirit of devotion, dedication, and service to our holy Church. I have always treasured the Faith as my most precious possession, and have honestly tried to live the Faith as I received it from God and from my saintly parents. God has given me many blessings in my long life, and I believe that I can honestly say that I have attempted to share them with others in His service. While I have never sought honors in doing so, I would be less than honest if I were not to tell Your Holiness that the honor you have bestowed upon me in naming me Count is a title which I shall cherish and attempt to be worthy of. Your Holiness may be sure of my heartfelt gratitude and renewed dedication. There is no way that I can adequately thank you for this, Your Holiness, except to assure you that I will do my best in the years that God will give me to service Him and His holy Church as best I can with the help of His grace.[20]

O'Shaughnessy went on to say he felt "great personal joy" to be associated with the institute: "We all look forward to the happy day when the building will be completed and this wonderful project will be under way, to contribute mightily to the unity of Christianity in our time. It is a great honor to be able to be associated with Your Holiness and the inspiration you have given to this project."[21]

The news of O'Shaughnessy's latest papal honors elicited many congratulatory letters, including one from Bishop James Shannon in Minnesota. "What worries me is that a Count must give up his 'no count' friends," Shannon wrote to O'Shaughnessy. "Now that you are royalty, how can you continue to fraternize with us commoners?"[22]

Hesburgh kept O'Shaughnessy up to date throughout the late 1960s and early 1970s about the institute. In one letter after an October 1971 trip to Jerusalem on the project, Hesburgh told O'Shaughnessy how the city's mayor had introduced him to a ninth-generation citizen who told him "that this was the most beautiful building built in Jerusalem for many, many years. I think you will agree with him once you see it."[23]

O'Shaughnessy and his second wife, Blanche, joined Hesburgh for a meeting with Paul VI in June 1972, months before the institute would be dedicated. O'Shaughnessy later described the audience in an interview with the *Catholic Bulletin*, which began its story with two quotations, "'It is the greatest thing that has happened in my reign,' Pope Paul VI told I.A. O'Shaughnessy, St. Paul philanthropist, speaking slowly in precise English. 'Then the Pope threw his arms around me and kissed me on both cheeks,' O'Shaughnessy said."[24]

O'Shaughnessy chose not to attend the dedication ceremony in September 1972, telling a *Miami Herald* reporter that he was satisfied with his earlier inspection of the site, and at age eighty-seven, "I don't get around as much as I used to."[25]

Monsignor Francis Gilligan, pastor of St. Mark's Catholic Church in St. Paul, made the trip to Jerusalem for the ceremony, thanks to funds contributed by his longtime friend and parishioner. "For many years God will bless you for what you have done," Gilligan wrote to O'Shaughnessy from Jerusalem, calling the institute's buildings "majestic" and its work "a symbol of the desire of the church to unite all Christians." In a second letter, Gilligan said, "Of all the buildings that bear the name O'Shaughnessy, this one will have the greatest influence since at the very spot where Christ taught, it brings together many of different faiths to grow in knowledge."[26]

PART IV

27

The Grand Old Man

You can never know how grateful my oldest daughter is to you.
I have a letter from her today which ends by saying,
"Life is beautiful." So again, you're magnificent!
—HAROLD CUMMINGS

As I.A. O'Shaughnessy approached eighty years of age in 1965, his friends and associates began to realize he wouldn't be around forever, and they honored him in a number of ways.

The grandest tribute may have been that held on June 18, 1966, when more than two hundred people crowded into the Minnesota Club "to pay homage to St. Paul's great Irish philanthropist," as one newspaper called him.[1] Present were fellow business executives, civic leaders, elected officials, and college presidents, including Father Theodore Hesburgh of Notre Dame, Monsignor Terrence Murphy of St. Thomas, and O. Meredith Wilson of the University of Minnesota.

But there was only one speaker, by plan—and it wasn't O'Shaughnessy. The committee overseeing the dinner had chosen

Bishop James Shannon, who recently had left the St. Thomas presidency, to speak. He read numerous telegrams from such people as President Lyndon Johnson and Vice President Hubert Humphrey. When the plaudits ended, O'Shaughnessy made a play for the microphone, but Shannon wouldn't give it up—one of the few times in his life that O'Shaughnessy was denied the stage.

After the dinner, O'Shaughnessy received a letter from John Myers, a longtime friend, who said he wanted to thank him for the great example he had set in how people should treat each other:

> It is not just your generosity which has meant so much, I.A.,
> but it is the spirit in which you have made possible these great
> works. The light touch which so characterizes your every
> action, the open friendliness which you exhibit to all, and the
> great Christian humility with which you infect all who come
> into close proximity with you—these are the qualities which
> number you among the truly great of this entire age. This letter
> calls for no answer—it is merely a very sincere expression of
> admiration and respect from one man to another.[2]

The *Minneapolis Star* story about the dinner noted that "Mrs. James Finn, a family friend from Coconut Grove, Florida, stood at Mr. O'Shaughnessy's side as the guests filed past to extend best wishes to the octogenarian," and the paper also published a photo of the two.[3] As it turned out, Mrs. James Finn was more than just a "family friend," and soon would be his second wife. O'Shaughnessy married Blanche Finn, an artist and the widow of an Army officer, in a chapel of the archdiocesan chancery in St. Paul, with Shannon presiding over the service.

~~~~~~~

O'Shaughnessy received two great honors in 1971.

The Minnesota-Dakotas region of the National Conference of Christians and Jews bestowed its National Brotherhood Award on O'Shaughnessy, who called it "one of the greatest things that has happened in my life." The conference cited his "vision, understanding and distinguished leadership in community, civic and religious affairs" and praised the way he had advanced "the welfare of his fellow citizens of all religious beliefs and cultural backgrounds."[4]

And the International Petroleum Exposition, meeting in Tulsa, Oklahoma, honored pioneers of the oil industry in choosing a "Grand Old Man" for each major sector on the basis of forty years of service. O'Shaughnessy was feted as the pioneer for refining, but he was unable to attend the event because of a cold.[5]

The City of St. Paul named the plaza on the south side of the new Civic Center complex after O'Shaughnessy in 1972. "I am delighted with the result," said Harold Cummings, chairman emeritus of Minnesota Mutual Life Insurance and a member of the Civic Center Authority, in a letter after receiving a thank-you call from O'Shaughnessy. "As quickly as I can find it I will stop by your office with a bottle of Twenty Year Old Grant's Scotch. I think you'll like it." Cummings handwrote a postscript at the bottom of the letter: "My grandson whom you recommended to Notre Dame is getting good grades!"[6] (Earlier that year, Cummings had sent another thank-you letter to O'Shaughnessy: "You can never know how grateful my oldest daughter is to you," he wrote, referring to the mother of the same grandson. "I have a letter from her today which ends by saying, 'Life is beautiful.' So again, you're magnificent!")[7]

O'Shaughnessy was so touched by the Civic Center honor that the following year—on his eighty-eighth birthday—he announced plans for the gift of a specially designed fountain for the plaza. He commissioned Ellerbe Architects of St. Paul to survey contemporary fountains around the country for design ideas.

Another distinction came O'Shaughnessy's way in November 1973 when *Corporate Report* magazine named Minnesota's twelve wealthiest citizens and listed him at number four, with a net worth of $110 million, behind only William McKnight and Richard Ordway of 3M fame, and Edward Osborn of Economics Laboratory (now Ecolab). The magazine admitted that its list "is *not* an authenticated, fully documented compilation; it is the best guess ever made," the result of four months of research and interviews. The magazine also conceded that O'Shaughnessy's wealth "is a well-guarded secret" and that he "has given away more money than many people who are regarded as wealthy collect in their lifetimes."[8]

O'Shaughnessy had spent recent years putting his finances—personal and foundation—in order. He sent a letter to the First Trust Company of St. Paul in 1968 and asked that it be filed with his will, in which he bequeathed his foundation stock in equal shares to his five children so they would have an equal voice in determining how to distribute funds:

> It would be natural that on occasion my sons and daughters
> may have diverse views as to the worthwhileness of various
> projects and programs. In particular each of my children may
> have a disposition toward making some disbursements in his
> local community. As a means of recognizing this point of view,
> I recommend, as a general policy, that each of my five children
> be responsible for recommending to the officers and Board of
> Directors the manner in which approximately one-fifth of the
> funds available for distribution are to be expended.[9]

Around 2000, the foundation directors, led by second-generation president Larry O'Shaughnessy, reexamined their grant-making procedures. A family retreat was held to share ideas, and a planning team led by a consultant explored and incorporated those ideas. Tim O'Shaughnessy, who succeeded his cousin Larry as third president of the foundation, worried that it would be difficult for the board to agree on a unifying theme and told *Philanthropy* magazine in 2010, "I never thought we'd get 10 Irishmen to agree on anything." They did reach agreement, and today the board, which includes two members from each of the five family branches, allocates half the grants, and each branch allocates 10 percent. The board also agreed on a focus area—K–12 education for disadvantaged children—in part because those grants "almost always pass what I call the 'I.A.' sniff test,'" said John O'Shaughnessy Jr., the founder's grandson and current foundation president.

Kaki O'Shaughnessy, the youngest of twenty-nine grandchildren of the family patriarch, agreed. "The only reason we're all here is because of grandfather," she told *Philanthropy*. "He is our common denominator."[10]

The foundation estimates that it has made more than $117 million in accumulated grants since 1941, with annual contributions ranging between $3 million and $4 million over the past decade.

28

The Epitome of Faith, Hope, and Love

All of us can be very proud that he was a dear part of our lives.
While we will miss him greatly—those twinkling eyes, that
spontaneous smile, that great heart—both we and our lives and our
institutions have been enriched by his presence and his great spirit.
—FATHER THEODORE HESBURGH

Death came quickly, and with little pain, to I.A. O'Shaughnessy.

He suffered a stroke on November 18, 1973, and was admitted to St. Francis Hospital in Miami, where he died at 4:05 p.m. November 21, the day before Thanksgiving. He was eighty-eight.

News of his death made front-page headlines, which called him a philanthropist and an oil millionaire. Obituaries told of his Horatio Alger–like rise from a modest life as the thirteenth child of a Stillwater bootmaker and homemaker to the nation's largest independent oil refiner and one of the most generous men in America. Survivors included his second wife, Blanche, three sons, two daughters, twenty-nine grandchildren, and twenty-three great-grandchildren.

His body was flown to Minnesota for a Mass of Christian Burial on November 26 at the Cathedral of St. Paul and a memorial Mass on November 27 at the College of St. Thomas. Burial was at Resurrection Cemetery in Mendota Heights, with his grave next to that of his first wife, Lillian, who died in 1959.

Thirteen years before his death, O'Shaughnessy had arranged for a family memorial at the cemetery, and the care that he took in helping to design the gravesite reflected his faith. All of the pieces came from a single quarry block of Vermont granite. The three bases represent the theological virtues of faith, hope, and charity. A Celtic cross soars fourteen feet high and stretches four feet wide at the arms. Two ledgers, one with Ignatius' name and the other with Lillian's, complete the memorial. Reads a description of the site:

> The single word CREDO carved by hand on the die is eloquent
> testimony to the faith of the people reposing in this plot. The
> family name O'Shaughnessy is incised inconspicuously on the
> bottom base. This cross epitomizes the true Catholic cemetery
> memorial which is erected first 'to the greater glory of God'
> and secondarily in memory of the family resting here.[1]

Faith, hope, and love also were the theme of the eulogy delivered by Father Theodore Hesburgh, president of the University of Notre Dame, at O'Shaughnessy's funeral. Noting that St. Thomas Aquinas had written that "a good man is one who knows the right things to have faith in, the right things to hope for, and the right things to love," Hesburgh asked, "How did I.A. O'Shaughnessy meet this test?" Hesburgh answered:

> He basically had faith in God. . . . He had faith in people . . . in
> his family . . . in his friends . . . and in God's providence, which
> saw him throughout almost 90 years of vicissitudes without
> end, some good and some bad, but all deepening the inner
> strength and solidity of his character.
>
> He wanted only what was good for his family, and
> he always put this above and beyond what he hoped for
> himself. . . . He hoped to be able to do good for others and
> dedicated his material success to that end, more than anyone I

have ever known.

It is not difficult, if you knew him well, to see clearly that he loved. First, God and the service of God as it was given to him to serve. He loved all of God's creations. . . . He loved life and laughter, a good game and a good joke, a good day with a brisk wind on the sunlit Florida water. . . . He loved being with his family and friends, loved giving away most of his income each year, loved getting others to give when they really did not want to, loved surprising those in need with a sudden solution to their seemingly impossible problems.[2]

O'Shaughnessy came to be a man of such faith, hope, and love because of the Christian spirit of his parents and the way they cared for the poor and less fortunate as well as their own family, Hesburgh said. That life of faith, hope, and love became so important for their youngest son "that for many years to come great things will be happening in the world, in Jerusalem, at universities and colleges, at hospitals, at orphanages, and at old folks' homes, in the lives of the young and the old, transformed by one man's generosity and vision." Hesburgh concluded:

All of us can be very proud that he was a dear part of our lives. While we will miss him greatly—those twinkling eyes, that spontaneous smile, that great heart—both we and our lives and our institutions have been enriched by his presence and his great spirit, and we will long be reminded that he passed this way on his path to heaven and eternal life. May he rest in eternal peace with God, and may we all rejoin him there one day.[3]

Monsignor Terrence J. Murphy, president of St. Thomas, told the memorial Mass the next day that he believed O'Shaughnessy deserved a chapter in the histories of both American industrial development and the American church. Murphy said he had encouraged O'Shaughnessy to collect his papers and tape an oral history, but to no avail. He took himself and his accomplishment so lightly, Murphy said, that he thought there would be of little value or interest to anyone: "It was this simplicity and unpretentiousness that made people so readily feel at home with him, whether they were extraordinarily successful people, ordinary people, or children. Pretentions, claims to exclusiveness [and] airs of any kind were quickly recognized by him whose own values were so sound, and his sharp wit instantly put things back in their proper perspective."[4]

～～～

In the days and weeks following his death, O'Shaughnessy was hailed far and wide. The *Catholic Bulletin,* the newspaper of the Archdiocese of St. Paul and Minneapolis, called him "a giant" and "an old-fashioned Catholic" characterized by "personal charm, a sharp Irish wit, a blend of humility and braggadocio, and a deep love of his family and his faith."[5]

The *Oil Daily* credited O'Shaughnessy's spirit, philosophy, vibrant personality, and fierce pride and drive with influencing and guiding the industry. Publisher Keith Fanshier, who had known O'Shaughnessy for three decades, defined him as "a humaniste, one who believed in his fellows, his country and its institutions, and also his industry. The nation in the difficult days ahead will keenly need more of such qualities in its people."[6]

The rector of the Ecumenical Institute for Advanced Theological Studies, which had opened in 1972 in Jerusalem thanks to O'Shaughnessy's gift of $4.5 million, wrote Blanche to extend his sympathy. "Everyone connected with the ecumenical institute knows that without your husband's magnificent generosity Tantur would not exist today," wrote Jean-Jacques von Allmen. "I am glad that he lived to see the building completed. . . . Among your husband's many benefactions, I think this one, situated in the Holy Land, so close to Bethlehem and Jerusalem, must have been especially dear to him."[7]

His friend James Shannon dedicated his "The Pilgrim Church" column in the *Minneapolis Tribune* to O'Shaughnessy, describing him as "one of God's great men." Shannon went on to say that O'Shaughnessy was a "unique" human person, and closed his column thusly:

The words of Ben Jonson adorn the cemetery marker of his
first wife: "Beneath this stone doth lie as much beauty as could

die." We need a Ben Jonson to fashion a comparable epitaph to the gentle man who is Ignatius Aloysius O'Shaughnessy. May flights of angels sing him to his rest.[8]

EPILOGUE

Granddad knew that we are all created in our relationship to God to represent God's love for his creation and to live a life of holiness by being good stewards. His good works were motivated by more than just his heart, but the Heart of God.

—GRANDDAUGHTER MICHELE O'SHAUGHNESSY TRAEGER

When it came time to determine a title for this biography, I immediately remembered three words in the closing comments of Father Theodore Hesburgh's homily at the funeral for Ignatius Aloysius O'Shaughnessy. Those comments bear repeating:

> All of us can be very proud that he was a dear part of our lives. While we will miss him greatly—those twinkling eyes, that spontaneous smile, that great heart—both we and our lives and our institutions have been enriched by his presence and his great spirit, and we will long be reminded that he passed this way on his path to heaven and eternal life. May he rest in eternal peace with God, and may we all rejoin him there one day.[1]

That Great Heart, I thought. *Perfect.*

Perfect because it reflected an incredibly generous and unselfish man—a self-made multimillionaire who not only "happily gave his money away," as a magazine headline once stated, but did so for the right reasons and to the right causes.

As I shared the title idea with family members, I received an e-mail from Michele O'Shaughnessy Traeger, the youngest daughter of I.A.'s oldest son, John. She was eighteen when her grandfather died.

"It sounds wonderful," she wrote, "but it spurred in me some thoughts about where his great love of humanity came from, and of course I realize that it was his Catholic faith." Stories over the years had "touched on his faith" but had not given enough weight to the subject, she said, and she wondered how much influence his parents had on him when it came to his faith:

> I believe that his great heart is rooted in them and their
> Catholic tradition and legacy, which is rooted in God's divine
> plan and THE greatest heart. Granddad knew that we are all
> created in our relationship to God to represent God's love
> for his creation and to live a life of holiness by being good
> stewards.
>
> Obviously this spirituality shaped his love of life, living the
> life of faith which was expressed in an outward way to inspire
> others to do the same. As you surely know, he didn't want the
> buildings at Notre Dame and St. Thomas to be named after
> him to be a promotion for himself, but rather to be used as an
> example for others to do the same. Many others have followed.
>
> His "Great Heart" was his way of sharing the blessings,
> the best exemplar of Christian principles in living the life of
> his faith. Good works, plus good faith, make it all the more
> powerful and blessed. I am hopeful that a sentence or two can
> be added in your book that makes it more than just obvious
> that his good works were motivated by more than just his
> heart, but the Heart of God.[2]

The sentence or two have been added.

ENDNOTES

Abbreviations Used in Endnotes

HL: Hesburgh Libraries, I.A. O'Shaughnessy files, University of Notre Dame, South Bend, Indiana

MHC: Minnesota History Center, I.A. O'Shaughnessy files, St. Paul, Minnesota

ND: University of Notre Dame

OFLC: O'Shaughnessy Frey Library Center, I.A. O'Shaughnessy files, University of St. Thomas, St. Paul, Minnesota

SCUL: St. Catherine University Library, I.A. O'Shaughnessy files, St. Paul, Minnesota

CST or STC: College of St. Thomas or St. Thomas College (now University of St. Thomas).

Prologue

1. James Shannon, "The Pilgrim Church," *Minneapolis Tribune*, December 2, 1973, 35A.

2. Bella Kelly, "Here's Mr. Giveaway Himself," *Miami News*, March 26, 1962, 1C.

3. Ibid.

4. Shannon, "The Pilgrim Church," 35A.

5. OFLC, Sister Alice Smith tribute to O'Shaughnessy, 120th anniversary of St. Joseph's Hospital, St. Paul, Minnesota, October 16, 1973.

6. Shannon, "The Pilgrim Church," 35A.

Chapter 1. The Best Man on the Team

1. John M. Lindley and Virginia Brainard Kunz, "He Loved a Tall Story: The Life and Times of I.A. O'Shaughnessy, The Man Who Happily Gave His Money Away," *Ramsey County History*, Winter 2004, 4–5.

2. Don O'Grady, "Oilman Has 'Irish Luck,' "*St. Paul Pioneer Press*, August 19, 1956, 1.

3. George Grim, "O'Shaughnessy: So . . . I Told Hesburgh to tell His Holiness to get off his pants," *Minneapolis Tribune*, January 30, 1972, 10A.

4. Lindley and Kunz, "He Loved a Tall Story," 7.

5. OFLC, Sister Victoria letter, 1951.

6. O'Grady, "Oilman," 1.

7. OFLC, transcript of *Ramsey County History* interview with Larry O'Shaughnessy, July 31, 2003.

8. OFLC, Leonard Rogge oral history, April and May 1977, 96.

9. O'Grady, "Oilman," 1.

10. Lindley and Kunz, "He Loved a Tall Story," 13.

11. *Record*, St. John's University, December 1, 1901.

12. Dunstan Tucker and Martin Schirber, *Scoreboard* (Collegeville, MN: St. John's University Press, 1979), 11.

13. Father Louis Traufner, *Worship and Work*, May 18, 1956, 3.

14. MHC, Box 7, O-misc. folder, O'Shaughnessy letter to John O'Leary, December 8, 1949.

15. MHC, Box 7, O-misc. folder, O'Shaughnessy letter to Father Walter Reger, September 27, 1961.

16. MHC, Box 10, thank-you letters 1954–58 folder, Father Dunstan Tucker letter, undated.

17. St. John's University archives, Collegeville, MN, Father Benjamin Stein letter to O'Shaughnessy, May 29, 1962.

18. Ibid., O'Shaughnessy letter to Stein, June 12, 1962.

19. Ibid.

20. Tucker and Schirber, *Scoreboard*, 11.

21. *Collegian*, CST, November 1905.

22. *St. Paul Pioneer Press*, September 14, 1905.

23. MHC, Box 2, D-misc. folder, Dr. Will Donahue letter to O'Shaughnessy, 1940.

24. "Son is following in father's footsteps," *St. Paul Dispatch*, December 18, 1925.

25. *Purple and Gray*, CST, December 1925.

26. MHC, Box 8, STC folder, Dan Herget letter to O'Shaughnessy, 1949.

27. MHC, Box 5, Mc-misc. folder, Donald MacGregor letter to O'Shaughnessy, October 12, 1964.

28. Ibid., O'Shaughnessy letter to MacGregor, October 14, 1964.

29. Joe Kimball, "I. A.'s checkbook still doesn't balance," *Minneapolis Star Tribune*, March 9, 2007.

30. OFLC, Rogge oral history, 97.

31. MHC, Box 3, F-misc. folder, O'Shaughnessy letter, 1951.

32. Lindley and Kunz, "He Loved a Tall Story," 16.

33. *Stillwater Weekly Gazette*, February 27, 1907.

34. *Collegian*, November 1905.

Chapter 2. Feeling Like a Millionaire

1. Lindley and Kunz, "He Loved a Tall Story," 17.

2. *St. Paul Pioneer Press*, October 11, 1908.

3. Ibid.

4. Lindley and Kunz, "He Loved a Tall Story," 18.

5. Grim, "O'Shaughnessy," 10A.

6. I.A. O'Shaughnessy Foundation, I.A. and Lillian O'Shaughnessy golden wedding anniversary album, John O'Shaughnessy letter, 1958.

7. Lindley and Kunz, "He Loved a Tall Story," 18–19.

8. "Globe Company Buys Site for Large Refinery," *Enid Morning News*, July 22, 1917, 1.

Chapter 3. A Good Industry to Get Into

1. Grim, "O'Shaughnessy," 10A.

2. MHC, Box 3, Globe Refining folder.

3. Ibid.

4. F. L. Jehle, *Globe Oil & Refining, Inc.* (1957), 1.

5. Ibid., 2.

6. "Globe Company Buys Site," 1.

7. Jehle, *Globe Oil & Refining*, 2.

8. Ibid., 4.

9. O'Shaughnessy anniversary album, Bob McDowell letter, 1958.

10. Jehle, *Globe Oil & Refining*, 5.

11. Patrick O'Shaughnessy, interview with author, January 28, 2013.

12. Jehle, *Globe Oil & Refining*, 6.

13. Ibid., 10.

14. Ibid., 9.

15. Ibid., 11.

16. Ibid., 12.

17. Patrick O'Shaughnessy interview.

18. Jehle, *Globe Oil & Refining*, 17.

19. Ibid., 18.

20. Ibid., 19.

21. MHC, Box 9, Thiess, Olson, Mecklenburger, Von Holst & Coltman folder, O'Shaughnessy telegram, June 1944, and law firm letter, August 1, 1955.

22. Jehle, *Globe Oil & Refining*, 25.

23. Ibid., 27.

24. Ibid., 42–44.

25. Globe Oil & Refining advertising and merchandising plan, undated.

26. Jehle, *Globe Oil & Refining*, 28.

27. "History, Lario Oil and Gas," *McPherson Daily Republican*, March 15, 1933.

Chapter 4. A Real Believer in America

1. Jehle, *Globe Oil & Refining*, 29.

2. Ibid., 30.

3. "St. Paul Man is Largest Individual Oil Producer; Building $1,000,000 Plant," *St. Paul News*, August 21, 1932.

4. Ibid.

5. "One of the Mid-Continent's Best," *McPherson Daily Republican*, March 15, 1933.

6. "'Happy Days Are Here Again,' is Theme of Globe Welcome," *McPherson Daily Republican*, March 15, 1933, 1.

7. Ibid.

8. "One of the Mid-Continent's Best."

9. "President O'Shaughnessy Sends Greetings," *McPherson Daily Republican*, March 15, 1933.

10. Jack Kolthoff, "New Globe Refinery Fulfillment of One Man's Dream," *Wichita Sunday Eagle*, April 9, 1933.

11. "Humble Start No Handicap to Francis Jehle," *Wichita Sunday Eagle*, April 9, 1933.

12. Patrick O'Shaughnessy interview.

13. "Globe is First to Adopt New Recovery Plan," *Wichita Beacon*, July 21, 1933.

14. Patrick O'Shaughnessy interview.

15. "Globe is First."

16. Jehle, *Globe Oil & Refining*, 37.

17. MHC, Box 4, H-misc. folder, Carl Haun letter to O'Shaughnessy, January 3, 1935.

18. Ibid., O'Shaughnessy letter to Haun, January 4, 1935.

19. Ibid., O'Shaughnessy letter to Haun, June 4, 1936.

20. Ibid., Haun letter to O'Shaughnessy, June 8, 1936.

21. MHC, Box 5, L-misc. folder, Rev. Steven Levin letter to O'Shaughnessy, November 16, 1938.

22. Ibid., O'Shaughnessy letter to Levin, December 7, 1938.

23. Ibid., Levin letter to O'Shaughnessy, December 15, 1938.

24. "M'Pherson Globe Refinery is One of Best in Country," *Wichita Eagle*, July 28, 1935.

25. Ibid.

26. "Old Oxford Oil Pool Gives Kansas Its Greatest Gushers," *Wichita Eagle*, September 17, 1935.

27. Lindley and Kunz, "He Loved a Tall Story," 27.

28. "John O'Shaughnessy is Made Manager of Lario Oil," *Wichita Eagle*, January 24, 1936.

29. Patrick O'Shaughnessy interview.

30. Jehle, *Globe Oil & Refining*, 34–35.

31. Patrick O'Shaughnessy interview.

32. MHC, Box 2, Deep Rock folder, B. L. Majewski letter to O'Shaughnessy, 1936.

33. MHC, Box 6, O'Shaughnessy letter to Williston and Minot, North Dakota, Chambers of Commerce, January 1938.

34. Patrick O'Shaughnessy interview.

35. Jehle, *Globe Oil & Refining*, 35.

36. Patrick O'Shaughnessy interview.

Chapter 5. Independent in Every Sense of the Word

1. Jehle, *Globe Oil & Refining*, 55–56.

2. Ibid.

3. "Globe Oil Gives Yule Bonuses to Its 600 Employees," *Wichita Eagle*, December 18, 1938.

4. Jehle, *Globe Oil & Refining*, 57.

5. Patrick O'Shaughnessy interview.

6. MHC, Box 3, Globe Oil & Refining of Illinois folder, Ralph Pierce letter to O'Shaughnessy, January 1949.

7. MHC, Box 7, P-misc. folder, Jerome Paddock letter to O'Shaughnessy, December 31, 1951.

8. O'Shaughnessy anniversary album, H. George Donovan letter, 1958.

9. MHC, Box 2, D-misc. folder, Donovan letters to O'Shaughnessy, December 1950, December 1971, and July 31, 1972.

10. Earl Lamm, "I.A. O'Shaughnessy Streamlines Operations for Postwar," *National Petroleum News*, November 8, 1944, 44, 46.

11. Patrick O'Shaughnessy interview.

12. MHC, Box 6, M-misc. folder, 1934 O'Shaughnessy letter to Globe employee.

13. Jehle, *Globe Oil & Refining*, 31–32.

14. "Globe Employees Favor Company Labor Methods," *Wichita Eagle*, April 12, 1937.

15. Jehle, *Globe Oil & Refining*, 32.

16. Ibid., 58.

17. Patrick O'Shaughnessy interview.

18. Lamm, "I.A. O'Shaughnessy Streamlines," 44, 46.

19. Patrick O'Shaughnessy interview.

20. MHC, Box 7, P-misc. folder, Lamm letter to O'Shaughnessy, November 1944.

21. Ibid., O'Shaughnessy letter to Lamm, December 23, 1944.

22. Ibid., Lamm letter to O'Shaughnessy, December 26, 1944.

23. MHC, Box 4, Fred Koch folder, Koch letter to O'Shaughnessy, December 16, 1939.

24. Ibid.

25. Ibid., Koch letter to O'Shaughnessy, October 7, 1941.

26. Ibid., Koch letter to O'Shaughnessy, December 1941.

27. Ibid.

28. Ibid., O'Shaughnessy letter to Koch, October 5, 1942.

29. Ibid., Koch letter to O'Shaughnessy, October 14, 1942.

30. Patrick O'Shaughnessy interview.

Chapter 6. "To Hell With the Profits. We Have a War to Win."

1. "Globe Has Processed 27 Million Barrels," *McPherson Daily Republican*, July 12, 1940.

2. "Globe to Build a 225-mile Gasoline Pipe Line to Iowa," *McPherson Daily Republican*, April 4, 1941.

3. Jehle, *Globe Oil & Refining*, 46.

4. MHC, Box 11, Globe Oil folder, 1942–43, George Parkhurst letter to George Woodruff, May 24,

1943, and C. K. Reiman letter to O'Shaughnessy, May 26, 1943.

5. Jehle, *Globe Oil & Refining*, 47, 49.

6. Grim, "O'Shaughnessy," 10A.

7. Jehle, *Globe Oil & Refining*, 40.

8. T. Glenn Harrison, "'We Have War to Win,' Boss Tells His Employees," *St. Paul Pioneer Press*, July 19, 1942.

9. Patrick O'Shaughnessy interview.

10. MHC, Box 8, R-misc. folder, O'Shaughnessy telegram to President Franklin Roosevelt, November 29, 1942.

11. MHC, Box 12, Petroleum Industry Committee folder, O'Shaughnessy letter, December 11, 1943.

12. O'Shaughnessy anniversary album, Bob McDowell letter, 1958.

13. MHC, Box 4, J-misc. folder, O'Shaughnessy letter to unnamed Chicago friend, December 22, 1941.

14. Jehle, *Globe Oil & Refining*, 41.

15. Keith Fanshier, "Salute to the Inevitable," *Oil Daily*, August 1943.

16. Ibid.

17. MHC, Box 7, *Oil Daily* folder documents, 1953 and 1957.

18. Ibid., Keith Fanshier letter to O'Shaughnessy, 1953.

19. MHC, Box 10, McDowell letter to O'Shaughnessy, July 24, 1943.

20. "General Offices of Co-Op Refinery to be Moved Here in Near Future," *McPherson Daily Republican*, July 31, 1943.

21. MHC, Box 3, Globe Oil & Refining Co. of Council Bluffs folder, E. L. Beeman letter to O'Shaughnessy, 1943.

22. "CHS co-op to expand refinery in Kansas, *St. Paul Pioneer Press*, March 13, 2013, 13A.

23. Lamm, "I.A. O'Shaughnessy Streamlines," 44.

24. Jehle, *Globe Oil & Refining*, 50–55.

25. Ibid., 58, 59.

26. Ibid., 59.

27. OFLC, Oil Workers International Local No. 517 letter to O'Shaughnessy, August 1954.

28. MHC, Box 10, thank-you letters 1953–55 folder, Archie Abrams Jr. letter to O'Shaughnessy, November 17, 1954.

29. Ibid., O'Shaughnessy letter to Abrams, November 30, 1954.

30. Patrick O'Shaughnessy interview.

31. MHC, Box 5, L-misc. folder, Lemont Teen Club letter to O'Shaughnessy, August 2, 1962.

32. Jehle, *Globe Oil & Refining*, 61–62.

33. MHC, Box 1, A-misc. folder, Aberdeen Petroleum Corp. and O'Shaughnessy letters, November 1959 and January 1961.

34. MHC, Box 4, J-misc. folder, Jehle letter to O'Shaughnessy, August 25, 1961.

35. Ibid., Jehle letter to O'Shaughnessy, December 26, 1961.

36. MHC, Box 10, thank-you letters 1963–64 folder, Jehle letter to O'Shaughnessy, January 6, 1964.

37. OFLC, Larry O'Shaughnessy, transcript of interview with *Ramsey County History*, November 14, 2003.

38. "Experience and Longevity: An Exceptional Track Record for 97 Years and Running," www.lariooil.com/history.

Chapter 7. Home and Family: A Refuge

1. Lindley and Kunz, "He Loved a Tall Story," 22.

2. Ibid.

3. O'Shaughnessy anniversary album, John O'Shaughnessy letter, 1958.

4. John O'Shaughnessy Jr., interview with author, September 20, 2012.

5. Lindley and Kunz, "He Loved a Tall Story," 28.

6. Larry O'Shaughnessy, transcript of interview with St. Thomas magazine, December 4, 2006.

7. OFLC, Larry O'Shaughnessy, transcript of interview with Ramsey County History, July 31, 2003.

8. OFLC, Rogge oral history, 103.

9. MHC, Box 6, Minneapolis, Northfield and Southern Railway folder, George Wright and O'Shaughnessy correspondence, October and November 1942 and 1943.

10. OFLC, Larry O'Shaughnessy transcript of interview with Ramsey County History, November 14, 2003.

11. Ibid., October 8, 2003.

12. MHC files, Box 9, W-misc., O'Shaughnessy letter, February 7, 1940.

13. O'Grady, "Oilman," 2.

14. Kelly, "Here's Mr. Giveaway," 1C.

15. Grim, "O'Shaughnessy," 10A.

16. John O'Shaughnessy Jr. interview, September 20, 2012.

17. OFLC, Larry O'Shaughnessy, transcript of interview with Ramsey County History, November 14, 2003.

18. O'Shaughnessy anniversary album, Stephen O'Shaughnessy letter, 1958.

19. Larry O'Shaughnessy, transcript of interview with St. Thomas, December 4, 2006.

20. MHC, Box 1, C-misc. folder, Catholic Daughters of America and O'Shaughnessy correspondence, September 1959.

21. MHC, Box 2, First National Bank of St. Paul folder, 1941 correspondence.

22. Grim, "O'Shaughnessy," 10A.

23. Ibid.

24. Barbara Flanagan column, Minneapolis Star, February 9, 1967, 1C.

25. MHC, Box 6, M-misc. folder, Barbara Flanagan letter to O'Shaughnessy, February 9, 1967.

26. MHC, Box 7, P-misc. folder, Val Peterson letter to O'Shaughnessy, December 1, 1949.

27. MHC, Box 7, P-misc. folder, O'Shaughnessy letter to Peterson, December 19, 1949.

28. Grim, "O'Shaughnessy," 10A.

29. Ibid.

Chapter 8. The Skipper

1. MHC, Box 5, Marileen folder, documents.

2. Ibid., R. Getchell Comstock letter to O'Shaughnessy, July 10, 1960.

3. MHC, Box 4, G-misc. folder, O'Shaughnessy letter, July 20, 1942.

4. MHC, Box 1, B-misc. folder, O'Shaughnessy letters to Austin Black, August and September 1969.

5. MHC, Box 7, ND folder, Father John Cavanaugh letter to O'Shaughnessy, March 1950.

6. MHC, Box 10, thank-you letters 1954–58 folder, Father Edward Joyce letter to O'Shaughnessy, March 1958.

7. Ibid., Father Theodore Hesburgh letter to O'Shaughnessy, March 1958.

8. MHC, Box 8, STC folder, Father James Shannon letter to O'Shaughnessy, March 1958.

9. Ibid., Shannon letter to O'Shaughnessy, March 2, 1960.

10. MHC, Box 7, ND folder, Joyce letter to O'Shaughnessy, May 1, 1961.

11. Ibid., Ara Parseghian letter to O'Shaughnessy, December 28, 1965.

12. MHC, Box 4, H-misc. folder, Hesburgh letter to Shannon, March 1969.

Chapter 9. The Most Excellent Oranges

1. Patrick O'Shaughnessy interview.

2. MHC, Box 3, Joseph Fitzgerald folder.

3. MHC, Box 5, Lake Wales Orange Grove folder, O'Shaughnessy letter to W. A. Varn, March 1931.

4. MHC, Box 4, Highland Park Service folder, Steve Loken letter to O'Shaughnessy, 1938.

5. Ibid., Jobbers Oil Products secretary letter to O'Shaughnessy, 1958.

6. Ibid., Curtis Anderson letter to O'Shaughnessy, June 12, 1942.

7. MHC, Box 3, F-misc. folder, L. M. Foster letter to O'Shaughnessy, 1937.

8. MHC, Box 7, ND folder, Arthur Haley letter to O'Shaughnessy, June 1942.

9. John O'Shaughnessy Jr. interview.

10. MHC, Box 8, R-misc. folder, O'Shaughnessy letter to M. L. Rawlings, May 31, 1938.

11. MHC, Box 5, Lake Wales Orange Grove folder, O'Shaughnessy letter to M. C. Dopler, October 1932.

12. Ibid., O'Shaughnessy and Dopler letters, August 19 and September 1933.

13. Ibid., O'Shaughnessy and Dopler letters, 1934 and 1940.

14. Ibid., O'Shaughnessy letter to Dopler, February 26, 1936.

15. Ibid., O'Shaughnessy letter to Lake Wales Citrus Growers Association, September 9, 1940.

16. MHC, Box 4, Highland Park Service folder, O'Shaughnessy letter to association, October 1962.

17. MHC, Box 5, Lake Wales Orange Grove folder, O'Shaughnessy and Dopler letters and grove reports, 1941, 1944, 1947–48, 1963–64.

18. Ibid., O'Shaughnessy letter, October 9, 1949.

19. MHC, Box 3, Joseph Fitzgerald file, January 1973.

Chapter 10. Olympic Gold Medalists

1. Mal Elliott, "Father of Zone Press Won '36 Olympics and Still Copied," *Wichita Eagle-Beacon*, 1B.

2. Rich Hughes, *Netting Out Basketball 1936: The Remarkable Story of the McPherson Refiners, the First Team to Dunk, Zone Press and Win the Olympic Gold Medal* (Victoria, British Columbia: Friesen Press, 2011), 63.

3. Ibid., 67.

4. History of Globe Refiner basketball teams brochure, 4.

5. Elliott, "Father of Zone Press," 6B.

6. Hank Kehborn, "O'Shaughnessy Backed First Olympic Cagers," *St. Paul Pioneer Press*, September 3, 1972.

7. OFLC, O'Shaughnessy and Sid Hartman letters, September 5 and 26, 1972.

Chapter 11. Win That Pennant or Else

1. MHC, Box 6, New York, Chicago and St. Louis Railroad Co. folder.

2. Al Ostrow, "Win That Pennant or Else, O'Shaughnessy Tells Tribe," *Cleveland Press*, July 1956.

3. Ibid.

4. *Commercial Dispatch* editorial, July 1956.

5. MHC, Box 1, Cleveland Indians folder, O'Shaughnessy letter to Ostrow, July 31, 1956.

6. Regis McAuley, "Tribe Rides Out Teacup Tempest," *Cleveland News*, July 17, 1956.

7. MHC, Box 1, Cleveland Indians folder, various fan letters to O'Shaughnessy, July 1956.

8. "Farrell OK with Iggy," *Cleveland News*, November 29, 1956.

9. Sidney Andorn column, *Cleveland News*, October 3, 1957.

10. MHC, Box 1, Cleveland Indians folder, Lawrence J. Kelly letter to O'Shaughnessy, September 13, 1958.

11. Ibid., H. E. Schell letter to O'Shaughnessy, October 15, 1958.

12. Ibid., William Daley letter to O'Shaughnessy, October 17, 1958.

13. Ibid., Craig Cullinan Jr. letter to Daley, October 23, 1958.

14. Ibid., Kelly letter to O'Shaughnessy, October 23, 1958.

15. Ibid., unnamed Chicago newspaper story, September 1959.

16. Ibid., Cleveland Indians financial statements.

17. Ibid., O'Shaughnessy letter to Cleveland Indians, July 20, 1961.

18. Ibid., O'Shaughnessy letter to Cleveland Indians, September 16, 1966.

19. MHC, Box 2, William Daley folder, Daley letter to O'Shaughnessy, November 1968.

20. MHC, Box 6, M-misc. folder, Milwaukee Brewers correspondence with John O'Shaughnessy, 1971.

21. Ibid., Milwaukee Brewers financial statements.

22. MHC, Box 4, H-misc. folder, William Bick letter to O'Shaughnessy, April 1962.

23. MHC, Box 4, H-misc. folder;
    and Box 10, thank-you letters
    1954–58 folder.

Chapter 12. Ambassador O'Shaughnessy?

1. Lindley and Kunz, "He Loved a Tall Story," 26.

2. "Globe is First."

3. OFLC, Robert Hannegan letter to O'Shaughnessy, February 13, 1945.

4. Ibid., October 16, 1945.

5. OFLC, John Hastings letter to O'Shaughnessy, January 12, 1945.

6. MHC, Box 1, C-misc. folder, documents, 1952.

7. MHC, Box 10, thank-you letters 1958–59 folder.

8. MHC, Box 5, Mc-misc. folder, Eugene McCarthy letters to O'Shaughnessy, July and December 1958.

9. MHC, Box 1, B-misc. folder, O'Shaughnessy and Harry Blackmun letters, September 1959.

10. MHC, Box 8, R-misc. folder, documents, 1960 and 1961.

11. MHC, Box 8, S-misc. folder, O'Shaughnessy letter to George Vavoulis, November 2, 1960.

12. MHC, Box 7, N-misc. folder, Richard Nixon letter to O'Shaughnessy, September 15, 1961.

13. OFLC, Hubert Humphrey letter to O'Shaughnessy, October 6, 1966.

14. MHC, Box 4, G-misc. folder, 1964; Box 6, M-misc. folder, 1968; Box 8, N-misc. folder, 1968; and Box 10, thank-you letters 1969–1973 folder; documents and letters, 1964, 1968, 1970, and 1972.

15. MHC, Box 10, thank-you letters 1969–1973 folder, letters, 1972.

Chapter 13. Honorary Citizen of Killarney

1. Kathryn Boardman, "Pair Gave Away Millions," *St. Paul Dispatch*, October 6, 1958, 4.

2. Ibid.

3. *New York Times*, June 24, 1957.

4. Boardman, "Pair Gave Away Millions," 4.

5. Ibid.

6. *London Times*, August 14, 1958.

7. MHC, Box 4, Killarney Estates folder, O'Shaughnessy letter to Michael Casey, June 8, 1959.

8. Ibid., O'Shaughnessy letter to John Ashe, November 1958.

9. Ibid., Gertrude Mathews letter, August 4, 1966.

Chapter 14. The Silver Link, the Silken Tie

1. O'Shaughnessy album, John O'Shaughnessy letter, 1958.

2. Ibid., Lucille O'Shaughnessy letter, 1958.

3. Ibid., Larry O'Shaughnessy letter, 1958.

4. Ibid., Donald O'Shaughnessy letter, 1958.

5. Ibid., Patrick O'Shaughnessy letter, 1958.

6. Ibid., John O'Shaughnessy Jr. letter, 1958.

7. Ibid., Barbara O'Shaughnessy letter, 1958.

8. Ibid.

9. Ibid., Michele O'Shaughnessy poem, 1958.

10. Ibid., Kathleen Penny letter, 1958.

11. Ibid., Father Theodore Hesburgh letter, 1958.

12. Ibid., Bob McDowell letter, 1958.

13. St. Thomas Academy archives, Mendota Heights, Minnesota, October 7, 1958.

14. *Minneapolis Star*, April 15, 1959.

Chapter 15. Here's Your Christmas Present

1. CST *Memorandum* newsletter, December 1973.

2. MHC, Box G-misc. folder, O'Shaughnessy letter to Archbishop John Gregory Murray, October 18, 1937.

3. Ibid., O'Shaughnessy letter to Murray, February 27, 1940.

4. OFLC, Father William Cunningham memo, 1932.

5. OFLC, Rogge oral history, 19.

6. "Here's Your Christmas Present," *Aquin*, CST, December 1939.

7. Al Wold, "One Pair of Wings for Mr. O'Shaughnessy," *Minneapolis Times-Tribune*, January 26, 1940.

8. Arthur Taylor, "Make Room for Mr. O'Shaughnessy," *Aquin*, January 26, 1940, 1.

9. "O'Shaughnessy Praised at Building Dedication," *Aquin*, January 26, 1940, 1.

10. Ibid.

11. Taylor, "Make Room," 2.

12. Ibid.

13. MHC, Box 8, STC folder.

14. Ibid.

15. OFLC, Rogge oral history, 21.

16. MHC, Box 8, STC folder, Father Vincent Flynn letter to O'Shaughnessy, December 24, 1946.

17. Ibid., Flynn letter to O'Shaughnessy, May 25, 1949.

18. Ibid., Flynn letter to O'Shaughnessy, August 1951.

19. Ibid., Flynn letter to O'Shaughnessy, February 1, 1953.

20. Ibid., Flynn letter to O'Shaughnessy, December 16, 1953.

21. Ibid., Flynn letter to O'Shaughnessy, May 13, 1954.

22. Ibid., Flynn letter to O'Shaughnessy, June 11, 1954.

Chapter 16. The Bond of Loyalty

1. OFLC, O'Shaughnessy Library brochure, 1959.

2. MHC, Box 10, thank-you letters 1954–58 folder, Shannon letter to O'Shaughnessy, May 17, 1957.

3. OFLC, Rogge oral history, 27.

4. MHC, Box 8, CST folder.

5. "O'Shaughnessy, St. Thomas and the Bond of Loyalty," *St. Thomas*, winter 2007, 29.

6. OFLC, Rogge oral history, 92.

7. MHC, Box 10, thank-you letters 1954–58 folder, Shannon letter to O'Shaughnessy, June 13, 1958.

8. OFLC, Shannon speech, O'Shaughnessy Library dedication ceremony, October 29, 1959.

9. Ibid., O'Shaughnessy speech.

10. Ibid.

11. Ibid.

12. Ibid.

13. OFLC, Nicholas Coleman letter to O'Shaughnessy, 1959.

14. MHC, Box 5, Mc-misc. folder, C. Agnes Rigney letter to O'Shaughnessy, April 16, 1953.

15. Ibid., O'Shaughnessy letter to John McKiernan, May 5, 1953.

16. Ibid., Rigney letter to O'Shaughnessy, May 5, 1953.

17. Ibid., McKiernan letter to O'Shaughnessy, May 7, 1957.

18. Ibid., O'Shaughnessy letter to McKiernan, 1957.

19. MHC, Box 8, STC folder.

20. OFLC, Rogge oral history, 42.

21. Ibid., 34.

22. MHC, Box 8, STC folder.

23. MHC, Box 10, thank-you letters 1963–64 folder, Shannon letter to O'Shaughnessy, April 25, 1963.

24. Ibid.

25. MHC, Box 8, STC folder, Archbishop Leo Binz statement, 1964.

26. MHC, Box 10, thank-you letters 1963–64 folder, Shannon letter to O'Shaughnessy, June 9, 1964.

27. Joseph B. Connors, *A Journey to Fulfillment: A History of the College of St. Thomas* (St. Paul: College of St. Thomas, 1986), 414.

28. ODLC, Rogge oral history, 57.

29. MHC, Box 10, thank-you letters 1969–73 folder, Monsignor Terrence Murphy letter to O'Shaughnessy, April 29, 1969.

30. OFLC, Murphy oral history, undated.

Chapter 17. A Bet on Notre Dame

1. MHC, Box 7, ND folder, O'Shaughnessy letter to Arthur Haley, 1941.

2. HL, undated document.

3. MHC, Box 7, ND folder, O'Shaughnessy and Haley letters, October 1941.

4. Ibid., O'Shaughnessy letter to Haley, December 1941.

5. Ibid., Haley letter to O'Shaughnessy, December 1941.

6. Ibid., ND letter to parents, July 1943.

7. Ibid., O'Shaughnessy letter to Haley, December 12, 1942; Haley telegram to O'Shaughnessy, December 17, 1942; and Haley letter to O'Shaughnessy, December 28, 1942.

8. HL, news release, December 1942.

9. MHC, Box 7, ND folder, O'Shaughnessy letter to Haley, October 1943.

10. Ibid., O'Shaughnessy and Haley letters, November 1944.

11. *Chicago Journal of Commerce*, July 23, 1943.

12. MHC, Box 7, ND folder, Haley letter to O'Shaughnessy, December 22, 1944.

13. Ibid., Cavanaugh letter to O'Shaughnessy, August 2, 1946.

14. Ibid., Cavanaugh letter to O'Shaughnessy, July 1948.

15. Ibid., Haley telegram and letter to O'Shaughnessy, November 1949.

16. HL, O'Shaughnessy Liberal and Fine Arts Hall brochure.

17. MHC, Box 7, ND folder, Cavanaugh letter to O'Shaughnessy, April 3, 1950.

18. Ibid., Hesburgh letter to O'Shaughnessy, April 1950.

19. Ibid., Haley letter to O'Shaughnessy, April 18, 1950.

20. HL, news release, May 11, 1950.

21. Ibid., Haley letter to O'Shaughnessy, November 13, 1950.

22. MHC, Box 7, ND folder, Hesburgh letter to O'Shaughnessy, March 30, 1951.

23. Ibid., Cavanaugh letter to O'Shaughnessy, May 23, 1951.

24. Ibid., Hesburgh letter to O'Shaughnessy, May 29, 1950.

25. Ibid., Cavanaugh letter to O'Shaughnessy, July 11, 1951.

26. Ibid., Hesburgh letter to O'Shaughnessy, February 4, 1952.

27. HL, O'Shaughnessy speech at Laying of the Cornerstone ceremony for O'Shaughnessy Hall, May 24, 1952.

28. Ibid.

29. Ibid.

Chapter 18. Spark and Torch

1. MHC, Box 7, ND folder, Hesburgh and O'Shaughnessy letters, July 24 and 29, 1952.

2. Ibid., O'Shaughnessy letter to Hesburgh, December 9, 1952.

3. Ibid., Hesburgh letter to O'Shaughnessy, March 10, 1953.

4. "I.A. O'Shaughnessy is Laetare Choice," *New York Times*, March 15, 1953, 77.

5. HL, O'Shaughnessy Hall brochure.

6. HL, O'Shaughnessy speech at dedication of O'Shaughnessy Hall, May 16, 1953.

7. Ibid.

8. Ibid.

9. MHC, Box 7, ND folder, Cavanaugh letter to O'Shaughnessy, May 19, 1953.

10. O'Shaughnessy anniversary album, Cavanaugh letter, 1958.

11. MHC, Box 7, ND folder, Edward Krause and Hesburgh letters to O'Shaughnessy, June 1954.

12. Ibid., Hesburgh letters to O'Shaughnessy, 1956 and 1958.

13. Ibid., Cavanaugh letter to O'Shaughnessy, December 1956.

14. Ibid., Cavanaugh letter to O'Shaughnessy, 1955.

15. Ibid., Hesburgh letter to O'Shaughnessy, May 21, 1956.

16. Ibid., Orange Bowl committee letter to O'Shaughnessy, October 27, 1964; O'Shaughnessy letter to Orange Bowl, November 4, 1964; and Florida judge letter to O'Shaughnessy, November 9, 1964.

17. Ibid., Joyce letter to O'Shaughnessy, November 10, 1964; and O'Shaughnessy letter to Orange Bowl, November 16, 1964.

18. Ibid., J. Michael O'Shaughnessy and O'Shaughnessy letters, November 10 and 23, 1959.

19. Ibid., Notre Dame news release, March 26, 1962.

20. Ibid., Haley letter to O'Shaughnessy, March 27, 1962.

21. Ibid., Hesburgh letter to O'Shaughnessy, November 16, 1962.

22. Ibid., Haley letter to O'Shaughnessy, September 6, 1963.

23. Ibid., Hesburgh letter to O'Shaughnessy, March 30, 1964.

24. Ibid., O'Shaughnessy letter to Haley, June 7, 1963.

Chapter 19. Steady Hand and Cool Head

1. Connors, *Journey Toward Fulfillment*, 368.

2. MHC, Box 8, STC folder, Shannon letter to O'Shaughnessy, February 1957.

3. James Shannon, *Reluctant Dissenter* (New York; Crossroad, 1998), 73.

4. MHC, Box 10, thank-you letters 1960–61 folder, Shannon letter to O'Shaughnessy, November 1960.

5. MHC, Box 6, M-misc. folder, Father John Roach letter to O'Shaughnessy, May 13, 1965.

6. MHC, Box 10, thank-you letters 1963–64 folder, Father John Lee letter to O'Shaughnessy, March 3, 1964.

7. St. Thomas Academy, *Kaydet* yearbook, 1972.

8. I.A. O'Shaughnessy Foundation report, 2013.

Chapter 20. The Hand of Aid

1. MHC, Box 10, thank-you letters 1965 folder, Kate Moorman letter to O'Shaughnessy, January 17, 1965.

2. *Minneapolis Tribune*, January 17, 1965.

3. SCUL, Sister Antonine O'Brien letter to O'Shaughnessy, December 30, 1953.

4. SCUL, O'Shaughnessy letter to Sister Mary William Brady, September 13, 1960.

5. MHC, Box 10, thank-you letters 1965 folder, James Cunningham letter to O'Shaughnessy, March 3, 1965.

6. SCUL, Cunningham letter to Sister Alberta Huber, March 15, 1974.

7. SCUL, *Currents* newsletter, winter 1975.

8. SCUL, Huber letter to Blanche O'Shaughnessy, December 1973.

Chapter 21. Opening the Doors to Knowledge

1. MHC, Box 10, thank-you letters 1963–64 folder, Fred Hughes letter to O'Shaughnessy, February 1, 1963.

2. MHC, Box 8, S-misc. folder, Alphonse Schwitalla letter to O'Shaughnessy, July 20, 1946.

3. MHC, Box 10, thank-you letters 1965–66 folder.

4. MHC, Box 5, M-misc. folder, Raquel Murphy letter to O'Shaughnessy, fall 1953.

5. MHC, Box 1, C-misc. folder, document.

6. MHC, Box 8, S-misc. folder; Box 5, L-misc. folder; and Box 1, C-misc. folder, documents.

7. MHC, Box 3, F-misc. folder, O'Shaughnessy letter to Fordham University, 1956.

8. MHC, Box 8, R-misc. folder, O'Shaughnessy letter to Father Maurice Van Ackeron, December 10, 1958.

9. MHC, Box 2, D-misc., O'Shaughnessy letter to DePaul University, October 1964.

10. MHC, Box 1, C-misc. folder; and Box 10, thank-you letters 1963–64 folder, correspondence with Cretin High School, 1939 and 1964.

11. MHC, Box 8, R-misc. folder, Sister M. Kateri letter to O'Shaughnessy, October 30, 1969.

12. MHC, Box 5, L-misc. folder.

13. MHC, Box 10, thank-you letters 1965–66 folder.

14. MHC, Box 10, thank-you letters 1958–59 folder, Bernice Roberts letter to O'Shaughnessy, March 10, 1959.

15. MHC, Box 8, S-misc.

16. MHC, Box 2, D-misc.

17. MHC, Box 8, S-misc.

18. MHC, Box 10, thank-you letters 1962 folder.

19. MHC, Box 1, C-misc. folder, Catholic Athletic Association letter to O'Shaughnessy, December 1950.

20. MHC, Box 8, S-misc. folder, St. Patrick's School letter, 1957.

21. MHC, Box 4, H-misc. folder, Louis Headley letter to O'Shaughnessy, August 21, 1956.

22. MHC, Box 6, M-misc. folder, 1946, 1951, and 1965 notes to Macalester College, and O'Shaughnessy letter, November 1957.

23. MHC, Box 6, Minnesota Private College Fund folder, Laurence Gould letter to O'Shaughnessy, 1955; and Box 10, misc. thank-you letter folder.

24. MHC, Box 10, thank-you letters 1962 and 1965–66 folders.

25. MHC, Box 5, L-misc. folder, O'Shaughnessy letter to M. D. Whitaker, December 19, 1957.

26. MHC, Box 6, Naval Academy folder, O'Shaughnessy letter to W. R. Smedberg, November 1957.

27. MHC, Box 10, thank-you letters 1954–58 folder, Naval Academy letter to O'Shaughnessy, 1958.

28. MHC, Box 8, S-misc. folder, O'Shaughnessy letter to Sioux Falls College, July 14, 1970.

Chapter 22. The Last Vigil Light

1. OFLC, Murphy oral history.

2. O'Shaughnessy anniversary album, Bishop Stephen Leven letter, 1958.

3. MHC, Box 8, R-misc. folder, Bernard H. Ridder Sr. letter to O'Shaughnessy, November 18, 1952.

4. Ibid., O'Shaughnessy letter to Ridder, December 9, 1952.

5. MHC, Box 4, House of the Good Shepherd folder, O'Shaughnessy and Mother Mary of St. Francis Xavier letters, October 1955.

6. Ibid., Mother Mary Paul letter to O'Shaughnessy, 1956.

7. Ibid., 1965 announcement.

8. MHC, Box 10, thank-you letters 1967–1971 folder, Sister Mary Louis letter to O'Shaughnessy, May 12, 1969.

9. MHC, Box 5, L-misc. folder, O'Shaughnessy letter to the Little Sisters of the Poor, July 31, 1944.

10. Ibid., Charles Ward letter to O'Shaughnessy, 1947.

11. Ibid., O'Shaughnessy letter to Little Sisters of the Poor, January 1961.

12. MHC, Box 1, C-misc. folder; and Box 10, thank-you letters 1953–55 folder, Sister Anna Marie letter, December 9, 1954, and Father Vincent Flynn letter, December 23, 1954.

13. MHC, Box 10, thank-you letters 1958–59 folder, Francis Miller letter to O'Shaughnessy, February 13, 1959.

14. MHC, Box 9, V-misc. folder, Mother Mary Jerome and O'Shaughnessy letters, April 9 and July 23, 1957.

15. MHC, Box 10, thank-you letters 1963–64 folder, Mother Mary Jerome letter to O'Shaughnessy, October 27, 1963.

16. Ibid., Mother Mary Catherine letter to O'Shaughnessy, October 27, 1963.

17. MHC, Box 5, L-misc. folder, Sister Leocreta letter to O'Shaughnessy, May 1953, and Robert MacFarlane letter to Sister Leocreta, May 11, 1953.

18. MHC, Box 10, thank-you letters 1953–55 folder, Sister Jane Marie letter to O'Shaughnessy, September 11, 1955.

19. MHC, Box 4, G-misc. folder, O'Shaughnessy and Rev. William Gelsdorf letters, July and November 1938.

20. MHC, Box 8, X-Y-Z folder, Sister Mary Samuel letter to O'Shaughnessy, March 1, 1957.

21. MHC, Box 4, G-misc. folder, Chicago bank executive's letter to O'Shaughnessy, December 1957.

22. MHC, Box 4, M-misc. folder, Most Rev. R. O. Geroz letter to O'Shaughnessy, December 1958.

23. MHC, Box 5, K-misc. folder, Father A. Simon and O'Shaughnessy letters, November 1967.

24. MHC, Box 5, Mc-misc. folder, O'Shaughnessy letter to Thomas McCann, November 1961.

25. MHC, Box 2, E-misc. folder, O'Shaughnessy and Wesley Methodist Church music minister letters, 1961.

26. MHC, Box 10, thank-you letters 1963–64 folder.

27. MHC, Box 10, thank-you letters 1967–68 folder.

28. MHC, Box 9, S-misc. folder, O'Shaughnessy letter to Monsignor Joseph O'Shea, November 2, 1972.

29. MHC, Box 1, C-misc. folder, O'Shaughnessy letter to Columban Fathers, 1957.

30. MHC, Box 7, O'Shaughnessy letter to Father Patrick Payton, June 1966.

31. MHC, Box 6, M-misc. folder.

32. Ibid., Father R. Martin letter to O'Shaughnessy, 1959.

33. MHC, Box 2, D-misc. folder, Father Edward Duff letter to O'Shaughnessy, 1961.

34. MHC, Box 4, H-misc. folder, O'Shaughnessy letter to Bishop John Treacy, November 1951.

35. MHC, Box 4, F-misc. folder, O'Shaughnessy letter to the Franciscan Sisters of the Sacred Heart, June 1963.

36. MHC, Box 6, M-misc. folder, O'Shaughnessy letter to the Sisters of Christian Charity, 1964.

37. MHC, Box 6, M-misc. folder, O'Shaughnessy letter to Father Terrence Moore, October 4, 1942.

38. MHC, Box 7, N-misc. folder, O'Shaughnessy and Father George Garrelts letters, fall 1961.

39. Monsignor James Lavin interview with author, November 30, 2006.

40. MHC, Box 4, Gilligan folder, Monsignor Francis Gilligan letter to O'Shaughnessy, April 1961.

41. MHC, Box 10, thank-you letters 1963-64 folder, Gilligan letter to O'Shaughnessy, 1962.

42. MHC, Box 8, S-misc. folder, Gilligan letter to O'Shaughnessy, undated.

Chapter 23. Public Need and Public Gain

1. OFLC, Smith tribute, October 5, 1973.

2. MHC, Box 6, Miller Hospital folder, O'Shaughnessy letter to Miller Hospital, 1970.

3. MHC, Box 5, Mayo Memorial folder.

4. MHC, Box 6, Minnesota Medical Foundation folder, various correspondence, including Dr. Ivan Baronofsky letter to O'Shaughnessy, October 1, 1951.

5. Ibid., solicitation documents and Owen Wangensteen letter to O'Shaughnessy, November 1956.

6. Ibid., Wangensteen letter to O'Shaughnessy, January 21, 1959.

7. MHC, Box 10, thank-you letters folder 1960, document.

8. MHC, Box 8, S-misc. folder, Murray letter to O'Shaughnessy, March 5, 1956.

9. MHC, Box 8, S-misc. folder, Sister Antonius Kennelly letter to O'Shaughnessy, April 6, 1956.

10. MHC, Box 8, S-misc. folder, O'Shaughnessy letter to Samuel Hunter, August 13, 1957.

11. Ibid., Hunter letters to O'Shaughnessy, January 16 and February 13, 1962.

12. MHC, Box 6, M-misc. folder, O'Shaughnessy letter to Marian Medical Research Foundation, October 10, 1961.

13. MHC, Box 9, U-misc. folder.

14. MHC, Box 8, S-misc. folder, O'Shaughnessy letter to Robert Slaughter, September 8, 1958.

15. MHC, Box 10, thank-you letters 1967–68 folder.

16. MHC, Box 1, B-misc. folder; Box 2, D-misc. and E-misc. folders; and Box 6, M-misc. folder.

17. MHC, Box 8, S-misc. folder, O'Shaughnessy letters and documents, 1957 and 1964.

18. MHC, Box 1, C-misc. folder, O'Shaughnessy letter to Children's Hospital ball director, June 1964.

19. MHC, Box 4, Hazelden Foundation folder, O'Shaughnessy and Peter Butler letters, September 17, October 2, and October 15, 1968.

20. MHC, Box 8, S-misc. folder, and Box 10, thank-you letters 1965–66 folder.

21. MHC, Box 9, V-misc. folder, William Grey letter to O'Shaughnessy, February 5, 1948.

22. MHC, Box 6, N-misc. folder, O'Shaughnessy letter to National Braille Press, November 2, 1942.

23. MHC, Box 1, American Red Cross folder.

24. MHC, Box 7, misc. documents, including O'Shaughnessy letter to Our Lady of Good Counsel Cancer Home, November 24, 1953.

25. MHC, Box 8, S-misc. folder, O'Shaughnessy letter to St. Paul Rehabilitation Center, 1957.

Chapter 24. Making a 1 a 2

1. MHC, Box 8, S-misc. folder, Carol Fiske letter to O'Shaughnessy, October 11, 1972.

2. MHC, Box 10, thank-you letters 1960–61 folder.

3. MHC, Box 6, M-misc. folder, O'Shaughnessy letters to Judson Bemis, July 20 and August 22, 1968.

4. Ibid., October 15, 1968.

5. MHC, Box 8, S-misc. folder, P. W. Fitzpatrick letter to O'Shaughnessy, September 1, 1959.

6. MHC, Box 8, S-misc. folder, Louise Otis letter to O'Shaughnessy, June 28, 1968.

7. MHC, Box 9, S-misc. folder, O'Shaughnessy letter to Thelma Hunter, May 13, 1964.

8. MHC, Box 8, S-misc. folder.

9. MHC, Box 4, G-misc. folder; Box 6, M-misc. folder; and Box 9, S-misc. folder.

10. MHC, Box 7, O-misc. folder, Arturo di Filippi letter to O'Shaughnessy, December 31, 1969.

Chapter 25. Just Saying Thank You

1. MHC, Box 2, D-misc. folder, O'Shaughnessy and Leo Durbin letters, 1957.

2. MHC, Box 1, C-misc. folder, O'Shaughnessy, Shannon and St.

John's University alumnus letters, 1961 and 1962.

3. MHC, Box 3, F-misc. folder, Leo Fecht letters to O'Shaughnessy, 1962 and 1964.

4. MHC, Box 4, K-misc. folder.

5. MHC, Box 2, D-misc. folder, Mrs. Vincent Doyle and O'Shaughnessy letters, 1941, 1947, and 1957.

6. MHC, Box 3, F-misc. folder, assistance letters, December 10 and 20, 1960.

7. MHC, Box 8, R-misc., assistance letters, August 1963.

8. MHC, Box 7, O-misc. folder, Helen O'Shaughnessy letter to O'Shaughnessy, August 17, 1957.

9. Ibid., O'Shaughnessy letter to Helen O'Shaughnessy, August 1957.

10. MHC, Box 10, thank-you letters 1958–59 folder, anonymous letter to O'Shaughnessy, March 12, 1959.

Chapter 26. Fulfilling a Papal Dream

1. Transcript of Ali Selim interview with Hesburgh, April 2011.

2. Ibid.

3. Ibid.

4. Ibid.

5. MHC, Box 7, ND folder, Hesburgh letter to O'Shaughnessy, August 4, 1964.

6. MHC, Box 10, thank-you letters September 1964 folder, Hesburgh memo, September 1964.

7. MHC, Box 7, ND folder, O'Shaughnessy letter to Hesburgh, September 29, 1964.

8. Grim, "O'Shaughnessy," 1A.

9. MHC, Box 2, Ecumenical Institute folder, December 1965 news release.

10. Ibid., Hesburgh letter to O'Shaughnessy, December 1965.

11. MHC, Box 2, Ecumenical Institute folder, Albert Outler report to Catholic Press Association, September 30, 1966.

12. Ibid.

13. Ibid.

14. MHC, Box 2, Ecumenical Institute folder, Hesburgh letter to O'Shaughnessy, May 23, 1966.

15. Ibid., Hesburgh letter to O'Shaughnessy, May 23, 1966.

16. Selim interview with Hesburgh.

17. Ibid.

18. Bernard Casserly, "O'Shaughnessy helps Papal dream come true," *Catholic Bulletin*, July 14, 1972, 1.

19. "O'Shaughnessy count," *Catholic Bulletin*, March 1967, 3, 15.

20. MHC, Box 8, Rome folder, O'Shaughnessy letter to Pope Paul VI, April 8, 1967.

21. Ibid.

22. MHC, Box 8, STC folder, Shannon letter to O'Shaughnessy, March 20, 1967.

23. MHC, Box 7, ND folder, Hesburgh letter to O'Shaughnessy, October 1971.

24. Casserly, "O'Shaughnessy helps Papal dream," 3.

25. Grace Wing Bohne, "They Went to Israel to See $4 Million Gift," *Miami Herald*, August 6, 1972.

26. MHC, Box 10, thank-you letters 196–73 folder, Gilligan letters to O'Shaughnessy, September 1972.

Chapter 27. The Grand Old Man

1. Betty Roney, "O'Shaughnessy to Receive Tributes June 18," *St. Paul Dispatch*, June 10, 1966, 16.

2. OFLC, John Myers letter to O'Shaughnessy, August 8, 1966.

3. *Minneapolis Star*, June 30, 1966.

4. Bernard Casserly, "Honor well-deserved," *Catholic Bulletin*, June 18, 1971, 6.

5. MHC, Box 7, I.A. O'Shaughnessy 1932–1973 folder, 1971 document.

6. OFLC, Harold Cummings letter to O'Shaughnessy, October 23, 1972.

7. MHC, Box 1, C-misc. folder, Cummings letter to O'Shaughnessy, 1972.

8. "Minnesota's 12 wealthiest citizens—and why *you* aren't on the list," *Corporate Report*, November 1973, 9–12, 30.

9. OFLC, O'Shaughnessy letter to First Trust Co. of St. Paul, October 17, 1968.

10. "I.A. O'Shaughnessy Foundation: A Legacy of Second Chances," *Philanthropy*, spring 2010, 10–12 and 60.

Chapter 28. The Epitome of Faith, Hope, and Love

1. MHC, Box 7, O-misc. folder, Osborne-Peterson Co. gravesite description, 1973.

2. Hesburgh eulogy, Mass of Christian Burial, Cathedral of St. Paul, St. Paul, MN, November 26, 1973.

3. Ibid.

4. Murphy homily, Memorial Mass, Chapel of St. Thomas Aquinas, CST, November 27, 1973.

5. Bernard Casserly, "He never lost touch," *Catholic Bulletin*, November 30, 1973.

6. Keith Fanshier, "I.A. O'Shaughnessy," *Oil Daily*, November 27, 1973.

7. OFLC, Jean-Jacques von Allmen letter to Blanche O'Shaughnessy, November 28, 1973.

8. Shannon, "The Pilgrim Church."

Epilogue

1. Hesburgh eulogy, November 26, 1973.

2. Michele O'Shaughnessy Traeger email to author, September 18, 2012.

INDEX

Index information under O'Shaughnessy, Ignatius Aloysius is divided into four sections: awards/honors/praise; opinions; personal life; philanthropy. IAO refers to Ignatius Aloysius O'Shaughnessy.

H